# LEON EVERETTE:
## THE GOOD, THE BAD, AND THE BLESSED

By

Hal Reeves

Hal Reeves

**LEON EVERETTE:**
The Good, The Bad, and the Blessed



Published by Spines Publishing Platform
ISBN: 979-8-89383-888-6

# CONTENTS

# INTRODUCTION

The story of Leon Everette Baughman is an interesting but complex one. Born in Aiken, SC, in 1948, Leon grew up in a transit family. His father was a construction union electrician who moved from job to job to find the best financial support available for his young, growing family. Later, in Leon's teen years, the family settled down in a small town called Ward, SC, which he would call home for the rest of his life.

Throughout his lifetime, he escaped numerous near-death experiences, as early as the age of three, to well into his adult life, most of which were brought on by his own irresponsible, reckless nature. To this day, he credits the grace of God and not luck as his reason to have escaped through all the potentially life-threatening tragedies.

He learned to play the guitar while on board a naval aircraft carrier during his two tours of duty in the Vietnam War. He served as a third-class aviation electrician during this time, and he and his amateur band won a talent contest while aboard the ship, resulting in what some call his initial rise to fame.

He got married while in the Navy, and after completing his tour of duty, he and his young wife, Kathy, settled down in their home state of South Carolina. During this time, he met some local musicians and formed a band playing for weddings, birthdays, and other special events. Having received high praise for his dynamic vocal skills, he decided on a solo career exploring the nightclub scene in nearby Augusta, GA. During this time, he changed his stage name to simply Leon Everette.

One night, while performing at one of the local nightclubs, Leon was discovered by an entrepreneur named Carroll Fulmer. After several tireless but unsuccessful visits to recording labels in Nashville, TN, and through persistent business practices, Carroll was finally able to get Leon a contract as an up-and-coming country music entertainer with RCA Records, one of country music's most prestigious labels.

During the early 1980s, Leon was one of the most sought-after recording artists in Nashville, having made eleven albums in just a few short years to reach the top ten on the Billboard Magazine charts. Throughout his career, he received nine gold albums, appeared in a variety of TV shows, performed on several occasions at the Grand Ole Opry, was an early spokesperson for a new soft drink called Mello Yellow, was inducted into the Rock a Billy Hall of Fame on the same day as Elvis Presley, and received many other country music and entertainment and lifetime achievement awards—too many to mention here. Sadly, due to anger issues and alcoholism, he ended his country music career in 1985 and returned to his home in Ward, SC.

At the time his country music career was over, he had saved enough money to invest in several business adventures as a new source of income. One of his most challenging investments was a popular nightclub in Aiken County, SC, called "Hurricane Central." Hurricane Central opened in the latter part of 1990 to standing-room-only crowds and was one of the most popular country music destinations in all of western South Carolina and eastern Georgia for years.

The anger issues and alcoholism weren't just limited to the downfall of his music career, as it was also one of the primary reasons for his and Kathy's highly contested divorce in the mid-1990s. Several years later, he met his now-wife, Diane, whose Christian influence convinced him to surrender his sinful life to become a disciple and follower of Jesus Christ. From that time on, he no longer performed solely country music but instead began a new career as a country/gospel artist.

During the decade of the new millennium, Leon's devotion to Christ led him to buy back Hurricane Central, which he renovated into a church for local worshipers. He currently serves as the minister of music, as well as the church administrator and the associate pastor.

One of his most proud achievements happened when he was seventy-three years old. He became one of the oldest, if not the oldest, members of Sony MC1-Nashville Recording Label to sign a recording contract as a country/gospel singer. He still entertains audiences all across the United States whenever he's called to perform, but wherever he goes, he goes there not only to entertain but also to tell his testimony and share his relationship with his Lord and Savior, Jesus Christ.

**Proverbs 3:5,6**

Trust in the LORD with all your heart,
And lean not on your own understanding;
In all your ways acknowledge Him,
And He shall direct your paths.

NKJV

*Dedicated to Sue Padgett
English Literature Teacher
Evans High School, 1968*

Chapter 1

**Not Just Another Day**

Circa 1951

**Langley, South Carolina,** is a quaint little town with the design of a tiny dot on any size road map. It sits quietly nestled about halfway between Aiken, SC, and Augusta, GA. Circa 1950, Langley was a small, tranquil, but prideful community with a home to a thriving cotton textile industry.

The Langley Cotton Mill, located in historic Horse Creek Valley, was one of the largest employers of the community. If you worked in the mill, you were all but sure to have steady employment. Otherwise, other longstanding jobs were mostly available in nearby Aiken, SC, North Augusta, SC, or a short drive across the Savannah River in Augusta, GA.

For Langley citizen Albert Baughman, steady work would be found through an IBEW (International Brotherhood of Electrical Workers) local union in downtown Augusta, GA. Albert's wife, Eula Lee, was a homemaker and the primary caretaker of their young three-year-old son, Leon.

Albert, or Al, as his co-workers and friends called him,

worked a forty-hour week with weekends off. That left Saturday and Sunday to run errands and attend church. Eula Lee was very much committed to the local church, so if they were going to run any errands, they would have to be done on Saturdays.

The weather in late April in this part of the south was generally very warm but not necessarily too humid. But one Saturday, April morning in 1951, the temperature fell to an unexpected twenty-nine degrees. To Eula, it was downright cold. Nevertheless, it was grocery shopping day, and if the family was to be fed, groceries had to be bought, as the pantry was running low on food supplies and other commodities.

Al had already pre-warmed the car, and he, Eula, and young Leon were now ready to go to the A&P Grocery store in nearby Aiken. Their drive to Aiken would be in their recently purchased 1946 Mercury Eight four-door sedan automobile. It was the couple's first car that they owned together, and it was a perfect fit to suit the needs of the young, evolving family. It had wide whitewall tires, a three-speed manual transmission, and a whisper-quiet motor. Although it wasn't considered a luxury model, it was just one step below the top of the Ford Motor Company's luxury line Lincoln model.

One unique feature of this style was the rear-hinged rear doors. Rather than the traditional front-hinged doors, which opened with the door swinging toward the front of the car, the rear-hinged doors swung open swinging to the rear of the vehicle.

The slang term for a door of this style was commonly known as the "suicide door." The term "suicide" was given because if the vehicle happened to be going at a certain speed and the door came open, the wind could potentially have enough draft to draw an object or individual out of the vehicle into oncoming traffic. The term was loosely used, and to this day, neither Al nor Eula had ever heard of such an awful thing happening.

As Eula gathered a few small toys and some snack food for

Leon, Al made sure the home was secure. Leon sat alone in the living room, intently watching The Howdy Doody Show on the family's black-and-white TV screen. After everything was in order, Eula scooped Leon up, and they all headed for the car.

Saturday was usually Eula's day to drive, as she was a stay-at-home mom while Albert needed the car to go to work and back during the week. She loved driving what she called "Al's other baby" every chance she got.

The road from home to Aiken was Highway 1. Although it was only a two-lane route, it was the major thoroughfare between Aiken and Augusta. For a small community, Highway 1 was a very busy roadway for commercial, residential, and farming vehicles. This was a time before the development of the interstate highway program, and major thoroughfares like Highway 1 drew immediate demands for commercial enterprises. The A&P Grocery just happened to be one of the more popular businesses along the route between Langley and Aiken.

The family was finally all set and ready to ride. While Eula drove, Albert rode in the passenger's seat, and little Leon had the whole back seat to himself. The back seat was like a little playground for Leon, as Eula made sure he had several of his favorite toys to keep him occupied along the way. With everyone now settled, it was time to head out north on Highway 1.

* * *

Meanwhile, it was just another Saturday morning in South Carolina for Jason Biggs. He'd just dropped off a load of pulpwood timber at a sawmill on the north side of Aiken. Now, he was heading south toward Augusta to pick up his next load for delivery. His pride and joy was his bright canary yellow 1941 model Peterbilt semi-truck hauling rig. The fourteen-wheeled, six-axle behemoth was a dream to drive, but to approaching traffic, it was an oncoming, rolling nightmare.

He'd made this same trip on many occasions with no vehicle incidents, speeding tickets, or overload violations whatsoever. This truck was his money maker, and he pandered to it as if it were a little child. He'd not been involved in any accidents to date, and he certainly didn't want one today.

* * *

The Baughmans continued their ride, listening to the radio and talking about things they needed at the grocery store. After just a short while, little Leon became unusually bored in the back seat and began to whimper and quietly sob.

"What's wrong, baby?" asked his mama, "We'll be there soon, and you can go for a ride in the grocery cart, okay?"

Leon momentarily quieted down just from hearing his mama's comforting voice. But after a few minutes, he once again grew impatient.

"Albert, why don't you give him one of those tangerines you brought from home? Maybe that will keep him occupied until we can get to the store," said Eula.

"That's a good idea," said Albert.

Albert immediately began peeling a tangerine, throwing the rind out the window little by little, then handed the peeled fruit back to Leon along with a paper napkin.

"Here you go, Leon," Albert said, "eat on this, and we'll wipe your hands and face when we get to the A&P, okay? Atta boy."

An eager Leon quickly reached for the tangerine. It was his favorite fruit, and it had been used before on other drives along the highway as a sort of pacifier to keep him calm and content.

"Eula, you might want to speed it up a little bit if you want to get there before dark," Albert teased. "Thirty-five miles per hour in a fifty-five-mile-an-hour zone is a bit slow, don't you think?"

"Oh, my, I didn't realize I was going so slow," replied Eula as she slowly pressed the gas pedal. "Then fifty-five it is."

After a couple of miles had passed, Leon had eaten most of the tangerine but noticed that his daddy had missed a small piece of the rind. Digging persistently at the remaining rind with his tender little fingers, Leon finally removed it from the rest of the fruit. He'd watched his daddy roll the window down and throw the peeling out the window along the way on other f amily outings. As he looked around, he saw two small handles o n the inside of the car door. He knew one of them must be the o ne to roll the window down. But which o ne?

He reached for the one closest to him and tried to roll it down, but it wouldn't budge. He tried stretching for the second handle, but it was too far away from him to reach. So, after several more unsuccessful attempts to roll the first handle down, he decided to stand on the floorboard behind the driver's seat and with both hands, quickly snatched the second handle toward him.

Without any warning, the door suddenly flew open. The oncoming wind was so strong, that as it hit hard against the door, it pulled little Leon from the back floorboard, his body hitting the inside of the door, then landing on the hot asphalt highway, uncontrollably tumbling and rolling along, and finally coming to a stop in a ditch on the opposite side of the road.

From the other direction, Jason Biggs' canary yellow pulpwood truck was quickly coming their way, just moments from an impact.

"Eula, pull over. Now!" shouted Albert.
Eula pulled the vehicle to the shoulder of the road as quickly as she could, slamming the brakes for a forceful stop.

"Oh, my God! Oh, my God!" a desperate Eula screamed, "Oh, my baby!"

As the semi grew closer and closer, Eula grew more and more frantic, feeling helpless, knowing that there was nothing she could do to save her baby from harm.

At first, Jason only saw an object being thrown from the vehicle. But as he got closer, he realized that it was an infant child. It had happened so fast. The baby went from the automobile to the road to the ditch in a matter of seconds. He only had seconds himself to react.

Without hesitation, he slammed on the brakes and swerved to the oncoming lane where Eula's car would have been riding, only to just miss a horrified father, Albert, running toward the potentially injured baby boy.

The semi had swung almost sideways, coming to a stop and blocking the road in both directions as Albert quickly reached little Leon. As he examined his only son, the first thing he noticed was blood protruding from his head. The infant's face, arms, and legs were also covered with road rash.

"Leon! Leon!" screamed Albert, but the baby would not respond—not even a whimper.

"Albert! Albert!" is he okay? "Albert, please!" cried out Eula.

"Stay right there, Eula, I'm coming," replied Albert.

Albert quickly reached into his back jeans pocket, retrieved a white handkerchief, and carefully draped it over young Leon's tiny, blood-soaked head.

Jason Biggs rushed to assist Albert, but there was nothing that he could do at this point. Feeling helpless, Jason guarded Albert against any oncoming traffic as Albert headed back to the family automobile.

"Are you and your wife okay?" asked Jason.

"Yes, obviously shaken up, but we're physically okay. I'm not so sure about him," responded Albert. "We're going straight to the Aiken Hospital."

As Albert reached his automobile, he said to Eula, "You hold him, and I'll drive, but whatever you do, do not remove that handkerchief! Do you understand?"

"Yes, Albert," replied a panicky Eula. "Please hurry! Please, Albert, let's go!"

Albert was insistent about not removing the handkerchief

because he didn't want her to see the devastating injuries to her precious son's bleeding head.

"Are you going to be okay?" Albert asked Jason.

"Yes, I'm fine. Go! Now! Get your son to the hospital. I will keep you and your family in my prayers," said Jason as the shaken family quickly fled away.

"Oh, my baby! Oh, my baby!" Eula cried as the car sped away to the hospital.

"Is he going to be okay, Albert?" she cried.

"Please, tell me he's going to be okay, Albert!" she exclaimed in panic and desperation.

She was so hysterical that she hadn't noticed that little Leon had not moaned, whimpered, or cried out loud.

Albert didn't know what to think, either. The baby wasn't responding audibly, but at least he could see his tiny chest move ever so slightly, showing a sign of a struggle to breathe.

"He's breathing, honey," Albert said in as reassuring a voice as he could compose under the circumstances. All the while, Albert was thinking that it was highly likely that Leon had suffered a concussion, which may lead to internal injuries, including brain damage. But for now, he was still alive and breathing.

* * *

Just a short distance away, Highway patrolman Joel Hamilton was parked on a side road off Highway 1, monitoring traffic, when he was suddenly approached by a passenger in an oncoming vehicle.

A man quickly brought his car to a stop, jumped out, and ran as fast as he could toward the patrol car.

"Officer, there's been a serious accident just down the road. I'm not sure if anybody was injured, but I'm sure they could use your help," said a concerned citizen. "I saw a semi-truck swerve into the oncoming traffic lane through my rear-view mirror as I topped the knoll just down the road. He appeared to be trying to avoid hitting someone or something in the road."

"Thank you. I'm on my way," replied Officer Hamilton.

As he pulled onto the highway a 40's model four-door Mercury came flying by in the opposite direction of the patrol car.

*Should I go to the accident, or should I chase after the speeding car?* Hamilton desperately wondered.

He was in a potential no-win situation. Was there an injured person in the speeding vehicle and possibly headed to the Aiken Hospital? Or were they fleeing the scene of an accident? Were there any potential casualties or serious injuries at the scene of the accident that needed immediate assistance? *Which way should I go?*

Then, without hesitation, he slammed on the brakes and made a hasty U-turn in an attempt to catch up with the speeding Mercury.

"Headquarters, this is patrol car 521. I'm in pursuit of a vehicle with a possible injured passenger or someone leaving the scene of an accident heading in the direction of Aiken on Highway 1 just north of Langley. I've been alerted by a motorist that described a serious accident on Highway 1 just north of the Langley city limits. Please have a patrol vehicle respond to the scene of that accident. I will continue in pursuit of the other vehicle and notify you of my results as they become available. Over," reported Officer Hamilton.

The high-speed chase was on. Patrolman Hamilton quickly deployed his flashing red lights and sounded the siren. The speeding Mercury had a reasonable head start, but it was no match for the newly designed high-pursuit Ford engine he was driving.

The Ford pursued as designed and quickly gained on the fleeing Mercury, but the Mercury seemed to have no intention of slowing much less stopping.

"Come on, man!" said the concerned officer. "Pull over!"

"Albert, there's a police car behind us; maybe he can help," said Eula.

"I'm not stopping. We can deal with him later. I'm going to the hospital, and I'm not stopping until I get there," replied Albert.

The patrol car reached within a few feet of the Mercury's rear bumper, but the driver refused to pull over. That's when Officer Hamilton saw an arm reaching out from the driver's side, signalling to come around.

As the Mercury momentarily slowed its speed, the patrol car pulled up alongside. Without hesitation, Albert held the wheel of the car with his left hand and held the limp baby in his right hand, exposing the blood-soaked handkerchief covering the injured child's head.

Officer Hamilton immediately knew why they weren't stopping—they were rushing that baby to the Aiken Hospital.

Without hesitation, Officer Hamilton pointed straight ahead and shouted, "Follow me!"

The patrol car quickly sped ahead and swerved in front of the speeding Mercury bound for the Aiken Hospital.

"Headquarters, this is car 521. I have made contact with the driver of the speeding vehicle heading north on Highway 1. From what I can tell, an infant child has been seriously injured, and they're trying to get to the hospital as quickly as possible. I am now in front of them, providing a police escort to the emergency department. Please notify the hospital of our situation, as we should arrive within the next few minutes. Over," Officer Hamilton requested.

Albert gathered his composure and closely followed the patrol car to the hospital. The patrol car was going at a speed that Albert had never experienced, but would it be fast enough to save young Leon? All kinds of thoughts rushed through his head. Now he understood by example that those doors his friends thought were so cool, were a potential death trap.

*I'm sure I locked those back doors,* he thought. *I don't know how it could have opened the way it did.*

Although he wasn't to blame, he couldn't get over the fact that it was still his responsibility to protect his only child. But, as hard as he had tried, this one time, he felt like he had somehow failed.

The flashing red lights and the sound of the siren had vehicles clearing the path of the speeding entourage to the hospital. When the hospital came into view, the patrolman saw that medical personnel were anxiously waiting for their arrival.

"We've got an infant child with a head injury and possibly other injuries, yet to be determined," exclaimed a serious-toned Officer Hamilton as he pointed to the Mercury parked just behind him.

"Thank you, officer; we'll take it from here," said one of the waiting medical professionals.

Albert quickly flung the door open and exited the vehicle with the injured child.

A nurse was already moving in his direction and reached with open arms for the bleeding baby.

"I promise, we'll take good care of your baby," she said. "Wait inside, and someone will advise you of his well-being as soon as we have a chance to assess his injuries."

A mentally strained and exhausted Eula hugged her husband, crying for the pain and suffering of her young son. They had no idea how long it would take to hear back from the emergency room personnel and had no way to prepare themselves for what the results would entail, but one thing was for certain; it would surely seem like an eternity before anyone would report back to them.

In the meantime, Officer Hamilton had one final duty to follow up on concerning the accident. He had already heard from headquarters that the scene of the accident had been secured without any further injuries or damages. Before he left the hospital, he took a statement from Albert, and it matched the description that the semi-truck driver, Mr. Biggs, had reported.

"I'm sorry for your son's injuries," said a concerned Officer Hamilton. "I'll continue to pray for his well-being, as well as for peace of mind for you and your wife. I will not be writing up a report for any traffic violations, but I will have to report how all the events transpired. But for now, that's all that I need, so remain here with your wife and hopefully, the doctor will report back soon."

* * *

Minutes turned into hours, as Alfred and Eula sat waiting for someone to give them some information about their son. Then finally, a doctor from the emergency department approached them with Leon's medical condition.

"Hi," I'm Dr. Roberts. "For now, it appears your son is going to be okay. He's in critical but stable condition at this time. Unfortunately, he experienced blunt force trauma to the head and is presently in a coma."

Upon hearing this news, Eula suddenly felt faint. Albert grabbed her and sat her down in a nearby chair.

"Ms. Baughman, are you alright?" asked the doctor. "Nurse, please assess Ms. Baughman's condition and grab a glass of water. She may be dehydrated."

"I know this can be a lot to take in for you, but we're doing all we can do to make your son as comfortable as possible," assured the doctor.

"All his vital signs are normal considering the extent of his injuries," the doctor continued. "X-rays to the head showed slight swelling around the brain, but that is common for a head injury such as his. The blunt force to the head caused a concussion, which causes swelling and therefore, limits the flow of oxygen and blood to the brain. I want to keep him here at the hospital in intensive care so we can observe him as the swelling in the brain subsides. I'm hopeful that as the swelling slowly recedes, he'll make a full, normal recovery. In the meantime, we'll keep you informed as soon as we have any further news to report. By the way, you may visit your son at this time.

"Nurse, please show Mr. and Ms. Baughman to baby Leon's room," requested the doctor."

"Of course. Right this way, please," said the nurse.

Upon seeing little Leon, Eula gasped and held her husband close. A blood-stained gauze bandage encircled his entire head. More bandages and gauze were used to cover his arms, face, and legs. What flesh that could be seen was obscured by road rash and/or bruises.

"This is going to take a long time, isn't it, Albert?" a worried Eula asked.

"Unfortunately, it looks that way, but the doctor seemed very hopeful," Albert encouraged.

Hours at the hospital turned into days, and days turned into weeks. But after almost three weeks, young Leon Everette Baughman was finally well enough to go home to be with his family. The recovery period was cautiously slow, but he had finally gotten back to a normal state of health. All his vital signs were positive. His reflexes were good, his hearing and vision were normal, and his appetite was hungry for his mama's home-cooked meals. Eula couldn't be happier than to go home and cook, as well as to have her entire family home altogether once again.

On the ride home from the hospital, Eula looked down at her precious Leon sitting on the seat situated between her and Albert. He still had minor bruises and scratches to heal, but he looked happy. *Praise God in heaven; he's going to be okay,* she thought in thankful prayer.

As she gazed into his still bruised and somewhat swollen, big blue eyes, she suddenly had a chilling, unnerving sense of warning. She couldn't help the feeling that the accident was some kind of maternal omen—one that would continue to remind her throughout her life that she would recall these series of events as a haunting, unforgettable memory.

Even more worrisome was her strong mother's intuition that this occasion would not be the last for her beloved son and that, regrettably, as hard as she would try, there was nothing in her motherly powers that she could do to always protect him from the unforeseen, potentially dangerous and harmful uncertainties of life.

Unfortunately for Eula, Leon's future daredevil antics and reckless behavior would lead to at least four more near-death experiences before he would reach the age of seventeen years old. But what was a mother to do?

Chapter 2

## The End of the Age of Innocence

Circa 1966

**Age of innocence:** *A time when a person or society exists in a state of childlike simplicity or naivety.* While it may apply to most people, some, of course, never seem to mature at all; they just grow older. The end of the age of innocence is generally accepted as the time when a seventeen-year-old high school student graduates and their twenty-first birthday, the unofficial socially accepted age as a young, mature adult. Most social circles agree that when this stage or phase in life comes about, one's innocence ends, and maturity begins. In simple terms, the innocently irresponsible grow up or evolve to become maturely responsible.

Some might argue that eighteen is the magic number marking the end of innocence. That opinion is well taken, but as previously stated, most sociology experts agree that the end is phased out over time and is not dependent on a hard number date or age. However, they also conclude that we have to consider that, as previously stated, the age of twenty-one is a good, practical biological barometer as a decisive indicator of one's fundamental maturity.

It should be noted that most social studies texts also teach that while a late-term teenager is an age when maturity begins to develop, some may not yet be experienced enough to accept responsibility for not only their social morés but also their personal choices, often resulting in careless or unpredictable behavior that may lead to unforeseen consequences. In other words, during this time, although they think they may "know it all," they do stupid stuff anyway and don't expect to be held responsible.

Having said all of this, there's still an underlying ideological buffer between a late teen and a mature adult—the year twenty. It's kind of like a Mulligan in golf. When playing golf, if you miss a shot, then you can use your Mulligan to do it over again and hope for better results the next time, and it won't count against you. In recreational golf, there is only one Mulligan given per round. There is also only one year twenty, so hypothetically, everyone can make the best of it without some mistakes counting against you because of your "innocence" or "immaturity." It's also during this time that we begin to become soberly mindful that once the scoring in the game of life officially begins, it will indeed be tallied and accounted for in the end.

The twenty-year-old immediately realizes that the world is indeed round and that the air we all breathe is shared across non-existing atmospheric boundaries. They've learned to accept that it's a free world controlled by societal rules and regulations, and by now, they have begun to choose or figure out where they fit in. It's like a wake-up call or a reality check to remind us that childhood and the teen years were fun for the most part, but now life is about to get real and very, very serious.

One quickly begins to realize that from here on out, at some point, they must do this "living-a-life thing" on their own. Either you have already, or you are about to now become the single most responsible person in your life. There's no going back except to recall mistakes you may have made in the past and use them to improve your chances for a better future.

As the hands of time seem unforgiving in their steady, forward momentum and their complete control of each day and night by never stopping, you soon learn that you need to establish a good personal foundation concerning all things related to not only prudent decision-making but also responsible living principles and personal choices.

Furthermore, as one's biological clock also continues to tick, the mysterious number twenty-one predictably approaches. Generally speaking, when twenty-one arrives, your innocent number is up. Socially speaking, from this time forward, your future is determined by the decisions you make and the actions you take to prepare your life for the things to come. You will unconsciously try to convince yourself that you need to grow up quickly. You're still the person you used to be, except now, terms of responsibility rely solely on your social and personal actions and decisions. The world at large can be cruel and unforgiving, but as for you and you alone, it all comes down to how you decide to live in it.

Unfortunately, the biological clock for seventeen-year-old Leon Everette Baughman went against all the usual teachings of high school and college social studies texts. To no fault of his own, his age of innocence would abruptly wind down long before his twenty-first birthday. The end of his age of innocence was not only being defined by a looming biological timeline but even more so by a man-made disaster—the ominous Vietnam War in Southeast Asia.

In 1966, the Vietnam War was as intense as it had ever been, and the need for more fighting bodies grew more demanding by the day. Some, mostly politicians, refused to even call it a war and instead insisted it was *merely* a conflict. Try to convince that narrative to a peace-loving seventeen-year-old boy living in rural South Carolina. You can call it whatever you want, but be it a conflict or a war, people on one side were killing people on another side.

Tens of thousands of innocent American young men were being sent into harm's way for armed combat against their will to fulfill a nominal quota for military warfare in a country most had never even heard of. To compensate for the rise of conscientious objectors and thousands of young men who fled to Canada for political asylum, the United States government was rumored to be planning for a possible military draft lottery based on the birthdate of young men between the ages of eighteen and twenty-six.

As was the case of many young men during this era, Leon's life was at a paradoxical crossroads. Should he take his chances with the impending draft lottery and hope that his number would be one of the last to be called and therefore, potentially not be needed to serve in the war in Vietnam? Or should he volunteer for military service due to his patriotism and love for his country? After all, serving and surviving was a remote possibility. Fleeing to Canada to avoid serving his country was out of the question. Neither would he join those who publicly protested the war and burned draft cards in the streets in front of municipal courthouses.

One can only imagine the emotional pressure and stress placed on a military-eligible young man during this time in our nation's history. None of his options were encouraging. Take a chance on the lottery and hope for a favorable outcome; get drafted by the lottery and serve without a full personal commitment; or do the honorable thing, volunteer for military service out of the love for his country. Either way, the dark thought that loomed in the back of every young man was the possibility of returning home from a crazy Asian war in a thick, black, zipped-up body bag with a name, rank, and serial number identification tag attached to it.

To make matters more complicated for Leon, high school and the world of academia had become less and less desirable. His primary reason for staying in school was his love of playing football. Up until this time, he had been a star running back for the Ridge-Spring-Moneta Highschool football team. His natural ability as a running back allowed him to set the record for the most rushing yards as a true freshman, a record that still stands today. And notwithstanding, there is always the other prominent interest for a young man staying in school—the female classmates. He was as popular with the young ladies as he was with his football teammates, but for different reasons, of course.

Unfortunately for Leon, due to the many moves his family made because of the nature of his father's transient employment, Leon fell behind in his education and had to be academically retained for a couple of years. Now, at seventeen years old and only a high school sophomore, this would be his last season of eligibility for continuing to play high school football because of his age. And without being able to play football, his desire to keep up academically literally failed him.

At just seventeen years old, the social pressures of staying in school and getting a good education and the thought of potentially going to war sent him into a deep, dark, angry state of depression. He became inhospitably mad at the world, and his social behavior began causing significant problems at home, at school, and with some of his closest friends.

His only way out, he thought, was to drop out of school, knowing he would become trapped between the potential of serving his country in an unpopular war and the remote possibility of living his life peacefully and safely on his own terms. But what galled him the most was the fact that the government bureaucracy had an important and potentially final say-so in deciding for him how his immediate future would unfold.

If it weren't for television, Leon may not have even heard of a place called Vietnam. It was so unknown that even the American news outlets were at odds on how to even spell the name of the country—Viet Nam or Vietnam? But the spelling didn't matter; all they seemed to want was an unnerving story from which to draw a viewing audience. Every time he turned the TV on, the war in Vietnam was wall-to-wall news coverage. In many cases, the actual brutality of war was being shown live and the dramatics were real and unscripted. Death, despair, and despondency became the mantra of the mainstream nightly news. At times, the drama was so intense that it became hard to tell if they were presenting the coverage for political purposes or TV ratings. Subsequently, they accomplished both.

For eighteen-year-old young men living in the United States, the morning and evening news played like a horror movie over and over. Having watched the devastating televised scenes night after night and day after day often caused horrific images to become impregnated in the part of the brain that could not become unseen. Watching the cries for mercy and help of a dying or critically injured American soldier and the contrasting shouts of anti-war protests created a perplexing dilemma of what to choose for any military-eligible young man.

To Leon's dismay, his disillusioned mind was full of thoughts that had no cohesion for rational reasoning on how to proceed forward for the betterment of his life. He didn't have any professional technical skills, and if he quit high school, he wouldn't be academically eligible to further his career in a technical college. He soon found himself in a no man's land of opportunity, as the darkest and most distant thought in the back of his mind of joining the military was becoming more and more of an alluring yet unnerving reality.

The end of the school year in 1966 meant a short summer break from the stress of academia that would give Leon time to make important decisions for his immediate future. During this time of despair in his life, the only person he could disclose his inner feelings to was his girlfriend, Kathy. They discussed all his options, and their love for one another finally led to a life-changing decision: he would quit high school, join the military, then get married after boot camp.

To them, they had figured out this "living-a-life thing" all by themselves. All their problems in the world had been solved with one (ah-hmm) thought-provoking decision. (I'm sure by now that you're thinking about the aforementioned dialogue about teenagers thinking they "know it all" but do stupid stuff anyway. Well, there you go.)

Mid-August meant pre-season high school football practice, and Leon wanted to make it his best season yet, as the possibility of quitting school was certainly a good likelihood. The coach was impressed by his hard-hitting, fast-running, and athletic fortitude. He'd never seen this type of energy from Leon before, but he liked what he was seeing. Little did he know, but Leon's inner frustration was the motivation for his seeming passion for hard-nosed football. Every time he touched the ball, he knew that this would be his last season, and he was going to make the most of it and enjoy it to its fullest potential.

During the fall of 1966, Leon finally reached his limit on anxiety, depression, and just plain outright frustration with the direction his life was going. He desperately needed a change, anything that would snap him out of the domineering doldrums controlling his everyday activity. So, about halfway through the football season, Leon and two of his high school friends decided to join the Navy on the "Buddy Plan." His two friends were seniors, and, like Leon, neither of them had any personal incentives for them to stay in school. As with Leon, the emotional stress of potentially having to go to war after graduating high school played an important role in their decision-making process. By signing up on the Buddy Plan, they would all go to boot camp together and then be assigned to their next duty station as determined by the Navy. For now, however, they would all keep it a secret between themselves until the last game of the football season was over.

Knowing that he would not be eligible to play high school football anymore, Leon left the football fieldhouse for the last time after the final game of the season. As much as he loved football, he knew that it would never be a special part of his life anymore. He felt so disheartened that he never even went back to turn his football equipment back in. It was also the last time that he would set foot on the school grounds, as he had now joined the Navy and was to report to boot camp in December to begin serving his country at the tender age of just seventeen years old.

He was now socially unoccupied and occupationally unemployed. He now had all the time in the world in his hands. But after a few days, he found a second-shift job at the Regal Textile Company in Johnston, SC, as a sewing machine mechanic. However, the people at Regal were unaware that he would only be there for a short term, and that the Navy would be notifying him in a matter of weeks of his obligation to report for boot camp.

In a surprise decision by the Department of the Navy, the three "Buddies" were given orders to report separately. No explanation was given, and there was no recourse for the three "Buddies" to refute the decision. One was told to report in December, another (Leon) was to report in January, and a third of the trio was to report in February.

Leon said his final goodbyes on January 24, 1967, as he headed for the Columbia, SC airport. There, he boarded a plane to Chicago, IL, before his final destination to the Navy Recruit Training Command, Great Lakes, in North Chicago, IL. At just seventeen years old, his age of innocence was officially over. His Naval recruit boot camp training would convince him of that daily for at least the next eight weeks.

Chapter 3

**Boot Camp**

**The long flight** to Chicago was mostly calm and uneventful for most of the trip. Then, about halfway into the flight, the captain made a potentially troubling announcement over the plane's PA system:

*Ladies and gentlemen, this is your captain speaking. We're getting severe weather reports from the O'Hare International Aviation Tower in Chicago that a possibly severe snowstorm is predicted to hit about the same time we make our landing. For safety purposes, please buckle your seat belts for the remainder of the flight. Also, please limit your movements inside the cabin for emergency purposes only. In addition, we may encounter some turbulence before landing, so put all portable personal items in a safe and secure location. As of right now, the landing strip has been cleared and is deemed safe for landing. I will notify you if there are any further developments. Thank you for your cooperation and for choosing Delta as your preferred flight carrier.*

Most of the plane's air route was primarily above the clouds where the sun was shining clear and bright. But the further north the plane flew, the more the blue skies turned to a sheep's wool white.

By the time the plane made its descent to O'Hare International Airport, it looked as if someone had covered the whole plane in a bright white fitted bed sheet. Visibility was zero throughout the challenging descent. Without a doubt, the pilot had to rely on instrument panel controls and constant contact with the aviation tower to make the plane's landing a safe one. Thankfully, the plane struck the runway with little disturbance to the passengers and slowly made its way to the terminal safely.

Leon disembarked the plane and joined a small group of other Naval recruits inside the concourse waiting area that were being assembled by a representative from Camp Berry. After a brief introduction and welcome, they were told that the roads were all closed due to a massive snowstorm that had hit the area. For the time being, there was no incoming or outgoing traffic to and from the airport. They were also told that their flight was one of the last planes taking off or landing at O'Hare, as well as the runway was now declared unsafe due to the unexpected accumulation of snow and icy conditions. Everyone in Leon's group had made it to Chicago just in time.

Little did anyone know at the time, but this wasn't just a regular seasonal snowfall. This storm was so severe that it would become known as the worst snowstorm in the history of Chicago—The Chicago Blizzard of 1967. It was rated as category 5, the highest rating for snowstorms as recorded by the National Weather Service.

Northern Chicago had been hit with an unprecedented record-dept of twenty-three inches of snow. The storm was a full-blown blizzard with 50 mph-plus northeast wind gusts creating drifts as high as 15 feet. The storm played havoc with all forms of travel from home to work and school. Because its severity had not been forecast by the local weather outlets, thousands became stranded in offices, schools, city buses, and other forms of transit. About 50,000 abandoned cars and 800 Chicago Transit Unit buses littered the streets and expressways.

The mayor of Chicago officially declared that the city was to be shut down for the safety of the citizens. Chicago's fleet of 500 snowplows and 2,500 workers was out in full force, and additional snow removal equipment was sent from Iowa, Wisconsin, and Michigan. Their efforts would seemingly be in vain as the blizzard continued its continual accumulation of snowdrift after snowdrift, often covering passageways that had previously been safely cleared for travel.

Meanwhile, like everyone else inside the airport passenger waiting area, Leon and the other recruits were stranded as well. While everyone else had the freedom to come and go anywhere inside the terminal, the recruits were confined to one small waiting area and only had permission to go to the restroom and get something to eat.

As the snow continued to fall and accumulate, they had no way of knowing how long they would be stranded. Then, after two miserable days of waiting out the storm, some of the roadways were declared travel-worthy, and the Navy sent a shuttle bus to pick up the recruits and take them to their destination, Camp Berry.

For the most part, Leon's scheduled eight weeks of boot camp went off without a hitch. His transformation from a boy without a cause to a man determined to have something to be proud of was going in a positive direction as he passed every daily challenge of the strenuous demands of the Navy's boot camp protocol.

Then, in the eighth and final week of training, his platoon practiced their marching routines and made final preparations all week for their weekend graduation. Unfortunately for Leon, before the week ended, another recruit provoked him into a fight, and it got seriously nasty. Leon had never started a fight in his life, but neither would he back down from someone who pushed him beyond the brink of his patience.

When the two recruits were separated, the Recruit Division Commander (RDC) investigated the brawl. There are violations of the Naval Code of Conduct that allow minimal corrective action, but fighting was not one of them. Leon and the other recruit were both disqualified from graduation and sent to the Naval "Mickey Mouse House" for two weeks of disciplinary punishment.

The Mickey Mouse House was a term used by the Navy as a place to temporarily house insubordinate recruits. But it was no playland and it certainly wasn't used for fun and pleasure. Wayward recruits, including serial troublemakers, those being disrespectful to their RDC, all-around goof-offs, and others were among some of the recruits Leon would join as he settled into his new training environment.

This small group of recruits would receive harsh punishment night and day for two weeks, including extended exercise regimens, kitchen police duties, forced marching, shoveling snow, cleaning floors, walls, etc., as well as additional naval drills and other punitive forms of physical and psychological punishment. The methods used to punish noncompliant recruits were not considered torturing, but they were, however, brutally effective both physically and emotionally.

Leon and the other recruit were escorted to the Mickey Mouse House by their RDC. As Leon neared the facility, he was immediately confronted by his new, temporary RDC.

"Well, well, well. What have we here, new meat?" asked the new RDC.

"He's all yours," said Leon's former RDC.

"Thank you," said the new RDC. "I'll take over from here."

The new RDC leaned into Leon's face and began his powerfully vocal introduction.

"Let me tell you, right now, Baughman, this is my house,

this is my street, and this is my neighborhood, and you don't belong here. Do you understand me?" asked the RDC.

"Yes, sir," said a nervously shaken Leon.
"Shut up, recruit. I do all the talking here," said the RDC. "Do I make myself clear?"

"Yes, sir," said a confused Leon.

"What did I just say, recruit?" asked the RDC. "Drop down and give me fifty push-ups right now. I'll be back in five to check on you."

Leon finished all fifty of his push-ups, but little did he know at the time that from here on out, this conversation would be cordial compared to the verbal abuse he was about to experience during his stay at the Mickey Mouse House.

After two grueling weeks of corrective action, Leon completed his stay at the Mickey Mouse House and was reassigned to a new platoon. His original platoon had graduated without him, and now he would be assigned to another platoon that had only two more weeks before their graduation.

Although Leon had endured the punishment at the Mickey Mouse without incident, he still had a lot of negative energy. Now, he was not only mad at the world but, more specifically, at the Navy as well. Not being one for having restraint over his aggressive nature, before his final two weeks were up Leon was sent back to the Mickey Mouse House for a second time for fighting with another recruit. It's not clear exactly what happened, but it was probably in part due to Leon's hot-headed temperament and his lack of self-control.

Upon his second arrival at the Mickey Mouse House, Leon didn't need to be introduced to the RDC in charge. When the RDC saw him approaching, he ran toward Leon, got into his face again and began a rant that could be heard from blocks away.

"Baughman, is that you again? What are you doing on my street? Why are you back in my neighborhood? Didn't I tell you that you don't belong in my house?" yelled the RDC.

"Well, I guess you must like shoveling snow, cleaning toilets, and swabbing and waxing floors. Well, I've saved some for a-holes like you and plenty more. Now, drop down and give me fifty right now," barked the RDC.

Leon once again completed his fifty push-ups, but this time, he knew what was in store for the next two weeks, and he wasn't looking forward to it.

Two weeks later, Leon was released from the Mickey Mouse House and transferred to another platoon that had just two weeks left before their graduation. Things went well for Leon for most of his final two weeks. However, the evening before graduation day, some of the recruits got into a playful, friendly pillow fight. Leon was careful not to get involved, as he was ready to get boot camp behind him. As he sat peacefully on his footlocker at the end of his bunk, shining his shoes, one of the recruits sneaked up behind him and clobbered him in the back of the head with a tightly wrapped pillow. Leon didn't hesitate as he ran the recruit down and began beating him until the RDC pulled him away.

Needless to say, the RDC was not happy with either of his recruits. They were just *hours away* from graduating from boot camp. All the RDC had taught them for the past two months was to always follow orders and stay out of trouble. For the most part, they had followed orders and were obedient recruits, but now they would have to pay a penalty for their momentary lack of discipline by not controlling their reckless emotions.

With less than fourteen hours to go, Leon would miss his third chance to graduate from boot camp. Instead, he would be ordered to serve a third round of penal duty at the dreaded Mickey Mouse House. For a third time, Leon was escorted to the Mickey Mouse House.

Once again, as the RDC in charge saw him coming, he met him before he reached the steps to the house.

"Baughman, do you like my street? Do you like my neighborhood? Do you like my house? Why are you back here again?I told you, you're not welcome here. Did you not understand me?" barked the RDC.

"Sir, yes sir," replied Leon.

"Oh, I see now," said the RDC, "You must like me. Do you like me, Baughman? Is that why you keep coming back? I must not be doing my job properly because if I was, you wouldn't be here, would you?"

"Sir, no sir," replied Leon.

"Well, since you like it here so much, I'll consider giving you double duty starting right now. Do I make myself clear?" asked the RDC.

"Sir, yes sir," replied Leon.

"Aw, just shut up and drop down and give me a hundred," demanded the RDC.

Later that week, the RDC entered the barracks area, where six disciplinary recruits stood at attention upon his arrival.

"Any of you scum bags like to drive trucks?" he asked. "I need three volunteers to go with me to the company headquarters building to do some hauling for the Admiral. Give me a show of hands. Who wants to volunteer?"

They all looked around in amazement as each one raised their hand. Who wouldn't rather be driving a truck? It was better than scrubbing floors and cleaning toilets, they all thought.

"Okay, Alverez, Marcelli, and Baughman, you're my drivers. Come with me," said the RDC. "The rest of you dirtbags fall in. You're coming as well."

As they arrived at the company headquarters building, sure enough, there was a dump truck and a pick-up truck parked in the street across from the company headquarters building.

"Ok," barked the RDC, "I need each of you to retrieve a shovel and my three drivers grab a wheelbarrow out of the back of that pick-up truck and report back to me. Now! Move it!"

After the three designated drivers got their respective wheelbarrows and everyone had their shovels, they immediately reported back to the RDC. Without hesitation, the RDC barked out and ordered, "Start shoveling the snow from the sidewalk leading to the steps of the headquarters building. Clean off those steps, and when you finish that, shovel the sidewalks all around this block, wheel it over to the dump truck, and load it up. I need this cleaned up before the Admiral returns. Do you understand?"

"Sir, yes sir!" they all replied.

"Oh," said the RDC to his "drivers," "Did you really expect to be driving a truck? I just asked if anyone liked to drive a truck. Recruits don't drive trucks; they drive wheelbarrows. Now get this snow off of my sidewalk before the Admiral gets back!"

The next two weeks were harsh and miserable, but young Leon made it without any incidents and was then reassigned to yet another platoon that had just two weeks remaining on their boot camp calendar. Leon was extra careful this time, as he followed orders, obeyed every command, and went out of his way to stay out of trouble. He was determined that this time, he was going to make it. He'd had enough of Naval boot camp, and he'd had more than his share of the Mickey Mouse House. This time, he was going to graduate!

He not only made it through graduation, but he also set a record at the time for the most number of weeks at the Navy's Mickey Mouse House (6 weeks), as well as the most number of weeks in naval boot camp history (14 weeks). His immature, Mickey Mouse-like behavior was over. His teenage innocence was forever gone. The immature, self-centered Leon, who entered the Navy as a young, naive boy, was now a graduate recruit and proud member of one of the most powerful fighting forces in the world.

He was now eagerly excited and ready to face his next Naval

challenge. As for his future outlook on life, well you might say his attitude was now "all on board", his mindset was in "ship-shape", and his next mission in life was now prepared for "anchors aweigh" for "smooth sailing" to his next naval destination.

Chapter 4

**The Sound of Music**

**On the long flight** home after graduating from Naval boot camp, Leon finally had some time to himself to clear his head about the decisions he had to make concerning his immediate and long-term plans. His initial plan was to spend eight weeks at boot camp, come home and get married, then continue his career as assigned by the Navy. However, his lengthy boot camp stay and the emotional trauma that he endured during those fourteen strenuous weeks had given him pause as to how to proceed when he returned home.

Upon his arrival at Columbia Metropolitan Airport, he was greeted by family and friends, including his fiancé, Kathy. They all immediately noticed something very different about not only his outward appearance but also his calm, quiet composure. Here now stood a lean, clean, but not so mean eighteen-year-old man that they hardly recognized but were happy and very proud of the improved transition that he'd made since they last saw him.

The following day, when Leon and Kathy finally had some quality time together, he didn't waste any time telling her that he had decided not to get married while on leave. It was a difficult decision because he knew how excited Kathy was and how happy she was thinking they were getting married in just a few short days. The last thing he wanted to do was break her heart, but for his and her well-being, he decided that it would be best to put his personal matters on hold by taking more time to assess his immediate and long-term needs, as he still had a significant amount of training waiting for him when he reported to his next Naval destination.

Kathy was heartbroken and upset, to say the least, but after a short while, she became more understanding and agreed with his decision. He had been through a lot since she had last seen him. She could tell by his new, unfamiliar demeanor that he was a new and improved version of the Leon she was engaged to before he left for boot camp. For the betterment of their present and future relationship, she agreed that it was in their best interest to postpone the wedding. Though she was disappointed in his decision, she would continue to support him in whatever it took to maintain their relationship.

After completing his leave, Leon reported to Fighter Squadron VF-121 at Naval Air Station (NAS) Miramar, California, to train for his military occupation specialty (MOS).

NAS Miramar is located about 14 miles north of San Diego. In 1986 there was a movie made there about the elite pilots who trained there and who, upon their graduation, using Naval slang, were called *Top Guns*. During his tenure at VF-121, he took intensive classroom and hands-on training for several months to become a certified Naval Aviation Electrician.

After successfully graduating as a Naval Aviation Electrician, Leon decided it was time for him and Kathy to get married. However, he was financially unable to afford to have her flown out to California, so he decided to make an important personal sacrifice. He would have his father, Al, sell his prized, turquoise 1957 Chevrolet Belair automobile, as well as his beloved horse, Blaze, to finance Kathy's flight and to also help in supporting their new marital beginnings.

Shortly after her arrival, Leon and Kathy were happily married in Coronado, CA. Then, in a surprise development, and after just three months of marriage, Leon was ordered to deploy to Vietnam. To make the situation more stressful for the young couple, during his last week in California, Kathy became pregnant, and she and Leon found themselves in a predicament beyond their control. With little time to spare, they immediately began making plans for her return to South Carolina and his deployment to Vietnam.

Needless to say, it was a very difficult time for both of them. Kathy would have to manage her pregnancy and deliver her baby without Leon's help and emotional support. And Leon would have the added pressure of feeling guilty for not being able to be there for Kathy, in addition to the emotional stress of focusing on his duty as a wartime sailor in Vietnam.

Shortly after Leon deployed to Vietnam, Leon's dad, Al, flew out to California and helped Kathy pack her possessions. Together, they loaded all her belongings into Leon's Volkswagen Beetle and a U-Haul trailer, after which they drove back home to South Carolina, where Kathy would be reunited with her parents until Leon's return home.

At the same time, Leon was aboard a Naval warship, the USS Coral Seas, full steam ahead, cruising toward the perilous waters off the coast of Southeast Asia—Vietnam. As he was getting acclimated to his new living quarters and working environment, Leon and his fellow sailors spent a lot of their time doing combat drills and exercises, as well as other Naval duties, to keep them mentally and physically prepared.

The cruise to the Tonkin Gulf would take anywhere between two weeks and a month, depending on strategic decisions made by the naval command headquarters. Nevertheless, the Navy made sure that their sailors and marines were very well-preoccupied throughout the entire journey.

The audible ambiance aboard the USS Coral Seas aircraft carrier was like a smorgasbord of sounds. No matter what time of day or night, complete silence and relaxed serenity were rare indulgences. The blare of PA system announcements, F4-Phantom jets taking off and landing, ocean waves crashing against the ship's side, the low-frequency mechanical hum of motorized machinery, and occasional laughter amid controlled rowdiness, are just a few of the never-ending sounds that contributed to the orchestra of noise in the thoughts and minds of every idling sailor.

One afternoon, while taking a break, Leon heard an out-of-place noise that caught his attention. After a short while, the sound became steady and louder.

*Now, what could that be?* he wondered.

It continued to tease his curiosity as there was nothing ship-related sounding about it, whatsoever. As he sat up on the side of his bunk, he looked down the long passageway to his left and saw a couple of men two compartments away rhythmically swaying. His curiosity finally got the better of him and as he slowly moved toward the direction of the sound, he realized what he was hearing was the sound of music.

The closer he got, the more pronounced the music rang out. He soon recognized that what he was hearing was the sound of a guitar, a banjo, and a laptop steel guitar playing. As he finally entered the compartment, he saw three fellow sailor musicians smiling, swaying, and strumming their instruments in a tanta-lizing musical harmony. The song was a familiar one and reminded him of having heard it many times on a local radio station back home. Then, after a brief instrumental session, one of the trio members began singing the lyrics to Glen Campbell's "Gentle on My Mind."

He recalled a time when DJs on the radio were discussing how the song was made popular by Glen Campbell in 1967 and how unusual it was that it was liked by almost anyone who'd heard it, yet the Adult Contemporary Music industry had the only chart that rated it in the top ten, peaking at number eight. Regardless, it was a huge crossover hit including easy listening, folk, country, and other genres of music of the American top forty.

The smooth-sounding vocals of a sailor named Terry Smith, along with the captivating instrumental accompaniment, struck Leon like a snared fish on a line. The more they played, the more he wanted to hear. These guys were having a really good time, and at the same time, making everyone around them less anxious and more at ease than they had ever been since being deployed to Vietnam. Little did he know at the time, but Leon would be hooked on music from that moment on. This initial exposure to musical entertainment, as simple as it was, would be the spark that would one day ignite the flame of his blazing musical career in the years to come.

Leon had always been a music lover from listening to songs that he'd heard on the radio, but this was the first time that he'd been exposed to it close up and in person. This style of hands-on playing music was entirely different from what he was used to, but boy was he loving it. The vibes from hearing the music and watching the musicians play seemed to be affecting everyone around with joyful emotions and positive reactions.

After a short while, Leon began to appreciate the music even more as he realized that he was not only hearing the music by ear, but somehow, he could feel it deep down in his soul, as well. He recalled times when he felt that something was missing in his life, and for now, this unexpected musical experience had the potential to fill that empty void.

As the days passed and they got closer to their destination, Leon felt a growing sense of excitement resulting from his brief but exhilarating exposure to what music can do to enlighten one's outlook on life. The thrill of watching the comradery of the musicians and their joyful expressions resulting from the fun they were having as they played their instruments gave him a wanting desire to do the same.

Leon's passion for learning how to play a musical instrument soon became obvious to the musical trio. He attended every possible musical session, and the trio recognized his desire to learn and agreed to invite him to join the fun. Since he wasn't a skilled musician, he decided to play along by slapping his knees, banging on the walls, or on anything that had a drum-like resonance to create a tempo. As simple as this may sound, it proved to be very advantageous, as he quickly learned to develop an artful style of rhythm of his own.

Leon was justifiably nervous yet joyfully appreciative as he began to hang out with his new musical friends at every available opportunity. Terry Smith graciously took Leon under his wing and began teaching him simple guitar licks and chords. It was a little intimidating at first, as Leon had never learned to play a musical instrument, but learning how to play the guitar was now becoming an unbridled passion. He began by learning simple finger positions on the guitar neck and strings, strumming along to the rhythm of the songs as he played them in his head. Then, after hours of dedicated practice, he slowly began learning how to master his finger coordination from simple guitar riffs to simple, cohesive song chords.

One day, as Leon was practicing alone with a borrowed guitar, he began singing a song in a low audible tone that he'd taught himself called "Love Me Tender," by Elvis Presley. Learning to play the song on his own gave him a much-needed boost in his confidence. He had been practicing as often as he could and it was beginning to show, as his finger positions on the guitar were almost perfect by now. He continued playing the guitar while softly crooning under his breath to the melody:

> *Love me tender, love me sweet,*
> *never let me go.*
> *You have made my life complete,*
> *and I love you so.*

As he sat on the side of his bunk, he began to quietly sing soulfully and confidently to himself. With his eyes now closed and his thoughts concentrating on the musical chords, he continued singing the melody while strumming the guitar with perfect hand-to-string coordination. Then, when he came to the final chorus, he was so intensely preoccupied with the song that his low-key voice suddenly sounded out loud with a dramatically passionate,

> *Love me tender, love me true,*
> *make all my dreams fulfilled.*
> *For my darlin', I love you,*
> *and I always will.*

As he slowly completed the final strum to the melody, he opened his eyes only to find an elated gathering of fellow sailors standing all around hollering and clapping in joyful jubilation as in celebration of their newly found vocal talent.

"Well, boys, it looks like the trio just officially became a quartet! We've got ourselves a new singer!" shouted one of the musical trio members.

Leon responded shyly but joyfully elated. It didn't dawn on him at the time, but this was his first performance before a live audience. The thrill of being an entertainer, even at this level, was so satisfying and exhilarating that he could hardly contain his urge for more of the same.

Over time, his confidence to sing out openly grew stronger as did his musical skills. His popularity among his fellow sailors was also growing in numbers beyond the small clique of musicians due to their fascination with his unique vocal style.

He was now a bonafide member of the band and spent every opportunity practicing and playing along with them. But he sensed that all was not perfect. The singing and guitar playing were fun, but he began to notice that he was a mover and a shaker. He wanted to shake, rattle, and roll, but the confined quarters of the ship prohibited him from doing so. It was difficult at times, but for the most part, he learned to bridle his emotional energy and made the best of an already positive experience. Nevertheless, he was content and having fun passing time with his new friends as the ship continued to carve its watery path toward the unpredictable waters of the Tonkin Gulf.

Chapter 5

## Olongapo

**When they finally** arrived and dropped anchor off the coast of Vietnam, the attitude of all aboard became more serious and combat-ready, as they were now officially in wartime mode in the middle of the enemy's territorial waters. The quartet's practice time together was now very limited, but they still gathered at every available opportunity. Fortunately, there were no combat-related issues that directly resulted in danger to those aboard the USS Coral Seas for the duration of their stay.

Finally, after six long months of tense emotional stress, the ship's crew members were granted an eight-day furlough for R and R, or rest and recreation. Leon and the rest of the quartet soon learned that their port of call would be Olongapo City, Philippines, which was about one thousand miles as a crow flies from the Gulf of Tonkin. The quartet agreed to stay together as a unit during their time at Olongapo, as traveling alone in a foreign country would be less adventurous as well as potentially more dangerous. Besides, none of the sailors had had a drink of liquor or any kind of alcohol since boarding the ship, and they expected to be heavily intoxicated once they got on dry land and between the four of them. Hopefully, at least one of them would be sober enough to make sure they returned to the base safely and on time.

After arriving at the Philippine naval base and having settled in their quarters, the quartet changed into civilian clothing and headed out for the dry land of the city of Olongapo. The first thing they saw as they left the base was a bridge that crossed what was known as the "Shit River" that connected the base to Olongapo. The river was a stagnant, barely flowing open sewage waterway that emptied into the nearby Subic Bay. Almost immediately after leaving the base, the smell was so bad that it was all they could do to keep from gagging. Even more disgusting were small boats floating along the waterway, with young boys diving in to retrieve coins tossed by the passing sailors and marines.

Upon arriving at the city limits of Olongapo there was an endless row of nightclubs and small business establishments on each side of the busy streets. The nightlife was much like a carnival atmosphere, specifically for adults only, including countless beautiful women walking along the streets and in clubs everywhere. To their delight, the overall atmosphere was more like a combination of a "sailors Disneyland" and an "oriental Las Vegas" without all the casinos.

No matter where you went, loud music blasted from every open doorway. At night, neon lights flashed on and off, lighting up the skyline, and the continuous sound of motorized vehicles constantly blowing their horns could be heard as if they were synchronized like a musical composition. The smell of spicy food filled the air with tantalizing aromas. And as you might expect, occasionally drunken sailors and marines could be found engaged in barroom brawls along the way at any given time.

After a long walk familiarizing themselves with Olongapo, the sailors decided to stop by a nightclub for a drink before returning to base. They didn't have to walk very far to find one, as there was one on every street and corner.

In addition to all the beautiful women, one thing sailors would always remember about Olongapo was its nightclub bands. No matter what club you visited, the quality of live music was immaculate. Although the singers would speak in a normal Asian accent, when they sang on stage, they sounded just like the original artist, no matter what culture or musical genre they came from. From Buck Owens to James Brown to The Beatles, they not only sounded just like the original artists, but they also mimicked their movements, as well.

It wasn't uncommon for a drunken sailor or marine to stagger to the stage and join in the fun by singing along with the club's band. On this occasion, an inebriated Leon and his friends did just that. After having more than a few drinks and after being entertained by the music of the club band, Leon abruptly stumbled to the stage and quietly spoke something to the band's lead singer. The band leader shook his head in agreement with whatever Leon had discussed and then went to all the other band members and quietly spoke something to each of them. Then, without hesitation, Leon grabbed a microphone, stood center stage, and motioned for the rest of his friends to join him on stage. As they staggered to the stage, Leon told them that they were going to sing a song and what else would a group of drunken sailors would say to that, except "okay".

Leon was so full of liquid courage that he couldn't control his excitement. All he wanted to do was show out and sing. This was his opportunity to release all the emotional energy that he had stored while singing aboard the USS Coral Seas. This time, he was going to sing, and he wasn't going to have to hold anything back. After making sure everyone on stage was ready, Leon spoke into the microphone and introduced his group.

"We're the USS Coral Seas Quartet," Leon drunkenly slurred, "and we'd like to do a song for you. If you know the words, feel free to sing along with us."

Then, right on cue, the band struck up a high-energy, clean sound of Credence Clearwater Revival's "Bad Moon Arising."

With the microphone in hand, Leon immediately took control of the stage, dancing and moving back and forth from one side to the other and then out into the audience. The other band members laughed and sang along, all the while giving him their support and encouragement. At the end of the song, the packed crowd stood in unison, applauding, yelling, and clapping, showing their appreciation for his performance.

Leon and his friends returned to their table and continued cracking jokes, laughing, drinking, and having more fun than they had had since joining the Navy. For a short while, Leon was pleasantly interrupted by sailors, marines, and beautiful women coming by to thank him and congratulate him on his spontaneous performance. A few of the ladies even asked him for his autograph, which he graciously wrote on a paper napkin at his table.

After the club band played a few more songs, the band's lead singer approached Leon and provoked him into doing another song. After a quiet discussion with the club band members, Leon agreed to sing not one but two more songs before going back to the base. For his first song, he captured the audience by their heart with a slow-dance song called "Can't Help Falling In Love." For his last song, he sang a fast-paced rock and roll song called "Jailhouse Rock," both by Elvis Presley.

The house lights were dimmed, leaving a sole spotlight shining on a spherical mirror ball, setting the mode for the upcoming song. Couples quickly flocked to the dance floor as Leon started singing "Can't Help Falling In Love." By now, Leon was either comfortable with performing or too inebriated to know any better. At one point, he ventured out into the table section where couples were sitting. As he held out his hand to ask a young lady to dance, a sailor sitting next to her abruptly stood in protest, but Leon quickly assured him that it was all in fun. After a short time of dancing, he returned the young lady to her table and politely motioned to her date as if to thank him for understanding, all the while continuing to sing.

Just over halfway from finishing the song, he went from table to table, grabbing paper napkins and wiping sweat from his forehead, then giving it to a swooning oriental beauty mesmerized by his natural charm and enchanting vocals.

When the song ended, he returned to the stage, and the band immediately struck up a high-energy version of "Jailhouse Rock." Without hesitation, Leon was all over the stage and out into the audience, singing with the passion of a rock star. And after the song was over, to his and his friend's delight, the crowd went wild.

As Leon returned to his table, one of his friends congratulated him and said, "Man, not only can you sing, but you can also entertain, as well! You're a natural-born performer, Leon!"

"You know what I think?" asked Leon.

"What's that?" asked his friend.

"I think you're probably just drunk, as am I," replied Leon. "I am only trying to have a fun time. It just so happened that everyone else is as drunk as I am and seemed to enjoy it as much as I did, but thank you anyway."

"I might be drunk," said his friend, "but I know what I just saw and heard. I seriously think you've got talent that you didn't even know you had. You've got the vocals down pat; all you need to do is learn how to perfect your guitar playing, and you might be able to do something special with your talent after your time in the Navy is over."

After an adventurous night out on the town, the tired, drunken foursome staggered their way back to the base safely and on time. The "lights out" announcement had long been announced well before their return.

When they awoke the next morning, they were still dressed in their civilian clothes, beer stains and all. But the previous evening would surely be a night to recall for each one of them, that is, if they hadn't gotten too drunk to remember.

The next day, after recovering from a hangover, Leon thought about what his friend had said the night before about perfecting his guitar skills. If he was serious about learning to play the guitar, then he needed to buy a guitar of his own. Later that afternoon, he and Terry Smith went back to Olongapo and found a musical instrument store. By this time, he was running low on money and couldn't afford anything expensive, so he found a nice beginner's guitar for a whopping twelve dollars. It wasn't much, but at least he didn't have to depend on borrowing someone else's anymore.

After R and R at Olongapo, Leon finished out his first tour of Vietnam in the Tonkin Gulf. As a 3$^{rd}$ Class Aviation Electrician, Leon remained steadfastly devoted to fulfilling his responsibility to service the complex electrical systems of F4-Phantom fighter jets and helicopters flying to and from Da Nang and the USS Coral Seas. Occasionally, he would have to fly by helicopter over enemy territory to service-disabled jets on the ground at the Da Nang aviation field. Although he was never involved in direct physical combat, the sounds of war and the visual memories of the casualties he witnessed remain with him to this day.

He was very fortunate that his first tour of Vietnam ended without incident, considering he was in a geographical location of one of the most dangerous places on planet Earth.

Finally, after thirteen stressful months, his tour of duty was over, and the USS Coral Seas was ordered to report back to NAS Miramar naval station in California. The thought of finally being able to go home was more than ecstatic, as he was not only going home to be with his wife but also his one-month-old daughter, Tammy, whom he had never met.

During the long cruise back to the United States, the mood and atmosphere aboard the ship were much more relaxed and unnerving. The quartet was able to spend more time together practicing their music, and Leon spent every opportunity to hone his guitar skills.

Then, one day, an announcement was made that anyone or

group that wanted to participate in a talent contest could do so on a given day. When the quartet heard the announcement, they immediately began rehearsing. After many hours of practicing, the quartet not only entered but won the talent contest, singing of all songs "I've Got a Tiger by The Tail" by Buck Owens.

Leon and the quartet's popularity grew exponentially after almost every sailor aboard the USS Coral Seas witnessed their winning performance. Little did they know at the time, but for now, they knew him as 3$^{rd}$ Class Aircraft Electrician Baughman, but in the years to come, they would come to know him as country music superstar, Leon Everette.

Chapter 6


**The G-Strain**


**As part of** his duty as a Navy Aircraft Electrician at NAS Miramar, Leon would occasionally have to go out to the aircraft storage and maintenance hangar and climb inside the Navy's F-4 Phantom fighter jets to perform routine electrical maintenance and diagnostic testing to ensure the craft's electronics were in a safe and operable condition. During one inspection, he noticed that someone had vomited inside the passenger, technically known as the Radar Intercept Officer (RIO) compartment of the aircraft.

"Look at this crap," he complained. "Why hasn't someone cleaned this mess up by now? What a wuss! If he can't hold it in, then he shouldn't be flying. I've serviced fighter jets in Vietnam and aboard the USS Coral Seas, but this squadron has more wimps than any military base I've ever seen."

Almost immediately, Leon was approached by a Top Gun pilot named Commander Jumper from York, SC., who overheard him complaining as he walked by the aircraft that Leon was servicing.

"Hey, sailor," said CMDR. Jumper, "This baby about ready to fly?"

Having been caught by surprise, Leon noticed the three commander bars on the approaching officer's uniform, stopped what he was doing, and quickly stood at attention and saluted him before answering.

As Leon stood at attention, the commander immediately noticed the name "Baughman" sewn on his uniform. He'd heard about a "hot shot," mouthy, 3$^{rd}$ class aviation electrician from his home state of South Carolina named Baughman and was pleasantly surprised to finally meet him. Baughman was known for his hot-headed, cocky attitude among his peers and was always making fun of volunteer co-pilots who became extremely airsick on their first training flight aboard an F-4 Phantom jet.

"No, sir, Commander," replied Leon as he completed his salute, "she won't be ready until someone cleans this mess up. I don't think you want to fly her while she's in this condition. The smell is disgusting! I don't know why they keep letting people with weak stomachs fly these things."

"Yeah, I know what you mean," replied CMDR Jumper, "but it's not uncommon for first-time volunteer aircraft electricians who want to get a flight certification to get airsick. Getting the certification looks good on your military record and can also be beneficial in future promotions, which means more money and potentially more privileges."

"Where are you from?" asked the commander.

"Ward, South Carolina, sir," answered Leon.

"The reason I asked is that I recognized your southern accent. I'm also from South Carolina. York, to be exact," replied the commander. "It's nice to meet you."

"Nice to meet you, as well, sir," said Leon.

Little did Leon know, but CMDR Jumper had been waiting for the opportunity to get Leon in his aircraft for a test flight demonstration for some time. He'd just never had the right time to do so. He was using this encounter to bait him into considering volunteering to fly with him so he could knock Leon down a notch or two from his mouthy, cocky attitude. Besides, he didn't appreciate a fellow South Carolinian disrespecting other Naval personnel with his brash attitude.

As their conversation continued, Leon thought to himself about what the commander had said about being promoted and making more money. If all you had to do was volunteer to fly in the backseat of a phantom jet with no qualifications whatsoever, then why not volunteer? What did he have to lose, he wondered, and what could possibly go wrong? This man is a Top Gun. Besides, he wasn't a wuss like some of the others who'd volunteered.

"How does an aircraft electrician go about volunteering to fly, sir?" asked Leon.

"Do you have someone in mind?" asked the CMDR.

"Yes sir, me," said Leon.

"I don't know. This is not for everyone. You've already seen what a wuss can do to a cockpit. It takes a special skill set to fly back there. Do you think you're up to it?" he asked.

In his usual mouthy, cocky way, Leon responded, "I know I'm up to it. I've ridden the biggest and badest roller coaster in the southeastern United States at Myrtle Beach a bunch of times, and I don't see how this could be any worse than that. I just don't see what's so hard about sittin' in there and ridin' along. Besides, the pilot is the one who's doin' all the maneuvering and stuff, right?"

"Yep," replied the commander with a smile, "just sit back there and enjoy the ride. That's all you have to do. There's nothing to it. Are you sure you want to do this?"

"Absolutely!" replied Leon.

"Okay, get approval from your immediate supervisor and meet me at the hangar maintenance control office at fifteen hundred, and I'll help you go through the enrollment process," said the commander.

"Aye, Aye, sir," replied Leon as he completed his farewell salute.

"I'll see you soon, Baughman," the commander chuckled to himself as he turned and walked away.

Leon's supervisor approved him for flight training and in the coming days, he attended oral instructions and hands-on classroom training exercises to familiarize himself with what to expect during the actual flight. After completing all of the oral, written, and physical requirements, he passed all of the prerequisites and felt confident that he was ready to fly.

Finally, the day arrived for the flight demonstration. Leon was already at the F-4 Phantom when the commander arrived. As the commander approached, Leon promptly stood and made a formal salute.

"Commander Jumper," greeted Leon.

"You can call me 'Desperado,' Baughman," replied the commander, as he returned the salute, "That's my call name as a certified Top Gun pilot."

"Yes, sir," replied Leon.

As they both positioned themselves inside their respective cockpits, the commander asked Leon if he was all secure and ready for takeoff.

"Any questions before we take off, Baughman?" asked the commander.

"Just one, sir, what's a Desperado?" asked Leon.

"Well, that depends," replied the commander. "In the old west, they were known as renegades or outlaws. But it's a Spanish word, and it means someone willing to do things that involve risks or danger, you know, like a daredevil."

"Ohhh," said a reluctant Leon as the overhead canopy was lowered into position.

The commander then began radio communication with the control tower and made all of the necessary flight protocols in preparation for take-off. As the aircraft approached the runway, the commander steered it ninety degrees to the right until it came to a complete stop at the very beginning of the long, straight asphalt pavement.

"Desperado, you are now clear for take-off. Have a safe and enjoyable flight. We'll see you when you return," said a voice over the radio headset.

"You ready, Baughman?" asked CMDR Jumper.

"I'm ready, sir," replied Leon.

"Okay, brace yourself for take-off," the CMDR warned.

Then, with the roar of the jet propulsion afterburners at maximum idle, the signalman on the ground waved a flag indicating "go" for takeoff, and in seconds flat, the aircraft raced down the runway reaching a speed of about four hundred miles an hour, as it left the ground.

At the moment of takeoff, Leon unexpectedly felt his body being uncontrollably pinned to the back of his seat as the aircraft became airborne over the crystal green waters of the Pacific Ocean.

"Baughman," said the commander, "are you alright?"

"Yes, sirrr," answered an almost breathless Leon.

All the while, Leon was being pushed back and down into his seat, fighting to make adjustments to compensate for the extensive pressure being exerted on his body.

"Baughman, did that roller coaster at Myrtle Beach have a loop-de-loop?" asked the commander.

"Yes sir," Leon slowly answered as he fought to get his breath and vocal cords synchronized to speak.

"Well, here's the Navy's version of the loop-de-loop. Brace yourself", warned the commander.

Then, without warning, the aircraft made a vertical maneuver at ninety degrees straight up to about ten thousand feet, leveled out upside-down going in the direction they had just come from, only to do a vertical dive, completing a wide, circular loop.

At this point, Leon was feeling a very excessive G-Force. He had been taught in classroom training the week before about how the pressure of acceleration can impact a body inside the cockpit, but he never imagined anything like this. He immediately began the breathing exercises he was taught to help overcome the discomfort, as well as to keep from passing out.

As part of his flight gear, he was equipped with an aviation "g-suit" or a flight suit worn by aviators who are subject to high levels of acceleration force. The g-suit is a specially designed device that is filled with air pressure to compensate for the opposing g-force on the abdomen and legs. Its purpose is to prevent a black-out and g-LOC (gravity-induced loss of consciousness) caused by the blood pooling in the lower part of the body when under acceleration, which can deprive the brain of blood.

G stands for gravity, and everyone on Earth feels 1G "pulling them down" at all times. When a high-performance aircraft executes maneuvers like turning quickly or speeding up super-fast, that change in acceleration pushes you back and down in your seat.

Under high G-forces, blood flows away from one's eyes and brain, and the heart starts pumping harder and faster. Leon was experiencing about 4-5G's, or about 4-5 times the normal pressure of gravity. Pilots call accelerations such as these "G-Strains" or excessive gravitational strain on the body.

The once mouthy, cocky sailor was now speechless. To make matters worse, he was feeling the urge to throw up. He fought as hard as he could, but the urge to puke was winning the struggle.

I ain't no wimp, he tried to convince himself. But no matter how hard he tried, the force of propulsion was beyond his control. He quickly became light-headed, dizzy, and almost to the point of passing out. Then, without warning, the aircraft made a barrel roll maneuver, causing the jet to spin linearly along the airborne pathway. At that point, Leon couldn't hold it back any longer.

All of a sudden, the oxygen face mask he was wearing quickly filled up, and the opposing oxygen supply caused the vomit to spew out uncontrollably. He momentarily broke the seal of the face mask to vent the vomit as it continued to gush all over himself and the entire cockpit.

"Baughman, are you alright?" asked the commander.

But there was no response from Leon.

"Baughman, are you alright?" the commander asked again.

"Not really, sir," Leon replied in a soft, weak, voice.

"Hang in there, Baughman. We've almost completed our maneuvers, then we'll be heading back to base," assured the commander."

As they made their rapid descent to prepare for landing, Leon couldn't help but puke again. To say the least, he had made a royal mess of that once pristine cockpit.

As the aircraft came to a complete stop, medics and fellow sailors rushed to Leon's rescue. The commander had radioed ahead of time that he had a "sick puppy" on board, which was naval aviation slang for a sick fellow sailor in need of medical assistance.

As the aircraft's canopy was raised, fellow sailors quickly removed Leon's helmet and oxygen mask. The first thing they noticed was his pale, olive-green complexion. Leon hadn't passed out, but he didn't know where he was, nor could he move on his own.

"Baughman, are you okay," asked a concerned CMDR.

Leon replied something inaudible, but the CMDR knew what he meant.

"Take good care of him, men," the CMDR ordered. "I'll check on him again during his recovery at Sick Bay."

As the CMDR walked away, he smiled, wondering if this experience did anything to change Leon's arrogant and cocky demeanor. Baughman was a good sailor; he could only hope that becoming a victim of his own condescending attitude would make him think twice before belittling anyone else, especially his Naval peers.

The ground crew of sailors had seen others in this condition many times before and had to physically remove Leon from the cockpit to a waiting ambulance. From there he was taken to Sick Bay where he would be cleaned up and given medical fluids to restore his well-being.

He was then taken home, where he stayed for the next three days until he finally recovered from the traumatic and humiliating ordeal.

He had been repeatedly warned by his flight instructors that this might happen, but he never thought that it would happen to him. As a consolation, he was also told that once you get airsick the first time, you'll never experience it again.

He had indeed learned his lesson. Without hesitation, he was rational enough to accept the fact that if it could happen to him, then it could happen to anyone. From his own experience, he realized that the unpleasant result of the air sickness wasn't due to anyone being a wuss or a wimp but, strangely, was more like a badge of honor as having achieved an act of bravery and courage.

He wasn't a Top Gun, but he was now a certified co-pilot for any future Top Guns. His greatest satisfaction was not just being certified to fly with Top Guns but also having their confidence and respect.

As unpleasant as that experience was, it didn't deter him from flying again. He would go on to fly many times during his naval tour of duty, but one thing he would never do again was to make fun of anyone who got airsick from flying.

Chapter 7

## Hope Denied

**After safely completing** his first deployment to Vietnam in 1968, Leon was ordered to report back to NAS Miramar in California. A few days after getting reacclimated to the base and having settled into his routine duties as an aviation electrician, Leon found a house to rent in nearby El Cajon, CA. After getting settled into his new home, he immediately made arrangements for his wife, Kathy, and his daughter, Tammy, to fly out from South Carolina to be with him.

The joy that Leon felt reuniting with his wife Kathy and their baby daughter was overwhelming, to say the least. For an often-disgruntled young man with known anger issues, this was probably the happiest he'd ever been in his life. He seriously thought that this was an opportunity to have a reset on life. He would make a genuine effort to be more loving and caring toward his wife, knowing that he was equally, if not more, responsible for stressful marital issues that had occurred during their brief and unfortunately, challenging marriage.

Sadly, the revived marital bliss didn't last for long. To the young family's regret, the Navy once again decided that they needed Leon more than his family did. After just six months of duty at NAS Miramar, he was ordered to be deployed back to the Tonkin Gulf, where he would spend his second and final tour of Vietnam. Once again, Leon's dad, Al, flew out to California to help Kathy prepare to drive back home to South Carolina until the termination of Leon's deployment.

Fortunately, there were no major issues that affected his duty while defending the perilous waters off the coast of Vietnam, and after completing his second tour of combat, he was once again ordered to return to duty at NAS Miramar in California.

Upon his return to California, he immediately made plans to rent a house in El Cajon and made arrangements for Kathy and the baby to fly out to be with him once again. This time, the house he was renting was technically a lease with an option to buy. He made a deal with the owner that allowed him to make repairs and remodel the home, whereas the monthly rent money would go toward payments on the home until he was able to afford a loan to buy the house outright. In addition, Leon also agreed to be responsible for the money used for materials and supplies to renovate the home.

The reunited family was once again living in marital bliss and enjoying the scenery, climate, and many attractions of sunny southern California. Leon and Kathy loved living in California so much that they began making plans to stay there after Leon's four-year term of Naval service was complete.

During this time, Leon attended a seminar on base for naval personnel who were qualified to take an early-out release from active duty. The course offered advice and counseling for sailors who were interested in employment opportunities upon their transition back into the world of civilian life.

One profession that attracted Leon's attention was law enforcement. It just so happened that the nearby San Diego Police Department was hiring and looking for qualified young men to join their force, and NAS Miramar was a favorite supplier of their recruiting resources. During this time, Leon met with one of the recruiters from the SDPD and expressed his interest in becoming a police officer. The recruiter took his contact information and assured Leon that he would contact him upon his release from the Navy.

To qualify for the SDPD, a candidate had to meet specific criteria, including a high school diploma. To Leon's advantage, he still had about six months of active duty left in the Navy, giving him plenty of time to get his future civilian life in order. He immediately made plans to earn a high school education equivalent and enrolled at night school at nearby Balboa High School, and after completing and passing the course, proudly received his official GED.

With just months remaining from completing his military career, Leon, Kathy, and their friends continued to remodel the house in preparation for making it their permanent home. Every day, Leon would go to work at NAS Miramar, and in the evenings and on weekends would work on replacing the kitchen cabinets, painting the walls and trim, and making structural improvements and changes throughout the house.

Finally, on September 15, 1969, at just twenty-one years old, Leon proudly received his honorable discharge from the Navy. The once seventeen-year-old naval boot camp rebellious misfit was now a lawful and excited civilian. He was overjoyed and humbly proud to have completed his service as a dedicated sailor and honorable fellow member of the United States Navy.

Leon was now unemployed and was using financial resources from his savings and the final check he received from the Navy to get by. As time went by, he finally got a call from the San Diego Police Department telling him that he had been accepted as a potential law enforcement candidate. All he needed to do was to fill out an application, come in for an interview with a recruiter, and last but not least, pass a physical examination.

Leon was thrilled to hear from the SDPD. The thought of having a steady job and a regular paycheck was very encouraging, to say the least. Everything that he and Kathy had planned for months was now coming to fruition. He was sure there wouldn't be any problems with the entry process, as he had just completed a four-year naval tour of duty with no physical or mental problems whatsoever. He was confident that he would make a good law enforcement officer, and now it appeared that his hopes and dreams were about to come true.

Leon didn't waste any time filling out an application to join the police academy. Shortly thereafter, he met with a recruiting officer for a formal interview. After reviewing the application, the recruiter assured him that everything was in order and that he didn't see anything that could prevent him from not being accepted. Leon was beside himself with joy as he was getting closer to the day he could start attending the police academy. However, he still had one last thing left to pass to meet all the prerequisites for qualification—his physical exam.

Leon was directed to a nearby medical facility on campus, where he would complete the final step in his application process. Upon arriving, he filled out the necessary paperwork, after which a nurse escorted him to a private room and took his vital signs, weight, and height. She recorded all of the necessary criteria in a medical chart and told him to wait until she could notify a doctor to come and complete the check-up.

After a short wait, the doctor came into the exam room and introduced himself.

"Good afternoon, Mr. Baughman. It's nice to meet you. I'm Dr. Gordon," said the doctor.

"Nice to meet you as well, sir," replied a confident Leon.

The doctor then proceeded to administer a thorough physical examination of Leon as the two made small talk and exchanged pleasantries.

"Mr. Baughman, as far as I'm concerned, everything looks good in your medical report as for your physical health," said the doctor. "However, there is one last thing that I need to verify before we proceed. Do you know how tall you are?"

"Yes, sir," replied a confident Leon, "I'm five foot eight inches."

"Would you mind standing?" asked the doctor. "My nurse measured you at five foot seven and one-half inches. If that's correct, then you're one-half an inch too short to qualify for the academy. Stand up for me, and let's take another measurement, please."

Leon stood, took a deep breath, and sighed. The doctor then used a medical grade measuring device to confirm his true height. The doctor had a perplexing expression as he reviewed the results of his measurement. To make sure of his assessment, the doctor measured one last time.

"I'm sorry, Mr. Baughman," the doctor lamented, "but you're only five foot seven and one half inches tall, and I'm not going to be able to give you a pass on your physical exam. Again, I'm sorry, but you're one-half inch below the required height to become a candidate in our academy."

"Five foot seven and one-half inches?" Leon scornfully replied, "I don't understand. I've been five foot eight inches throughout the past four years of my Naval career! Measure again!"

"I'm sorry, Mr. Baughman, but this measuring device doesn't lie. I wish that there was more that I could do for you, but it is what it is," the doctor replied.

Finally, after an intensely heated back-and-forth conversation of disagreeing views over a discrepancy of just one-half inch, Leon stormed out of the building in a maddening rage and utter disappointment. Sadly, his hopes and dreams of starting over in the civilian world on a positive note had been abruptly terminated, resulting in a nightmare of heartbreaking rejection.

His immediate and long-term family plans had just been devastated in a matter of mere minutes by a city-slicker doctor who had the deciding factor in controlling his destiny but refused to deviate from the binding terms of what Leon considered a minor technicality. The once sacred hope of a secure, idyllic future that had kept him striving toward achieving a more perfect and happy family life had been crushingly denied by societal dictates beyond his ability to challenge.

The recent joy and personal satisfaction that he'd experienced after completing his tour of duty in the Navy was now replaced by sadness and dejection after returning to the lifestyle of civilian society.

Perhaps a better way of describing this moment in time can be exemplified by borrowing a few lines from legendary author Charles Dickens 'A Tale of Two Cities':

*"It was the best of times, it was the worst of times…
we had everything before us, we had nothing before us…"*

As with the literary example so artfully described by Mr. Dickens, Leon's opposing emotions of joy and sadness simultaneously collided, resulting in his once prideful character being hauntingly devastated by the essence of the darkness of betrayal of one's *hope denied*.

Needless to say, Leon arrived home in an angry mood of frustration with a heavily burdensome heart. His will was broken. Negativity and depression filled his thoughts and emotions. He'd always been able to overcome adversity, but this experience was a battle he couldn't win on his own. The rules and regulations that defined the criteria for becoming a law enforcement officer were written inflexibly and indelibly in black and white. For this binding document, there weren't any lawful means to defend oneself from the terms of qualification, not even in the slightest shade of a gray area.

Meanwhile, Kathy anxiously awaited Leon's return. She was so happy for him, as she knew how much becoming a law enforcement officer meant to him. In addition, she knew that he was looking forward to being able to have a steady and reliable job to support his family to ensure a respectable quality of life for their present and future lives. In her mind, there was no way he could be denied qualifying.

"Hey, honey, how'd it go?" Kathy asked as Leon entered the home.

Before he had a chance to answer, she could see the look of anger or heartache on the expression on Leon's face, as well as his edgy mannerisms.

"Not good. Not good at all," replied a reluctant Leon. "It was downright awful. They turned me down because I wasn't tall enough. I measured one-half inch too short to meet the minimum height requirement, and that a-hole doctor wouldn't give me a pass."

Trying to hide her disappointment, Kathy was shocked by the sudden turn of events. She never had the slightest inclination that things would turn out this way. Neither had she ever seen such hurt and anger from Leon's unnerving disposition. She needed to find a way to calm him down, and quickly.

"It's okay, honey," said a sympathetic Kathy, "We'll figure this out. This is just a bump in the road, and we've got a long way to go."

"We've got a long way to go, all right. We're going back to South Carolina," Leon replied, as he bluntly and disrespectfully cut into her response.

"What do you mean, we're going back to South Carolina? We haven't even discussed this," answered Kathy.

"There's nothing to discuss," said an arrogant Leon. "I've already made up my mind."

Realizing that he was firm on his decision and that there was nothing she could do to make him reconsider, Kathy asked, "So, when are we leaving?"

"As soon as we can pack and tie up some loose ends around here, which shouldn't take long," Leon replied.

"What about the house?" asked Kathy.

"What about it?" answered Leon. "It's just a house. We'll just stop what we're doing and leave it as is to the owner."

"But we've still got repairs to complete," said a concerned Kathy.

"No, we don't," snapped Leon. "I've done all I'm going to do around here. We're dropping everything in California and are heading back to South Carolina as soon as possible."

Sure enough, after a few days, they loaded up their car and prepared for the long journey back to South Carolina. The ride home must have been tense and unnerving for Kathy, as she would be confined in an automobile on the road with an irate Leon traveling thousands of miles for days on end. For her, their arrival in South Carolina couldn't come soon enough.

One can only imagine the hurt and disappointment of the once optimistic but now disheartened couple. Their hopes and dreams had been shattered—their joy deprived by unforeseen forces and circumstances. Their once-promising future was now a present uncertainty. Perhaps their unfortunate fate can best be described as a paradoxical moment in time that can be summed up by borrowing more lines from the aforementioned Dickens' classic, 'A Tale of Two Cities':

*"...it was the season of light, it was the season of darkness,*
*it was a spring of hope, it was the winter of despair..."*

Chapter 8

**The Terrible Twenties (Part One)**

**After arriving home** in Ward, SC, from the long, exhausting drive from California, Leon and his family moved in with his parents until they could get settled and were able to find a place of their own. Unfortunately, the anger and disappointment from his California experience still haunted him and continued to occupy his thoughts and emotions. To say the least, his attitude and disposition were difficult for those around him to deal with, and nothing anyone could say or do seemed to help in improving his temperament.

It did take a while, but eventually, Leon's demeanor calmed down and became more tolerable, but not necessarily always desirable. He was uptight and edgy. His mood swings were uncontrollable and unpredictable. He could be calm and cordial at times, but at other times, without provocation, he would snap at the slightest thing that he deemed annoying or displeasing to him.

It was during this time that he began having dark thoughts about decisions that he'd made in the past that he thought were the cause and blame for his disgruntlement in life. Up until this time, his experience in the Navy was the best thing that had ever happened to him. So, why did I have to spoil everything by getting married and having a family? He would ask himself over and over. In his mind, he and Kathy should have never made that decision, especially at such a young and irresponsible age. Nevertheless, here he was, just twenty-one years old, unemployed, broke, and mad as hell at the world.

Since Leon and Kathy were living in the same household as his dad, Al, and his mama, Eula Lee, it was quite obvious to his parents that there was a potentially damaging strain on the young couple's marriage. Leon had become selfish, obnoxious, and downright hateful at times toward Kathy, and she seemed to have little to no recourse except to avoid him when he got into one of his hideous moods.

Al was careful not to interfere with their relationship, but at the same time, was also concerned about Leon's grouchy attitude and lack of responsibility. Leon simply had too much time on his hands, and the idleness was taking its toll. Leon desperately needed a job, and that was one thing that Al thought he might be able to do to help him out of his doldrums.

When the timing was right, Al had a long, serious, heart-to-heart, father-to-son talk with Leon about his present situation. Al was careful not to overstep his boundaries concerning their marriage but instead concentrated on Leon's idleness and unemployment. After a successfully inspiring conversation, Leon agreed with Al that he did indeed need a job and was appreciative of Al volunteering to do whatever he could to help. Leon confessed to his bad behavior and told Al that he would try his best to improve his attitude and that, hopefully, finding a steady job would be a good start to improve his life, as well as his marriage.

Al was a well-known and very respected member of the IBEW Local Union in Augusta, GA, and he knew people in positions of authority that might be able to help him get Leon accepted into their apprenticeship program. After several meetings with the Business Agent and the Apprenticeship

Committee Chairman, Al was able to convince them that Leon would make a good electrician's apprentice. Leon applied for and was accepted to join the union, and the following fall, at the beginning of the next semester of school, Leon started his electrical apprenticeship classroom studies.

Leon now had a renewed, optimistic confidence in his step, as he was now excited for the opportunity to potentially become a journeyman electrician. The electrical trade was one of the leaders among all the crafts in the construction industry and one of the highest, if not the highest-paid, profession among its peers.

Leon started his first job as an electrician's apprentice at the construction of the new University Hospital in Augusta, GA., in 1970. The original University Hospital was established in 1818 and was the second oldest hospital in Georgia, but it desperately needed to be replaced to update and modernize the quality of medical care for the surrounding community.

Leon's responsibility as an electrician apprentice was to work under the supervision of a journeyman electrician, from which he would also learn the skills of the trade. His primary responsibility in his first job was to install fluorescent light fixtures in the many stairways throughout the hospital. To his surprise, there were a lot of stairways on the many floors of that building, but he loved his job, nevertheless.

One day, after being on the job for about a year, he was helping his journeyman pull some electrical wire from an electrical panel on a lower floor to one of the floors above.

"Leon," said his journeyman, John, "I need you to go down to the electrical control room in the basement and find panel number 7A. When you find it, feed the "fish tape" into the spare conduit like we did yesterday on the last panel, and I'll connect the new wire to it so you can pull it down into position."

A fish tape is a tool used by electricians to insert into one end of an electrical conduit (or pipe) and "fish" or push it through to the end of the conduit so a person waiting on the other end can attach a new electrical wire to it for it to be safely pulled back through the conduit.

"Here," John continued, "take this walkie-talkie and let me know when you're ready to get it started. I've already checked their batteries, and they're fully charged. But before you go, let's do a soundcheck to make sure these things are working properly."

John pressed the call button on his walkie-talkie and spoke into the receiver, "Leon, do you read me? Over."

Leon responded, "Loud and clear. Over."

Leon grabbed the fish tape and the walkie-talkie and headed for the electrical control room. When he got there, he was surprised to find that overnight, the construction insulators had stacked their new thermal insulation sheets directly underneath the panel he needed to gain access.

"What the heck is this crap?" he asked. "Those idiot insulators have blocked my access to the panel that I need to get to."

By union rules, the materials, tools, etc., of one craft can't be moved or altered by members of another craft. Only someone from the insulators union was allowed to move the insulation blocking the electrical panel, but Leon didn't want to waste time notifying them, as John needed him to fish the tape through as soon as possible.

Not knowing what to do, he tried contacting his journeyman, John.

"Hey John," Leon called on the walkie-talkie. "Do you read me?"

There was no response to his call.

"John, do you read me?" repeated Leon.

Although he tried several other times, he never got a reply. He assumed it was probably due to not being able to get a good signal from being down in the basement where the signal may have been impeded by the thick concrete walls and floors above.

He knew John may have been getting impatient, so instead

of going back upstairs to explain his dilemma, he decided to climb on top of the insulation, gain access to the panel and fish the tape through the conduit as originally planned.

When he finally positioned himself on top of the insulation, he opened electrical panel number 7A to find not one but two unmarked conduits. Not knowing which one to access, he tried contacting John, but once again, there was no reply.

Leon's frustration with the walkie-talkies was growing, as he knew they were working fine just a few minutes before he went to the basement.

After several more calls with no reply, he decided to try to push the fish tape through the conduits one at a time, using a process of elimination. Hopefully, John would grab the metal tape once it was exposed on his end, and if, after pushing all the fish tape through, John hadn't received it, he would try the next conduit until he had found the right one.

"Well, here goes nothing," Leon said to himself as he started the fish tape into the first conduit.

Then, suddenly, without warning, there was a loud "boom" sound and a bright flash of electrical sparks and smoke coming from the panel box. Leon had struck a live wire with the metal fish tape and had been electrocuted and thrown across the stack of insulation, ending up on the floor below.

"Oh, no!" John said out loud upon hearing the loud blast from below.

"I think Leon's hit a live wire. Call for a medic and meet me in the electrical panel room in the basement," he shouted to a nearby fellow worker.

John and other nearby workers raced to the basement to check on Leon, hoping for the best yet fearing the worst.

"Leon. Leon!" John shouted as he knelt beside a dazed and confused Leon. "Are you alright?"

"I think so," replied a shaken Leon. "What happened?"

"I think you hit a live 440-volt line inside the panel box.

Were you standing on this insulation when you accessed the panel box?" asked John.

"Yeah, I had to. I couldn't get to it any other way, and I tried contacting you, but I couldn't get a response from you, and I didn't know what else to do," Leon answered.

"Can you sit up?" asked John.

"Yeah, I think so," replied Leon.

"How do you feel?" asked John.

"I'm a little light-headed, but I think I'm okay," said Leon.

"Okay, let's get you up and go to the first aid station and have someone assess you, alright?" asked John.

Fortunately, Leon was treated for minor burns on his hands and given some aspirin for his headache. Other than having a nasty taste of copper, which would last for the next three days, his recovery went very well.

After assessing the situation, John determined that if Leon had not been standing on the stack of insulation, he probably would have been killed by electrocution. The insulation had prevented him from being grounded, thereby breaking the full potential of a load of a 440-volt electrical power surge.

Leon didn't blame anyone but himself for the incident and took full responsibility for his inexperienced actions. The outcome could have been more horrific, to say the least, but all-in-all, it proved to be a good lesson learned, albeit learned in a problematically dangerous way.

The young twenty-one-year-old Leon had defied death yet again. Up until this point in time, there had been at least five other near-death misses in his life due to accidents, bizarre encounters, and downright recklessness.

Unfortunately for Leon, the decade of his twenties had just begun and unbeknownst to him, there were a lot of other unpredictable grim, and bleak circumstances that would affect him before the decade would end.

The next series of events may or may not be near-death experiences, but as far as his personal life and marriage, the trials and hardships of an already young and rocky relationship were easily predictable. Harsh words, hurtful feelings, personal rejection, and abandonment of marital responsibilities were just a few of the many ill-fated hardships that were yet to come.

The decade of his twenties had only just begun, and before it would end in the years to come, Leon would often look back and dispiritedly recall the woeful circumstances and ill-fated events that occurred during this time in his life that he would come to regrettably remember as *The Terrible Twenties.*

Chapter 9

## The Terrible Twenties (Part Two)

**In the early days** of 1970, Leon reacquainted with some old friends who, like himself, happened to enjoy playing music as a pastime. They were far from being skilled musicians, but they were pretty good, nonetheless. All in all, they were just good old boys hanging out, playing music, and having a good time. Once they found out that Leon was also an amateur musician, they invited him to join them. Leon was more than happy to oblige them. He was overjoyed by the potential of having music become a part of his life once again.

At this low point of time in his life, this is what Leon needed to help overcome some of the adversity that he had experienced in the recent past. He'd missed playing along with his buddies in the Navy as well as the camaraderie and personal satisfaction that only music could provide. Although he didn't have an addiction to music, it was, however, the one thing that brought him joy and fulfillment. It was like an elixir or medicine that, when taken by just the right dose, would give him peace of mind and personal satisfaction that no form of drug or psychological therapy could provide.

Equally important was the fact that, over time, Kathy noticed the change in his attitude and disposition after just several practice sessions with the group. On alternating practices, they would gather at Leon and Kathy's house and Kathy could see firsthand how music was a positive influence on his life. To make a good situation a better situation, she would encourage him to keep playing with the band, as she was surprisingly becoming a fan of his unique vocal talent as well as his style of music.

Al and Eula Lee were more than pleased to see that Leon had found a new lease on life by once again embracing the magical impact of music. More importantly, they also noticed an improvement in his relationship with Kathy during this time and presumed that it was possibly due to stress relief from playing with his musician friends in his free time.

To show their support and offer encouragement, they decided to reward him for his positive attitude and improved demeanor. Al began asking his friends and co-workers about the types of acoustic guitars that most musicians loved to play. He didn't want just any guitar; he wanted one with a quality sound that would last and potentially become an heirloom. He finally got lucky and talked to a man who owned a music store in Augusta who convinced him into buying a "like-new" D35 Martin guitar.

"Mr. Baughman," said the store owner, "when a skilled guitar player hears the mention of a D35 Martin, they stop what they're doing, and their eyes light up. This guitar is the gold standard for longevity, quality craftsmanship, and pristine sound. It can play any mood or style of music and is entirely crafted by hand by some of the most skilled woodworkers in the industry. Furthermore, as the taste of a good quality wine improves with age, so does the sound of this guitar. Have a seat, and let me demonstrate how this baby sounds."

The store owner then checked to make sure that all the

strings were in tune, then began to play "I Walk the Line" by Johnny Cash. The sound was almost angelic to Al's ears. Surely, this is the one he'd been looking for.

"It's by no coincidence that I picked that particular song, Mr. Baughman," said the store owner. "This is the same make guitar that Johnny Cash uses. It also happens to be the same make guitar that Elvis Presley used, as well."

"Well, if it's good enough for Elvis, then it's good enough for me," Al laughed. "I'll take it! Thank you. Thank you very much."

Later that evening, Al and Eula Lee presented Leon with his new guitar. To say the least, Leon was overwhelmed with joy. He was already familiar with the reputation of the D35 Martin guitar and knew that his parents must have invested a substantial price to purchase it. Maybe one day, he thought, I'll be able to use this guitar in some way to show my appreciation for their generosity.

In the meantime, the group continued to practice whenever they could, and after many successful sessions, they realized that they had gotten to be pretty good. Once they felt completely confident in their ability to perform, they began discussions of continuing as an officially organized band. Leon stood out as the frontman or lead vocalist, and it was decided by all members of the band that he would be the leader of what would become known collectively as "Leon Baughman and The Lonely Strangers."

As time went by, the band got better and better and more confident with their instrument playing and vocal skills. Finally, after many practice sessions, they ventured out and began playing at local birthday parties, weddings, and holiday events free of charge. At the time, being able to perform in front of strangers while having fun at the same time was payment enough for their time and effort.

Then, in December 1970, they were invited to play at the IBEW Local Union Christmas party. It would be their first venue for a paid performance. To say the least, it was a huge success. Without a doubt, Leon's exceptional vocals and mesmerizing stage appeal became the main attraction for the band's notoriety.

For many of the pleasing partygoers, the name of the band would be forgotten in just a few days, but the name Leon Everette Baughman would remain with them for the months and years that followed, that is, until the day that he would legally shorten it to simply, Leon Everette. And that name, they would remember for a lifetime.

To his friends and co-workers, everything seemed to be going well for Leon during this time in his life. Music was not only a major influence on his life, but it was also a life changer as well as a lifesaver. His anger issues became fewer and far between. His overall demeanor seemed genuinely pleasant, and his once bitter tone was less harsh and more cheerful. He had a steady job that paid very well, and He and Kathy now had their own home, and in a few short years, welcomed newborns Kim and Duane into the family.

Although there were still some off-and-on rough patches during their marriage, for the most part, Kathy continued to be supportive of Leon's love of music and appreciated the positive change that it brought to his mannerisms. She also appreciated the time he was spending at home and didn't seem to mind the times he was away practicing with the band.

But just when it seemed that things were going well for the young couple, Leon began visiting the local nightclubs to watch and listen to the bands in nearby Augusta, GA. Needless to say, because of this, he began spending more and more time away from his family and neglecting his responsibilities as a supportive husband and loving father.

Regardless of what others thought of Leon's seemingly lack of responsibility, he always had a legitimate reason for his actions. Leon's answer to all the naysayers was that he had a good job and was making good money that comfortably supported his family's needs. To him, it was Kathy's responsibility to maintain the house and take care of the kids while he was away at work. In his self-centered mind, in a sadistic albeit sincere way, he thought that it was his place to be the breadwinner and the buyer of the diapers and Kathy's place to be the breadbaker and the changer of the diapers.

His reason for going to the clubs was to gain experience by meeting accomplished band members and watching them perform. Watching and learning from bands that had already polished their skills would result in lessons he could learn from to use in taking his music skills to a higher level, thereby potentially being able to be more supportive in the long run of his family's needs. Nevertheless, Kathy saw it as an excuse, while Leon saw it as a motive. Predictably, the friction between the once-loving couple was getting warmer and warmer.

On some occasions visiting the nightclubs, Leon would ask to sing along with the house bands on songs with which he was familiar. His voice, stage presence, and confidence got better and better each time he performed. After a while, Leon didn't have to ask for permission to sing anymore. The house bands liked his singing so much that they began approaching him when they saw him in the audience and, as a courtesy, would invite him to come up to the stage and sing along with them.

On one hand, Leon was spending a lot of nights away from home and neglecting his responsibilities as a husband and father. On the other hand, he was getting a lot of good public exposure, and word of mouth was supporting his talent from club to club. It didn't take long until everyone in the nightclub scene, including owners, workers, and patrons, knew the voice behind the name Leon Everette Baughman.

By now, Leon had begun to stay later and later at the clubs, just hanging out with friends and members of the bands that he had met over the past few years. Unfortunately, the once seemingly harmless social gatherings would lead to unsuspecting moral issues in his life. Along with the casual fun and conversations, he began drinking more and more alcohol, which, over time, would become more and more problematic for a variety of reasons. But for now, this was the least of his worries, and he had a lot of worries, but nothing could prepare him for his next unavoidable but self-inflicted crisis.

Chapter 10

**The Terrible Twenties (Part Three)**

**Sometime during his** mid-twenties, Leon's dad, Al, approached him about a potentially great job opportunity. Plant Urquhart, a subsidiary of South Carolina Electric and Gas (SCE&G), an electrical power generating plant in nearby Beech Island, SC, needed electrical instrumentation mechanics. Al reasoned that even though Leon didn't have any experience as an instrument mechanic, he did have enough knowledge of electricity to qualify for the position. The position paid very well, more than an electrician apprentice, and had great benefits, as well as the potential to be a lifetime employment opportunity. Besides, the job at the University Hospital would be ending soon, as construction was getting close to completion.

So, Leon filled out an employment application, sat for an interview, and a few days later, to his astonishment, he got a phone call notifying him that he had the job. He immediately notified his employer that he would be quitting his job, and two weeks later, started working for SCE&G as an instrument mechanic.

He loved his new job. It paid very well. It was a good, clean working environment, the co-workers were friendly, and the actual workload was far less physical and stressful than that of being an electrician's apprentice.

During this time, "The Lonely Strangers" band changed membership and became known as, "Leon Everette and the Ever Readies". It was also during this time that Leon noticed that some people were having a hard time pronouncing his last name, Baughman, correctly. Some were calling it "Bo-man," whereas the correct pronunciation was "Bault-man." Although some distant family members were outspoken about him dropping the family surname, he never meant any disrespect to the family whatsoever. It was simply a business decision made on behalf of the band. Regardless, whenever people heard the entire name of the band, all they remembered and all they would talk about was "Leon Everette," and that's all that mattered.

Leon Everette and the Ever Readies were now becoming regulars at the local nightclubs. Their popularity grew immensely, as they always seemed to draw larger than normal crowds, which resulted in their being in high demand wherever they performed.

Originally, the band started out wearing circa mid-1970s flashy-style polyester suits, including bell bottoms, shirts with frilly lace fronts and sleeves, and glossy black patent leather shoes. But over time, they decided to change their wardrobe to match the general attire of the club patrons, which usually meant something more casual, including jeans and either cowboy shirts or just plain T-shirts, wide leather belts with flashy belt buckles, and of course, the latest style cowboy boots.

Due to various reasons, and after a short run of fun and enjoyment, the band decided to go their separate ways. Some had families that were growing and had to cut back on practicing and playing due to obligations at home, while others had to move out of state due to employment requirements. In the end, Leon, now twenty-nine years old, was the sole member that continued playing music either solo or with local club bands. Having a natural talent for music, he could fit in with any house band, and besides, he had higher expectations—he wanted to see what Nashville had to offer.

Going to work from Ward, SC to Beech Island, SC, then to Augusta, GA, to perform at the Holiday Inn Lounge at night made for quite a stressful day. To compensate for the time restraints on his daily schedule, he decided to rent a motel room at the Holiday Inn and use it as a secondary residency. Kathy wasn't necessarily fond of this idea, but for the time being, and as long as it would only be for a short term, she would go along with his decision.

He would often go to work and work all day, then go to the Holiday Inn and take a short nap and freshen up, then go to the club and play his regular music sets, then come back to the Holiday Inn and sleep, then go to work the next day, and to keep Kathy happy, would return home to spend the night on occasions.

Leon continued his job at SCE&G and things were going very well for a good while, that is, until he decided to venture out and explore the music scene in Nashville, Tennessee. To say the least, Leon's job at SCE&G was becoming a reality of being in serious jeopardy. He was now going to Nashville two to three times a week and the stress and strain of being on the road were catching up to him both physically and emotionally.

His once already tiring routine was now even more exhausting, as he would leave the Holiday Inn Lounge after his music set, drive six and one-half hours (on a good night) to Nashville and park behind a Gulf gas station, sleep in his car until late morning when the gas station owner would awaken him, take a sink bath in the gas station restroom, walk around Nashville trying to get an interview and/or audition with record label executives, drive back to the Holiday Inn, and spend the rest of the shortened night, then go to work or skip work altogether the following day.

Needless to say, this routine put an awful strain on his relationship with his boss, co-workers, and Kathy. When he did show up for work, he was often late, and on several occasions, his co-workers would find him sleeping in the restroom on the commode or in a dimly lit storage supply room.

The stress from going back and forth to Nashville had finally reached its peak, and his mind and body were taking their toll. There's no doubt that Leon wanted to quit his job, but at the same time, he was too scared to quit, knowing he didn't have anything else to fall back on financially. In addition, he wasn't going to work because he liked it anymore but would go solely for the simple purpose of financial survival.

To add to his growing frustrations of rejection and disappointment from his unsuccessful trips to Nashville, his home life and relationship with Kathy were also deteriorating. But it was no fault to her, as he had no one to blame but himself.

It's a wonder that Leon lasted as long as he did on the job. He'd been reprimanded on several occasions, as well as threatened to be fired, but he was well-liked and a very good worker when he did show up for work. But, in his heart, he knew that the day would soon come when he would probably do something out of character or make a mistake that was beyond anyone's control to prevent him from being fired. He knew that his disregard for standard employment practices was pushing his superiors to their limits of responsible management and didn't understand why he'd not been fired before now.

One of Leon's co-workers, named Lenny, was a sixty-something-year-old man who was known to be cantankerous, old-fashioned, and didn't appreciate younger workers telling him how to go about doing things, no matter if their suggestions were practical or not. Lenny loved to give orders but would be difficult with anyone who tried to give him an order or advice on how to go about solving a work-related mechanical problem. In his mind, if he oversaw a project, it was his way or no way of getting the job done—and at the time, he was the mechanic, and Leon was merely the mechanic's helper.

On the other hand, Leon was now twenty-nine years old and was a very knowledgeable worker. For the most part, he would follow the lead of his supervising mechanic by carrying out his responsibilities as a mechanic's helper. He was always willing to learn but didn't mind speaking up when he thought he had a better idea about how to go about getting a job done. But Lenny viewed him as a young pup who came across as being a cocky, insensitive know-it-all. Needless to say, there were probably more bad days than good days when he and Lenny were working together.

One day, Leon and Lenny were assigned to install a brand new $25,000 instrument control panel in the plant's main operations control room. In today's money, that would be a cost of over $100,000, easily. The new control panel was an updated version of the instrumentation system that controlled the operation and function of the pumps, generators, and other mechanical machinery throughout the plant's power-generating system.

Lenny's supervisor showed him where the new panel was to be installed and gave him the specifications supplied by the vendor on how to properly install it. To Leon's dismay, Lenny, being a hard-headed know-it-all, discarded the written instructions and began assembling the panel on his own.

Leon remained close by and made himself available in any way that Lenny needed help but was careful not to upset Lenny in any way, as this was a very important piece of equipment for the future stability of the plant's operation.

After a short time had passed, Lenny became frustrated because he was having a hard time trying to determine how to configure some of the parts for the new panel. When Leon would suggest referring to the instructions, Lenny would snap and talk down to him in a hateful, demeaning tone of voice.

After several cordial attempts to get Lenny to let him read the instructions, Leon could see that Lenny had made up his mind and that he wasn't going to take anyone else's advice on how to proceed.

Finally, Lenny succumbed to Leon's appeal to help. However, he'd still not read the instructions.

"Here, hold this bracket up right there while I mount the panel board to it," ordered Lenny.

Leon followed his instructions as given, but Lenny was still having a hard time making the pieces go together.

"I think I see what's causing the problem," suggested Leon. "I don't think that piece goes on this bracket. I think it goes on another part of the assembly."

After several unsuccessful attempts to make the pieces go together, Leon was getting tired of holding the heavy bracket in place and spoke up once again.

"Lenny, it's not going to work that way. I think I might know how it goes. Let me show you what I have in mind, and if it doesn't work, we can try something else," Leon urged.

"I don't need you to tell me what to do or how to do it," snapped Lenny. "When I tell you to do something, do as I tell you to do it, even if it's wrong!"

By this time, Leon had had about all he could take from Lenny's despicable attitude and failure to properly install the new equipment. As badly as he wanted to help, he remained as calm and composed as he could trying not to make a bad situation a worse situation. But everyone has their limitations, and Leon was on the very brink of his.

Lenny finally lost his composure and began tossing tools, cursing the new panel, then bolted out of the room in a maddening rage.

In the meantime, Leon remained standing alone in the room, still holding the panel bracket in place as Lenny stormed out.

"Where are you going?" asked a frantic Leon.

"Anywhere but here, for now!" replied Lenny.

"Well, what do you want me to do with this bracket and panel?" Leon demanded.

"I don't care. Throw it in the river for all I care!" answered a furious Lenny as he walked away.

"Did you say throw it in the river?" asked a perplexed Leon.

"Yeah, throw the damn thing in the river!" Lenny sarcastically replied.

"Lenny, wait a minute, we can do this!" Leon pleaded.

Lenny shouted something back to Leon, but Leon couldn't discern what he said, as he was too far away, and the noise from the mechanical machinery was too loud for him to hear.

So, there stood Leon, still holding on to the heavy bracket, having done nothing wrong, but instead had done everything that he had been told to do to help in any way possible, only to be talked down to and now left stranded, and treated like a low-life scumbag. To say Leon was mad at this point is an exaggerated understatement.

About fifty yards away, in the back of the plant, flowed the Savannah River. It was the primary source of cooling water for the plant's operational needs. Leon never had any reason to go near it, but after what he'd just been through, he thought that it was time to take a stroll to the riverside.

"Where are you going with that panel?" asked the plant's operations manager as Leon was leaving the room.

"I'm going to throw it in the river," Leon calmly replied.

"Throw it in the river. Are you crazy?" exclaimed the operator.

"Well, you can call me crazy all you want to. At this point, I don't care. I'm just doing what my supervisor told me to do," answered Leon.

"Leon, you can't be serious!" yelled the operator.

"Watch me!" Leon said as he left the room.

By this time, the operator was on the phone calling security.

"Security, an employee is walking toward the river on the backside of the plant with a very important and expensive piece of equipment. He's threatening to throw it into the river. Send someone to stop him! Now!" demanded the operator.

A couple of security personnel left their posts and ran

toward the back of the plant, where they saw Leon approaching the river carrying the instrument panel.

"Stop right where you are!" one ordered.

Leon looked back but didn't slow down as he casually walked toward the river.

"Leon, don't do it! Don't do it! I didn't mean it!" cried Lenny as he came running out of the back of the plant.

"I'm just doing what I was told, Lenny. You insisted that I follow your orders, no matter if what you told me was the wrong thing to do, so I'm just following your orders," answered a frustrated Leon.

"Leon, please don't," pleaded Lenny.

Leon momentarily hesitated, then as security got closer, he shouted, "I'm doing this because this is what you told me to do, Lenny.

"You said to throw the damn thing in the river. You also said for me to do as you said, no matter if it was wrong. So, I'm doing this for you, Lenny!"

Then, with a powerful lunge, Leon threw the control panel as far as he could into the swiftly swirling waters of the Savannah River.

As everyone approached, all they could do was watch as it calmly floated downstream over rocks and eddies along the fast-moving, cold-water currents.

Within minutes, Leon was apprehended by two security personnel, escorted off the job site, and fired on the spot, never to set foot on the property of SCE&G ever again.

Leon sat in his car in a state of numbness for a short while before leaving the plant's parking lot. Thoughts of the demise of his immediate future began to overwhelmingly haunt him. He was now out of a job and unable to support his family. He also couldn't afford to stay at the Holiday Inn any longer and the only place he could go now was back home. To make matters worse, he still had to confess his actions to Kathy. But his darkest thought was how would she respond?

Furthermore, there would be no more trips to Nashville. For now, the hope of making it big-time in Nashville was merely a reality beyond his financial and personal abilities.

So, here he was, now at twenty-nine years of age, once again unemployed, broke, and mad as hell at the world, just like he was when he had the same depressing feeling at twenty-one years of age back in California.

What was he to do now? He didn't know it at the time, but he would take it one day at a time and somehow make the best of a very bad situation. Leon didn't always win the difficult battles in life, but he would never shy away from a struggle, nor for the opportunity to be able to fight again another day.

The past ten years had been full of disappointments, rejections, and heartaches, but his reunion with music was far away, the highlight of the decade. Had it not been for his love for music, he may have been worse off. On the other hand, if it had not been for his love of music, he may have been better off.

Regardless, it was all in the past at this point, and it seemed that the only good news, if there was any, was the fact that he'd finally reached the end of a once-promising but unfulfilling decade.

Nevertheless, he still had a long life to live and many dreams to follow. As with many other country music amateurs seeking professional recognition, his struggles in life would continue—some to win, others to lose. But finally, it was an end to an era of many disappointing lessons in life from which to learn and improve oneself. Yes, the once seemingly unapproachable end had finally come at long last to his often low-spirited but always unforgettable age of *the terrible twenties.*

Chapter 11

## Humble Pie

**The drive home** from his last day on the job at SCE&G was a long and quiet one for Leon. He didn't want to go home, but this time, he didn't have any other options. He was exhausted and depressed from the trips back and forth to Nashville earlier in the week, and now, after a long, problematic last day at work, all he wanted to do was to be left alone and go to bed and get some much-needed rest.

He tried to convince himself that his bout with exhaustion and disappointments in Nashville was taking a toll on his mind and body and that this was all a bad dream. But deep down, he knew that on this occasion, he had surely messed up big time. The damages he had done were both irreversible and unforgivable. He also acknowledged that everything that happened on that fateful day was, for the most part and in the end, totally irresponsible on his behalf. He was hard-headed, short-tempered, and slow to rationally respond to uncomfortable or difficult situations. In just one day, he'd gone from having an open road to a potentially successful life to a dead-end street on a road to nowhere.

Now self-humiliated and at the lowest point in his life, he

headed home, not knowing if he'd be welcome to go inside or have the front door slammed in his face. Regardless, there was no other place to go. This was his only choice, yet far and away, not his preferred choice. Nevertheless, he would eat his humble pie and take the criticisms from his scorners, recover from his adversities, and move on until he could find something positive in his life to help him overcome his present, humiliating situation. Although this experience was a major setback, and to his credit, he had never been a quitter and he certainly wasn't quitting now.

Upon Leon's arrival, Kathy was taken aback by what she saw as he entered their home. Leon stood strangely stiff and unspeaking before her with an appearance of a man that looked like death warmed over. She stood confused, facing a man with a look deeper than just being sad, the epitome of loneliness, and with the morbid expression of defeat, all compressed into the mind, body, and soul of a lost, desperate, undeniable person of self-inflicted despair.

He was shocked but appreciatively surprised when she welcomed him back into their home. Still traumatized by all that had just happened that afternoon, he struggled to find the right words to say. No matter what he would say, it surely wouldn't be acceptable or good enough to please Kathy, or so he thought.

In his best effort to utter the slightest phrase of a sentence, he tried to explain his unannounced visit by trying to make a joke, saying, "Well, it looks like I'll have to get into music after all. I just got fired from SCE&G."

"You got what?" asked a confused Kathy.

"Yeah, I messed up in a bad way at work today, and they fired me on the spot," replied Leon.

About that time, their children came running from the back of the interior of the house, shouting, "Daddy's home! Daddy's Home!"

Leon quickly hugged them all and sat with them for a little

while, then asked them to go play in a nearby room so he and Kathy could talk.

After the kids were settled, Leon explained to Kathy the details of what had happened earlier that day. Although Kathy was not happy about his being fired, surprisingly, she was somewhat sympathetic to his situation.

"So, what are you going to do?" she asked.

"Well, all I know that I can do, for now, is to play as often as I can at the clubs to make enough money to pay the bills and get by and in the meantime, try to find a job that will be more stable and better paying," he responded. "One thing I'm not going to do is to go back to Nashville. As hard as I tried, I couldn't get my foot in the door at any of the recording labels, and I've made up my mind that I'm not going back again."

That was exactly what she had hoped he would say. Maybe if he would quit wasting his time away from home going to Nashville and not getting any support from any of the people in the know there, he would possibly spend more time at home.

She didn't like the idea of him continuing to play at the local clubs, but perhaps she could tolerate it if he would come home at a reasonable hour at night and spend more time with the kids when he wasn't working. In addition, he would have to either stop completely or cut way back on his alcohol consumption. She wasn't going to put up with a drunkard in her house whatsoever.

Leon agreed to all the terms and conditions that Kathy demanded and began booking club events and other social engagements as often as he could. The pay wasn't great, but it was enough to pay the bills and put food on the table.

He later found a job with a tree surgeon business during the day and continued to play the clubs at night. To help ends meet, he worked as a laborer doing most of the grunt work for the tree removal company foreman. Nevertheless, he reported to work on time, remained sober, and gave his employer a good day's work for a good day's wages.

As the summer was coming to a close, he began thinking about quitting the music business altogether, as the nightly gigs and the daily work routine were becoming repetitious and exhausting. To make matters worse, there were also times that he and Kathy were beginning to have more and more petty arguments, thus putting additional stress on their already strained marriage.

With no other opportunities for a well-paying job close to home and with the ever-growing strain on his marriage, Leon finally decided that when the summer season was over, he would drastically cut back or possibly quit the nightclub scene altogether. All that he needed was one good break with a fresh start with someone who could help him in Nashville. But that had been his dream for months.

He supposed that miracles happened in life for a reason. It didn't have to be anything extravagant, just something to fulfill a need for most people. But, then again, sometimes people can be a miracle to others by just being themselves. Tonight, he would perform as he had done many nights before, only this time, he was hoping that someone else was expecting a miracle and that he, in just a small way, could be a part of it. The show must go on, and tonight, he would, once again, give it his all.

Chapter 12

## Who is That Man?

**One warm summer** evening in 1978, as Leon crossed the Savannah River on his way from his home in Ward, SC., to Augusta, GA., he thought that this night would just be another gig on a small stage in front of a lively but small crowd. He hadn't long left his regular day job as a laborer for a tree surgeon business, only to freshen up, change clothes, get a bite to eat, then head out to perform his scheduled appearance at a newly opened local country music nightclub called "The Good Times Club".

Just another gig, he thought, the same songs, a different club, a few drinks, and hopefully, see some new faces and meet some new friends, and most importantly, get a much-needed paycheck. Little did he realize it at the time, but that night, he would not only meet a new friend, but he would also meet someone that would change the course of his life forever.

Upon arriving at the club, he was pleasantly surprised when he noticed something he'd never seen before. The club marquee read:

## Tonight Only
## Leon Everette Live!

He parked his car, grabbed his guitar and case, and headed for the club entrance. He had arrived early on purpose, as he always liked to settle in and get acclimated before he was scheduled to go on stage. As he entered the doorway, he noticed a clock on the wall to his right that read eight o'clock. His timing was perfect. He would use this time to observe the people and atmosphere and familiarize himself with the place until he had to go on at nine.

He sat his guitar case down at the end of the bar and made a waving motion to the bartender. "How you doin'," he said, "I'm Leon Everette. I'm scheduled to perform at nine tonight. Is the manager here?"

"He's in his office," said the bartender.

"Monica," said the bartender to a nearby waitress, "would you let Sam know that Mr. Everette is here to see him?"

"Sure," said Monica, "Mr. Everette, if you'd like, you may sit here at this booth while I let Sam know you're here. May I offer you a drink while you wait?"

"Thank you, Monica," Leon replied. "You can call me Leon, and yes, can I get something with Vodka?"

"One finger or two?" she asked.

"Oh, just one thanks," said Leon.

"Coming right up, *Leon*," smiled Monica.

As Leon sat in the back corner booth, he could see the whole interior of the club. "For The Good Times," by Ray Price was playing on the jukebox, and a few couples were slow dancing, smiling, and making small talk as the vinyl forty-five RPM played to its conclusion. It was a generously populous crowd, but far from full capacity.

Although the club building was not new, the ownership of

the club had changed, as well as the name of the club. This was the club formerly known as "The Holiday Inn Lounge." The interior had been completely renovated and was very well maintained compared to other local clubs he'd played. Like many other clubs, it did have the stench of cigarette smoke and the aroma of spilled beer, although it was missing the sticky floors, scantily clad waitresses, and obnoxious clientele. But then again, the interior was brand new, and the night was still very young. The usual "fun crowd" didn't usually begin to show up until around nine o'clock anyway. But for now, they all seemed to be enjoying themselves as the jukebox ejected Ray Price and grabbed "Take This Job and Shove It" by Johnny Paycheck.

It wasn't long before the manager's office door opened, and a fifty-something-year-old man approached Leon's booth. It was Sam Caldwell, a well-known and well-respected businessman in the nightclub circle not only in Augusta but throughout the state of Georgia.

"Hey, Leon, how you doin'? It's good to see you," Sam said as he reached out to shake Leon's hand.

"It's good to see you, too, Sam," said Leon.

"Now, we've got you scheduled for nine o'clock, is that right?" asked Sam.

"Yes sir," replied Leon.

"Thank you very much for doing this for me," Sam continued, "I've heard a lot of good things about you. I'm excited to hear you sing, and I hope you enjoy your time with us this evening.

"As we discussed a couple of weeks ago, you'll be performing three twenty-minute sets with a fifteen-minute or so break in between," said Sam. "After your last set, stop by the bar, and the bartender will have your check ready for you as you leave."

"Thank you, Sam," replied Leon. "I do appreciate you giving me this opportunity."

"You're very welcome, Leon. If I don't get to speak with you later, I hope to see you again soon," said Sam as he returned to his office.

As Sam approached his office doorway, he paused and looked back at the crowd. The expression on his face showed his delight, as he thought it already looked like a larger-than-usual crowd for this time of night. Did the marquee outside have anything to do with a crowd this size so early in the evening? It remained to be seen, but so far, so good.

Little did Leon know, but Sam had done his homework. He wasn't a successful businessman by just going with the flow. Sam made waves and demanded the very best club atmosphere and quality entertainment for his clientele. He'd heard from his regular customers, time and time again, about Leon's singing ability and stage presence when performing at other local clubs. He'd made phone calls to other club managers inquiring about Leon, and sure enough, it was unanimous, Leon was a dynamic singer and a quality performer that could surely draw a crowd. Sam was soon convinced that booking Leon meant banking money. And drawing a crowd in a nightclub meant putting more money in the business' bank account.

Leon wasn't aware of it at the time, but because of all the favorable comments he had heard about Leon, Sam had his maintenance crew advertise that Leon would be performing two weeks prior. More specifically, the day he confirmed a contract with Leon, the marquee read:

**By Popular Demand**
**Leon Everette Live**
**One Night Only! August 17th**

In a cunning business move, Sam had the marquee changed on the day of Leon's arrival to make it look like the general public had only one chance to see Leon live that weekend. It was a Thursday night, and their contract stipulated that if Leon's performance met certain criteria, i.e., a minimal crowd total, was pleasing to the crowd, and of course, a minimal profit was received due partly to the quality of the entertainment, then the contract would be extended for two more nights. If any of these prerequisites weren't met, then Sam had the right not to extend the contract.

Sam was aware that his regular clientele also visited other clubs in town and that word of mouth was the best form of free advertising. Displaying the "one night only" marquee two weeks early meant that the clientele would see it and talk to their friends when they visited other clubs. The more they talked about what they read on the marquee, the better his chances were to ensure a larger-than-usual Thursday night crowd.

To the public eye, if they wanted to see Leon Everette live at this nightclub, then they only had one night to do so. In addition, a good Thursday turnout meant the beginning of a potentially successful three-night weekend for his business. The strategy wasn't about being deceptive or dishonest. It was about being a good businessman, not only for himself but for Leon as well, as larger-than-usual crowds seemed to be an emotionally charged incentive for performers to do their very best for the club's patrons.

As the clock moved closer to the nine o'clock hour, Leon made a stop by the restroom to freshen up before going live on stage. Inside, his body was tired from the long, hard day at work, but he knew he had to make sure his outward appearance didn't show his fatigue. He splashed cold water on his face, performed facial muscle exercises, and gargled his vodka-laced drink, all in hopes of putting on a pleasing expression as he introduced himself to the audience.

* * *

In another part of the club, Carroll Fulmer was sitting at a table near the stage with some of his friends from Aiken, SC. Carroll was a very successful businessman who grew up and went to school in Aiken County but now lived in Orlando, Florida. He and his wife were with a couple of old high school friends while they were in the area for a few days, having recently attended the twenty-fifth-year celebration of their high school reunion.

Carroll and his wife, Barbara, met and dated throughout their high school years in Ridge Spring, SC. During this time, Carroll was voted "most likely to succeed," and Barbara was voted "class queen." They married right after high school and Carroll started a produce delivery service that turned into one of the largest independent freight hauling companies in the southeastern United States. He was a small-town country boy that had worked hard using honest business practices, evolving to become a self-made multi-millionaire.

Carroll and his small party were just out for a night on the town, having a few drinks and reviving old stories and memories from their past, when Leon readied himself on the stage.

"How y'all doin' tonight?" asked Leon. "I'm Leon Everette, and I appreciate you all being here, so let's get this party started, shall we?"

Applause, whistles, and rebel yells answered his introduction.

As the lights grew dimmer, Leon began his rendition of Waylen Jennings' "Good Hearted Woman" which started mellow but ended up with a high-energy vibe that had the dance floor packed with rhythmic romping couples. The audience roared with satisfaction as the song ended, giving Leon a much-needed boost of confidence.

Leon continued his set singing some old as well as some new country music songs, as Carroll sat in awe of what he was hearing and seeing.

"Who is this young man?" he asked his friends.

"That's Leon Everette," his friend Tom replied. "He's from over in Ward, SC, not far from where you grew up, Carroll. He's well-known in this community, but that's all I know about him. I agree with you though; he's very good."

"No disrespect, Tom, but very good doesn't do him justice," replied Carroll. "He's got one of the most dynamic voices I've ever heard. Why isn't he in Nashville?

"I don't know," said Tom, "Why don't you ask him yourself? I'm sure he'll be taking a break pretty soon."

"I might just do that," said Carroll.

Carroll was mesmerized as Leon continued his charismatic crooning performance. His friends became oblivious to him as his sole concentration was on Leon's movements, vocals, and confidence as he continued singing and interacting with the audience. But when Leon began the intro to Conway Twitty's "Hello Darlin," he lost his customary low-key composure. Without hesitating and having momentarily lost his self-control, he stood up and yelled out, "Sing it, son!"

Barbara, Tom, and Tom's wife were momentarily taken aback as laughter and applause erupted from everyone at their party. Carroll usually had a soft-spoken, mild-mannered, smooth-composure-type temperament. It would take something really special for Carroll to come out of his normal, down-to-earth personality. This was one of those moments. Leon was that special, and Carroll could not get enough of him. The more Leon continued his mastery of the stage, the more Carroll knew he had to introduce himself.

Carroll watched closely as Leon exited the stage after finishing his first set of the night and walked toward his booth in the back corner of the club. He noticed a waitress nearby and motioned for her to come over.

"Hello, ma'am," Carroll began, "I was wondering, do you happen to know what Mr. Everette is drinking tonight? I'd like to buy him a drink and ask him over for a quick introduction. Do you think he would mind?"

"I don't think he'd mind at all," she replied, "but I'll ask."

As the waitress spoke with Leon, Carroll grabbed an extra chair from a nearby table.

The waitress soon returned and said, "Mr. Everette would love to meet with you, and thanked you for the drink. He'll be over as soon as he freshens up a bit. And by the way, he's a very casual type of guy. I'm sure he'd prefer you to simply call him Leon."

"Thank you very much," said Carroll, as he gave her a generous tip for her service and kindness.

After a quick stop in the restroom, Leon headed over to visit Carroll and his party. As he made his approach, Carroll stood up out of respect and introduced himself and everyone at the table. Leon took a seat next to Carroll, and they began their first conversation.

"Leon," Carroll began, "Tom tells me you're from my part of the country. I grew up, went to school, and got married in Ridge Spring. That's just a stone's throw from where you're from in Ward.

"Listen, I know you'll have to prepare for another set of songs shortly, so I'll get straight to my point. Leon, why on earth aren't you in Nashville? All those songs you performed sounded as good or better than the original artists. Am I right, Tom?"

"I most certainly agree, Carroll," replied Tom. "Leon, you have a great stage presence and an outstanding singing voice. I agree with Carroll. Why aren't you in Nashville?"

"Believe me, I have been to Nashville," Leon responded. "I've been there so many times that I can tell you every bill-board that's passed along the highway going and coming. I tried so hard just to get my foot in the door of a recording label's producer's office that I finally had to stop due to road fatigue and mental exhaustion. Besides, not knowing anyone and being rejected over and over by low-level shysters that I did meet on the streets finally led me to just flat-out give up. Nashville is a tough town, Mr. Fulmer, and I don't have any contacts or connections there. It's really hard for me to describe to you just how difficult it is to make it there on your own."

Without even blinking an eye, Carroll responded, "Well, I don't know anyone there either, but I do know my country music, and you sound a lot better than a lot of what I've been hearing on the radio lately. Furthermore, I don't know anything about the music industry either, but I do know that money talks, and money is no object to me. Would you be interested to continue this conversation when you have more time to discuss it with me?"

"Sure, Mr. Fulmer," replied Leon, "I'd be delighted to meet with you. Tomorrow's Friday and I have to work at my day job, and if things go well tonight, I'll be back here tomorrow night. So, would you like to meet on Saturday around noon at the Aiken Diner in downtown Aiken?"

"I'll be there," replied Carroll. "By the way, I'll be in town through the weekend. Here's my contact information. Please, give me a call if something comes up or you change your mind."

"Thank you all for all of your kind words," Leon said to Carroll's friends. "And thank you for the drink, Mr. Fulmer."

As Leon stood up to return to the stage, Carroll stood, smiled, shook his hand, and said, "Leon, thank you again for taking the time to meet with me. By the way, I like to keep relationships casual. Please, call me Carroll."

Needless to say, that was a conversation that Leon didn't see coming. He'd had requests from people before offering to buy him a drink and have a short conversation, but this one was especially interesting.

However, he didn't want to get his hopes up too high, as he'd been hurt and disappointed by false hope in his past. But then again, this man seemed sincere and forthright and claimed that money was no object and said himself that Leon should be in Nashville. Little did he know at the time, but this would be the first of many conversations with Mr. Fulmer that would lead to his eventual success as a country music superstar.

* * *

In the meantime, Sam stood unnoticed at the doorway to his office, looking out all around his club. His customers were having a great time. He could tell by their body language that they were glad to be in his club tonight. The waitresses were all busy bringing in orders for drinks from an overly crowded bar and serving them to customers with cash-in-hand tips waiting for their return. Four bartenders were working feverishly, trying to keep up with all the drink orders. Over at the entrance, the doorman was busy keeping people from coming inside, as there was now a standing room only inside.

Then by a businessman's instinct, his clever mind went to work. Friday's marquee, he thought, will read, "Back by Popular Demand, Leon Everette Live!" And Saturday's marquee will read, "Final Night, Leon Everette, Live!" His only regret was that he didn't have enough space on the marquee to put, "Come Early, Standing Room Only!"

After slowly making his way through the many closely placed tables and chairs, Leon stepped up on the stage and looked out across the now-capacity crowd. He then noticed Sam at the back of the club looking wide-eyed and smiling from ear to ear, signaling a celebratory two thumbs up. To Leon, this meant not only a paycheck for tonight, but most assuredly, two more before the weekend would be over.

* * *

As Leon drove home, all he could think about was the conversation that he had with Mr. Fulmer earlier that evening. Mr.

108

Fulmer presented himself as a man that could be respected, but then again, he could also have been a slightly drunken good ol' boy dressed in a fancy, high-dollar business suit talking like a big-shot businessman showing off in front of his friends. Nevertheless, Mr. Fulmer had indeed given the impression of being sincere with his teasingly but optimistic invitation. All things considered, only time would tell, and Saturday was just two short days away, and it couldn't come soon enough for an emotionally rejuvenated Leon.

Leon was apprehensive about telling Kathy about Mr. Fulmer as he didn't want to get her hopes up only to potentially be disappointed about the possibility of having been told false information. But, at the same time, if Mr. Fulmer was factual in his statements, then it would be the best news they had ever had throughout their somewhat rocky marriage. Saturday was just two days away, and only time would tell if what Mr. Fulmer said was, as a matter of fact, true or false.

Leon couldn't contain his excitement. He had to tell Kathy just to see what her reaction would be. As it turned out, she too, was skeptical but agreed with Leon that he should show up and meet with Mr. Fulmer just in case he was serious. What did he have to lose? Only time and an expectation of disappointment, to say the least. Besides, that seemed to be Leon's most promising attribute.

* * *

When Leon arrived at the Aiken Diner, Mr. Fulmer was already there waiting for him in a private corner booth in a quiet location away from the heavy traffic coming and going to and from the restaurant entrance. As Leon entered the restaurant, Mr. Fulmer motioned to get his attention in case Leon didn't see him as he came inside. Leon walked toward the booth now feeling much better about the situation. Mr. Fulmer had shown up as promised. Perhaps there is something to be hopeful for about this, after all.

Mr. Fulmer stood and reached out to shake Leon's hand as he approached the booth.

"Thank you very much for taking the time to meet with me, Leon. Please, have a seat," said Mr. Fulmer.

"Thank you, as well, Mr. Fulmer," replied Leon.

"Please, call me Carroll. As I told you before, I like to keep relationships among acquaintances trusting and casual," said Carroll.

"Okay, well, thank you, Carroll," Leon said with a friendly smile.

Leon immediately felt at ease with Carroll from the get-go. Carroll was so nice, sincere, and down-to-earth. He was easy-going, and when he spoke, his tone was such that you felt compelled to listen, as whatever words were coming out of his mouth would surely be something that you would want to hear.

"Leon, I don't want to waste your time here today, but I'll take as much time as you will allow me to explain to you why I asked you to meet me here today," said Carroll. "But before I do that, please allow me to tell you something about my personal and business background.

"As I told you the other night, I was raised and went to school in the same part of South Carolina as you, in Ridge Spring-Monetta, not far from where you live in Ward, SC. I grew up in a farming community and, as a seventeen-year-old young man, decided to start my own trucking business hauling produce for local farmers to grocery stores, farmer's markets, and other food outlets in our community, then eventually, across the state. When I first started my business, I barely had enough money to fill my delivery truck with gas.

"As the demand for my services expanded, my business began to grow as well, and in 1961, I purchased two B61 Mack Trucks and began hauling freight and produce up and down the eastern seaboard. That was just under twenty years ago, and now I own the largest independent trucking company in the eastern United States. I don't drive anymore, but I now have an entire fleet of freight trucks, and I pay drivers good money to haul products back and forth up and down the eastern seaboard daily.

"I've said all of that just to tell you this. As I said, I started with little to nothing, and now I'm worth millions of dollars. I'm not boasting, Leon. That's just a fact."

Leon sat quietly, listening to every word, and nothing sounded phony at all. In addition, this was supposed to be a casual meeting, but Carroll was dressed in a full-blown business suit. Leon began putting two and two together. Carroll was a businessman through and through. This man was truly the real deal.

"I've learned that to have a successful business, you have to be entirely honest with people and give them your best effort for what they bargained for or for what they've invested in," Carroll continued.

"So, I've asked you to meet me here to propose a potentially financially lucrative business deal with you. Leon, I'm serious when I say you are a diamond in the rough, just waiting for someone to find you to take you to the next level of country music stardom. And I want to be that person who helps you to get there.

"Leon, like you, I don't know anything about the country music business nor anyone in the business of country music that I could call for advice. But I do know that money talks, and as for me, I have plenty of money. So, money is not a problem.

"In addition, I think that by most people's standards, I've been a very successful businessman all my life. If I have a good product, I know how to promote it and successfully sell it to potential buyers and/or investors. Promoting is my niche, and I'm very good at it. If I don't believe in a product, then I won't waste my time on it.

"The first thing I'd like to do is get familiar with Nashville, then start looking for quality leads that may point us to places of interest to potentially get the ball rolling, so to speak. Does this sound like something you'd be interested in pursuing with me?"

By this time, Leon was all eyes and ears, beaming with excitement, and felt as if he was floating on air above the soft, padded seat below him and he wasn't anywhere near ready to come back down to earth. He wanted to hear more!

"Absolutely! I'm interested, Carroll. What do you have in mind?" Leon asked with excitement.

"Well, I've discussed this with my wife, and she's all on board. I suggest that you do the same," said Carroll.

"Oh, that won't be a problem," answered Leon, "I will discuss it with her, but I know she'll be as excited as I am to hear of the opportunity you're proposing."

"Okay, good. Here's what I propose. I have a privately owned plane. It's a Cessna King Air, and it's quite roomy and comfortable. It seats up to eleven passengers with plenty of cargo space.

"Give me about a week to take care of some business responsibilities back home, and I'll call you later in the week and let you know when I'll be able to meet you. I'll have my pilot fly my wife and me to the Saluda County Airport, and you can meet us there. And from there we'll fly straight to Nashville.

"I'll have a rental car ready and make all other accommodations ahead of time so that everything will be taken care of before we arrive. And by the way, I'll be footing the entire bill. It won't cost you a thing but your time. How does that sound?"

"That sounds great! I can hardly wait. I'll be ready anytime you are," said an excited Leon.

"Since you already know your way around Nashville, you can give my wife and me a tour of the city and point out places that you know are potential resources for quality information about how to get started in the music industry business. If you lead the way, I'll do all the talking. Are you okay with that?" Carroll asked.

"Absolutely, Carroll!" answered an appreciative Leon. "I look forward to hearing from you soon. Have a safe and pleasant trip on your way back home."

"Thank you for meeting with me, Leon. I look forward to seeing you in about a week, as well," said a pleased Carroll.

Leon gleamed with joy as he drove down the two-lane rural back road toward home. He could hardly wait to tell Kathy the potentially promising news. He was just a week away from going back to Nashville, the same place he'd just declared the week before as a place he never had any intention of visiting again. But this time, although it would be for the same purpose, the lodging conditions and travel arrangements would be entirely different, and most importantly, at no cost to him.

Was he looking forward to returning to Nashville once again after so many unsuccessful attempts on his own? You better believe he was—he was ecstatic!

Chapter 13

**Nashville**

**Carroll Fulmer was** pretty much beside himself in a state of elation all the way home on the flight back to Orlando, Florida. His wife, Barbara, was equally excited as she could see and feel the enthusiasm that Carroll displayed after his successful one-on-one meeting with Leon. If Leon's talent could be pursued as a viable product, then Carroll Fulmer was the perfect person to successfully promote and sell that product.

"Barbara, I have a really good feeling about Leon," Carroll said. "He seems like a very down-to-earth young man who just needs to get his foot in a small crack in the doorway of an office of someone in a position of authority to give him either an interview or an actual audition. It sounds as if he's tried everything he can do on his own but hasn't been given a fair shake or opportunity by anyone he's met in Nashville. I can only imagine how frustrated he must be after so many unsuccessful trips back and forth only to be shut out completely."

"I agree," answered Barbara, "and no matter what you decide to do to help him, I just want you to know that I'm one hundred percent behind you. So, from here on out, just go with your instincts. That's always been the best course of action your whole life, so why change now? This young man needs you, and you have a deep desire to make him known all across our country, so put together a plan of action and do what you do best; go sell this man to the world of country music!"

Barbara's support had always been a positive influence on Carroll's decision-making in past business ventures, but this simple spousal pep talk put his energy into overdrive in his quest to help Leon go from the ground floor to potentially through the roof of the country music industry.

Using his trucking industry success as an analogy, he knew that there would be potential roadblocks and unexpected sharp turns along the way, just as there were before he made his first commercial haul. However, he also knew that when the going gets rough and the road gets bumpy, the best thing to do is to just "keep on truckin," as every road has an intersection at some point, and if the going gets to be too overwhelming, just take a detour and go another route, but whatever you do, never leave the road.

In addition, you'll never find success on a road that you know goes nowhere because that road stops at the end of a dead-end street. The best way to reach success is to stay focused on where you're going, always keep your eyes on the road and always make sure you have enough fuel to complete the journey.

The following day, after arriving back home, Carroll went to work at once to get his business responsibilities in order before leaving for Nashville. Fortunately, he had three sons and a daughter who was more than capable of managing the trucking business while he was away. A few days later, after discussing his new venture with his family and finalizing business details, Carroll called Leon and told him that he had everything in order and to meet him at the Saluda County Airport around two-thirty the following Wednesday afternoon.

Carroll called his pilot, and asked him to ready the plane and gave him all of the details of the trip. He then made all the lodging and rental car arrangements for their arrival in Nashville.

When the following Wednesday arrived, the pilot was ready and waiting at the municipal airport in Orlando, standing beside the freshly cleaned, fuel-filled plane. Carroll and Barbara quickly boarded their Cessna King Air, excited to get started on their new adventure. It was especially exciting for Carroll, as he could hardly wait to see the expression on Leon's face when they arrived at the Saluda County Airport.

* * *

Meanwhile, on a rural road leading out of Ward, SC, Leon and Kathy were making their way to the Saluda County Airport.

"Do you think they're gonna show up at the airport?" asked a nervous but excited Kathy.

"Well, he hasn't let me down so far. I'm confident that he's a man of his word. The only reason why they may not be there is that they may have had a delay or something," said a confident Leon.

"Did you pack everything that you think you'll need?" Kathy continued to nervously ask.

"Think so," said Leon.

"Extra underwear?"

"Yep."

"Toothbrush and toothpaste?"

"Yep."

"How about clean socks? You always need fresh, clean socks when you do a lot of walking."

"Kathy, relax. I think I've got everything that I need. Besides, if I'm missing something or if I run out of something, there are plenty of places in Nashville to shop," said a reassuring Leon.

* * *

Upon their landing at the Saluda County Airport was an eagerly waiting Leon and Kathy. As the plane came to a stop, Leon was overtaken by the excitement of going back to Nashville, a place where he recently said he would never visit again. But this time would be different, as he had finally met someone who truly believed in him and was willing to put his life on hold not only to potentially get Leon's life in order but also to help start his career as a country music entertainer.

As the plane's side door opened, Carroll welcomed Leon aboard. Leon said goodbye to Kathy and eagerly climbed the steps leading up to the plane's entrance. Once onboard, Leon was amazed at the plush interior of the plane. The seats were individual leather high-back, heavily padded recliners designed for luxury, comfort, and relaxation. Toward the rear of the plane, some seating areas had a portable dining table that could also be used as a business desk. The cargo area was equally impressive, as it had more than enough room for the pilot and three passengers' luggage and carry-ons. And the most impressive feature of all was a direct view of the pilot's compartment highlighted with all the gauges, bells, and whistles that an instrument control panel could ask for.

"Welcome aboard, Leon," said a jubilant Carroll. "It's good to see you again."

"Hey, Leon," good to see you," Barbara chimed in.

"Thank you so much. It's good to see y'all again, too. I am so grateful for this opportunity. You don't know how much this means to me," said an appreciative Leon.

As the plane completed its ascent and leveled off above the cloud line, the pilot completed his check-in with the control tower and announced to the passengers that the weather in Nashville was ideal and that their direct flight should take about two hours or possibly a little less.

Carroll offered Leon some snack foods and drinks and showed him around the plane's passenger compartment and restroom, then they both sat down for a casual conversation.

"Leon, here's what I have in mind for this trip," said Carroll. "Hopefully, it'll be the first of many to follow. Since neither one of us knows anyone to contact for advice, and since you are familiar with the layout of Nashville, why don't you show Barbara and me around so we can get acclimated to the area?

"I've planned this trip as a fact-finding venture and not necessarily one to conduct actual business, although I won't turn down an opportunity if one presents itself. I'm primarily interested in gathering information about people to talk to and places to go to get us into a studio for an interview or possibly an audition for you.

"But don't get discouraged if we're not successful this time. I promise you, I won't stop, no matter how many trips we have to make, until I come face to face with someone in the know about this business. Then, after I've had a satisfying business discussion with a legitimate music expert, we will know where we stand and will have more information on how we should proceed. Are you okay with that?"

"That sounds like an excellent plan, Carroll," Leon replied.

Carroll had intentionally planned their arrival in Nashville on a late Wednesday afternoon. His reasoning was to get a feel of the city's activities during the workweek, as well as the weekend, then fly home the following Sunday afternoon.

After checking in to one of Nashville's prestigious hotels and getting settled in, the threesome headed out for an evening dinner at one of Nashville's finest restaurants. During dinner, Leon described some of the things that they would see as they discussed their plans for their tour of Nashville the next day. After dinner and a few adult beverages, they headed back to their rooms for the night. They would all sleep well, knowing that tomorrow could be big, but it definitely would not be a bust.

Thursday morning, as they drove along in their rental car, Leon told them his story about his many unsuccessful trips to Nashville. He showed them the Gulf gas station that he jokingly called his Nashville Hotel, where he would park and sleep in his car, awaken the next morning and take a sink bath in the gas station restroom, then walk the streets all day hoping to find any form of lead or someone to help him fulfill his desired goal.

Carroll hadn't heard that story before, and having heard it, he became more encouraged to want to help Leon even more. His heartstrings began tugging at his emotions. Leon had sacrificed so much time and effort to have received absolutely nothing except for rejection and grief in all his many trips to Nashville. Right then, Carroll convinced himself that he was going to do his best to see that someday Leon would be so successful that he'd be able to own that Gulf station if he decided he wanted to buy it.

After driving around and noting all the potential landmarks for doing business, they decided to walk alongside one of the main streets in Nashville called Broadway. Broadway was to Nashville as "The Strip" is to Las Vegas. Bright Neon signs lit up the night, and country music blared from the doorways of the many nightclubs and bars along the way.

This was the country music capital of the world. Cowboy boots, cowboy hats and larger-than-large belt buckles were the dress of the day. Occasionally, one would have to watch where you stepped, as the splatter of chewing tobacco adorned the sidewalks as a stroke of paint adorns the canvass of an artist's rendition of a country-western prized depiction of art.

On many street corners, as well as store-front sidewalks, acoustic guitarists and violinists (or locally called fiddlers) played and sang to their passing audiences, hoping for donations for their talents to pay a bill or, in some cases, buy their next meal. Their ultimate hope was the same one that Leon was searching for; that special someone who would have the authentic industry clout to recognize their talents as a potential county music entertainer.

As they continued their walk, they would stop and visit some of the bars along the way. Carroll cordially yet cleverly approached waitresses, bartenders, and musicians, inquiring about where to go and who to see about getting into the music industry. Although he wasn't successful in getting the specific information he was hoping for, he did get somewhat familiar with some of the terms of the music industry as well as how the vernacular slang is spoken among those who were also in pursuit of stardom but had yet to achieve that status. Having talked to the many unsuccessful amateur musicians, at least now he knew where not to go.

By the time Sunday rolled around, Carroll had had enough of this visit to Nashville. It wasn't very productive, but it was educational, and they all had a good time. He didn't expect much progress toward his ultimate goal, but at least he had a better understanding of how the Nashville music scene works and where to go and where to not go to get the results for what he'd come for.

* * *

On the flight back home, Carroll had a heart-to-heart talk with Leon about what he thought about their trip to Nashville.

"Leon," Carroll said with a soft, fatherly, yet business tone, "now, don't get discouraged about our lack of results from our time in Nashville. I know we didn't get what we came for, but believe it or not, I have a better understanding now of what we're up against, and I think I may have an idea of where we may need to go to find what we may need.

"Furthermore, I think I may have gotten enough information on a couple of potential prospects that may be a good start for us to pursue on our next trip back to Nashville. I've made notes of the names of some of the record label companies, and when we get back home, I'm going to make some phone calls and see if I can find someone to help me get an invitation to meet with some of their upper-level executives.

"So, when we get back home, go about your normal routine

and wait for my next phone call. In the meantime, I'll be in contact by phone with some of my business associates that may be able to help me get the information I need so we can do this again. Are you okay with that?"

"Yes, sir," Carroll, Leon replied with an appreciative tone.

* * *

Shortly after landing in Saluda, Leon was greeted by an anxious but excited Kathy. On their way back home, Leon explained the details of the trip and what their next move would be. Kathy was apprehensive at first, as she wasn't one hundred percent sure if all these trips were going to be worth their while or not. But then again, she thought, what else do we have to lose?

Less than two weeks later, Leon got a call from Carroll.

"Leon, pack your bags; we need to go back to Nashville. I've got us an appointment with the top two country music song-writers in Nashville, and they've agreed to meet with us Thursday morning at nine o'clock, Nashville time. Do you think you can make it, or do you need more time?" Carroll asked.

"Absolutely, I can make it!" Leon enthusiastically replied.

"Great," Carroll said. "I'll pick you up at the Saluda Airport Wednesday afternoon at two o'clock."

"Okay," said Leon, "I look forward to seeing you Wednesday."

Carroll had done his homework. He'd made contact with some of his close business associates and explained his desire to get an interview with top record label executives in Nashville, and as expected, he got what he'd asked for.

His associates had made phone calls to their associates who made phone calls to their associates until they were satisfied that they had the information that Carroll had asked for. Carroll's associates let it be known that he was a man on a mission and a man that knew that when he had a product to sell, he would go to the ends of the earth to find a way to promote it.

Word soon got out to the Nashville music elite that there was a very respectable, prominently successful businessman from Orlando, FL, that was representing an unknown potential country music talent that was looking for an opportunity to prove himself by way of an interview or an audition, or both. After receiving this news, those in positions of authority became cautiously excited, for a quality referral of a new talent meant more money for their company, not only for record sales but also for the potential of commercial endorsements and product memorabilia.

The next time Carroll Fulmer would step foot in Nashville, he wouldn't have to track down anyone or plead with anyone about who to see or where to go to do business—this time, those who had all the clout and power in the Nashville music industry would not only be expecting him but their doors would be flung wide open as a grand gesture of a warm, welcoming invitation.

Chapter 14

**"Quiet Please, Recording in Progress"**

**On their second** trip to Nashville, Carroll took the lead, and Leon followed his direction. Through his business associates, Carroll had successfully made an appointment to meet with two of Nashville's top songwriters and composers—Jerry Foster and Bill Rice.

Foster and Rice weren't just your everyday good ol' boys country music songwriters. They were members of the "Who's Who" and the "Elite of the Elite" crowd in Nashville. They had made a name for themselves by writing and composing a plethora of hit songs for the likes of Charlie Pride, Jerry Lee Lewis, Hank Williams, Jr., Mickey Gilley, as well as many other successful country music artists.

Foster and Rice dominated the early 1970's ASCAP (American Society of Composers, Authors, and Publishers) awards by taking home a total of twenty-one awards in 1972 and 1973 alone. They were often complimented as being the "Rogers and Hammerstein" of country music. In the years to come, they proudly proclaimed that being enshrined in the Country Music Hall of Fame was their greatest honor and life's achievement. It was safe to say that if you wanted to make a name for yourself in the country music industry, using a Foster and Rice composition would probably be a good start.

Upon landing in Nashville, Carroll and Leon went straight to Foster's and Roger's music studio. Never one to be late for a business meeting, Carroll made sure they were there in plenty of time. Upon their arrival, Carroll went straight to the receptionist's desk and announced his and Leon's appointment. The receptionist politely welcomed them and offered them a seat in the adjoining lobby.

To their surprise but not a disappointment, the building had been designed using a classic style of architecture having a quaint, old-fashioned interior that would make any country music fan feel comfortable and right at home. The waiting room had a warm, pleasantly charming "Grand Ole Opry" character as well as a heavenly aura of country music divinity. The furniture was comfortable and very nice, but not necessarily luxurious. The displays of the many country music Grammys and other awards and the walls covered with photographs, both color and black and white, of country music stars dating back to the 1940s seemed to beg for someone to hear their illustrious story.

After a short wait, Carroll and Leon were escorted to another room by the receptionist.

"Someone will be with you shortly," said the receptionist. "May I offer you a beverage or a snack while you wait?"

"No, but thank you," Carroll and Leon replied.

Eager to meet their potential new clients, Mr. Foster and Mr. Rogers entered the room. As they met with the two local country music icons, Carroll and Leon sat attentively quiet as Foster and Rice introduced themselves and began to tell the details of their production process.

"Gentlemen, welcome to Nashville. Better known as 'Music City'." said Mr. Foster, as both he and Mr. Rogers gave them both a firm yet warm handshake. "And right now, you're sitting in the very heart of the city."

The casual, inviting welcome immediately put Carroll and Leon at ease. Their nerves were still a little jumpy but would be much more tolerable from here on out. Foster and Rice were there to talk business, but they made Carroll and Leon feel as if it was a reunion of old friends.

"We've got a catalog of a variety of songs that we've prepared for you," Foster continued. "What we'll need from Leon is to find the right fit for his vocal range. Leon, since you don't have any demos for us to critique, how would you best describe the style of voice that you have for country music?"

"I don't know how I would describe my voice, per se," answered Leon, "but the best example that I can relate to is Narvel Felts. I've always admired his style, and he's my favorite singer of all time. If I had to describe my voice, I'd say that it's in the same category or range as Narvel's."

"That's quite a compliment to yourself if it turns out to be true," Mr. Rice chimed in. "Narvel is one of my favorites as well. I hope you won't disappoint us because if you indeed have the talent anywhere close to that of Narvel, then we may be able to help you get off to a good start. Give us a few minutes to scan our song catalog, and let's see if we can find one that we think may be a good fit for you."

As the prestigious songwriting duo momentarily left the room, Carroll and Leon sat in awe of even more gold records, country music awards, and pictures of country music stars of the past and present adorning every wall in the plush executive office suite. In the audible background was the faint sound of music from an adjoining sound recording studio, wherein all probability, an artist was in the process of recording a song.

After a short time, the songwriting duo once again entered the room. This time, the primary composer of the two, Mr. Rice had an acoustic guitar with him.

"Well, gentlemen, I think you may be in luck." said an excited Mr. Rice. "We found several songs that we think you may like which may also be a good fit for Leon's vocal style.

Please allow me to strum a few chords and sing a verse or two for you. And if this one doesn't work for you, we'll try until we do find one for you. Sound good?"

In unison, Carroll and Leon replied with an excited, "Absolutely!"

Mr. Rice sat down in a nearby chair, positioned his guitar against his chest and on his lap and began strumming and singing to the melody and words of a song the duo had composed called "Over".

As Mr. Rice continued his demo of the song, Carroll looked over to see a wide-eyed, smiling ear-to-ear, Leon enthusiastically nodding his head in a positive response to what he was hearing.

"So, what do you think, Leon?" asked Mr. Rice after ending his sample of the song. "Do you feel comfortable with the lyrics and the melody? Because if you do, we're going to the production studio and do a take or two with you singing it, then we'll evaluate the results and go from there."

"I absolutely love it!" Leon responded.

"Okay then," said Mr. Foster. "There's a recording production underway at the moment, but they're almost finished with their session, and when they do, I'll send someone back to get you, okay? In the meantime, please help yourself to some snacks and drinks, and in case you need them, the restroom is just down the hall on the right."

Carroll and Leon, both appreciatively acknowledged them and patiently waited for their return. After about half an hour or so, a female receptionist entered the room, and introduced herself, and said, "Gentlemen, please follow me. Mr. Foster and Mr. Rice are ready for you in the sound recording studio."

Foster and Rice already had their in-house studio musicians, backup vocalists, and soundboard operator prepared for the song that was to be recorded by Leon.

Mr. Foster led Carroll to a quaint but plush enclosure on the opposite side of the recording sound booth. Carroll sat behind and to one side of the soundboard operator and his elaborate music recording and editing control panel.

The sound control room was equipped with all the latest equipment and accessories necessary for making high-quality sound recordings. On the wall adjoining the sound booth was a large, clear glass or plexiglass window for viewing the artists as they played their instruments and sang their songs for the recording.

As he sat down, Foster reached toward the soundboard and flipped a switch, which turned on a lighted sign above the entrance and exit door that read, in bold, red-colored letters, "Quiet Please Recording in Progress."

At the same time, Mr. Rice escorted Leon to the sound recording booth to make him feel comfortable as he prepared him for his posture before a suspended microphone to get a quality "soundcheck" before recording. He then strategically placed a sheet of paper on which the lyrics were printed on a music stand in front of Leon and adjusted the stand to fit Leon's height. After Leon became comfortable with the melody and the lyrics, they proceeded to start the recording.

Leon followed all of Rice's instructions, and after they were satisfied that they had a good sample of his voice, the instrumentals, and the background vocals, they proceeded to make the actual recording of Leon's first official single record called "Over."

Carroll sat and listened in awe as Leon began to sing. Leon's vocals were, indeed, an ideal match for both the melody and lyrics. The sound quality of the instruments played by the studio musicians was precise and flawless. When the background vocalists came in, Carroll had chills all over from the divine-like harmonies that accompanied the truly alluring sound of Leon's unique voice.

Carroll, having a penchant for success, was pleasantly amused as he closely watched Foster and Rice's positive reaction as the recording came to an end.

Foster then reached for a switch to the sound booth microphone and spoke to Leon.

"Leon, that sounded great!" said an excited Foster. "We'll do a few more takes to perfect some of the things that I think we can improve on; then at some point in time, we'll run it through our mixer and production process to fine-tune anything that we may notice that we need to change before we finalize it for distribution. But, as far as your part, I think you nailed it!"

Carroll and Leon then took a restroom break as Foster and Rice met alone in the sound booth, combing through their catalog of songs. When Carroll and Leon returned, they motioned for them to sit with them, as they had some good news that they thought would be worth their while.

While holding his finger in-between a couple of sections of the catalog to mark saved pages, Foster began speaking, "Hey y'all, I think we may have some good news for you. While you were away, we found a couple more songs that we think Leon may want to consider recording. We were so impressed with "Over" that we'd like for him to record a couple more songs called, 'Giving Up Easy' and 'My Lady Loves Me.' What'd you say, Leon?"

"I'd love to!" replied a jubilant Leon.

Needless to say, Carroll and Leon stayed in Nashville and finished recording the final two songs. Once again, Foster and Rice were very encouraging with the results.

Afterward, they flew back home to wait for a call from Foster and Rice to let them know that the final results of mixing the tracks were completed. The process would take time, as the schedule for this procedure was backed up significantly, but they had promised that they would expedite the results as quickly as they could.

Leon was finally leaving Nashville for the first time since his many trips there, having now completed his original motive for going there all those disappointing times before. He had not only gotten his foot in the door for a sit-down interview, but he had also gotten an audition that led to him getting his first official country music recording. He could hardly wait to tell Kathy, family, and friends about the good news.

Surely, by now, there were conversations within the brick-and-mortar walls in and around the confines of Music City, of a new name in town that had the potential to become the latest in a long line of country music legends and entertainers, and his name was Leon Everette.

Chapter 15

**It's Not "Over" Yet**

**All the time** and effort put into making the demo in Nashville was finally completed and sent to Carroll for his approval. Carroll could hardly wait to call Leon, as he was so excited and happy having heard the results of the three songs on the newly formatted demo called a cassette tape.

"Leon, I just received and listened to the demo from Foster and Rice," an excited Carroll said. "My friend, Foster and Rice were right when they said that 'you nailed it'! And the musical accompaniment and background vocals were equally amazing. No doubt, those two know their business. This is a high-quality, professional sound. I can hardly wait to hear it on the radio!"

"So, what do we need to do now?" asked an equally excited Leon.

"Now that we have our demo, we need to go back to Nashville and sit face-to-face with someone in authority at a recording label business," replied Carroll. "Let me make some calls and after I can confirm an appointment, I'll let you know when we need to go back."

"Sounds good," replied Leon, "I'll be waiting for your call."

Carroll didn't waste any time, as he already had a shortlist of record label companies in Nashville and their phone numbers. The one thing that he did not have was the specific names of persons in authority whom he needed to make an appointment with.

Nevertheless, he began making cold calls, and one by one, the only person he was able to talk to was the receptionist, and she would take a message and his phone number only to say that someone would return his call as soon as possible.

To his dismay, he never received a call back from any of the recording label executives whatsoever. Although he thought he'd done everything that needed to be done to get a proper interview, he soon realized that since he was new and an unproven manager in the business, he was being placed at the end of a long line of managers working to achieve the same results. He admitted to himself that he was new to the business and he still had a lot more to learn, but he wouldn't stop until he had achieved his goal.

Having hit yet another dead end, he then resorted to once again calling his associates in hopes of finding a recording executive that would schedule a face-to-face interview with him and Leon to listen to the demo. After a few days, one of his contacts eagerly called him with news that an appointment was scheduled for him with a highly esteemed executive of Capitol Records named Jim Foglesong.

Jim Foglesong was no amateur executive when it came to the country music industry. Under his leadership, over ninety country songs reached the number one position on the country music charts, with performers like Merle Haggard, Barbara Mandrell, Reba McEntire, Conway Twitty, Loretta Lynn, and many, many others.

The day finally arrived when Carroll and Leon were to meet with Mr. Foglesong. They were so excited yet had to work hard to suppress their joy to present themselves professionally. They now had their demo cassette and felt confident that it would be their "golden ticket" for an opportunity to help get them to the next level in the country music industry. Carroll just knew that once Mr. Foglesong heard Leon's voice, he would immediately be impressed.

"Good morning, gentlemen," said a cordial Mr. Foglesong. "Welcome to Capitol Records. You come highly recommended. I do apologize, but I'm on a tight schedule. What do you have for me?"

"We have a demo tape of Leon singing three songs written, composed, and produced by Foster and Rice," Carroll proudly answered. "Now, I know you're a busy man, and your time is limited, but I'd appreciate it if you'd just listen to the first song and give us your professional opinion."

"Sure, I'll do that for you," replied Mr. Foglesong.

Carroll handed Mr. Foglesong the demo tape and he inserted it into his cassette player. After about ten seconds had played, he quickly ejected the tape, saying, "I don't hear anything special here. I can find a hundred singers down on Broadway that sound like that. Singers like that are a dime a dozen in Nashville. Now, I'm always looking for a product that I can sell, and frankly, I don't think I can sell that. But thank you, gentlemen, for coming, but I don't think we're going to be able to do business at this time."

Now, Jim Foglesong was a very well-respected and successful businessman in the music business, to say the least. He was not known for being rude or flippant whatsoever. However, if Jim Foglesong had an imperfection in judging talent, it was probably his spontaneous, quick-trigger decisiveness that sometimes resulted in his missing out on quality, worthwhile clients.

Carroll and Leon looked at one another in astonishment and disappointment. Carroll had a product that he was confident he could sell, yet this man had not only indirectly ridiculed his decision-making ability but had seemingly made a mockery of him. Leon thought his voice was unique, yet this man thought that it sounded common and was plentiful among the masses.

But the most annoying thing of all is the fact that he'd only listen to a mere ten seconds of the recording, and that felt pretty much like a slap in the face.

The dejection that Carroll and Leon were feeling was disheartening, to say the least. Over time, they would learn that this was a common fallacy or character trait of Jim Foglesong. As effective as he was in finding and helping launch successful careers of exceptional vocalists, he was also known for his quick dismissal of new or unknown outsiders to the industry. To his credit, he had a tight business schedule consisting of interviews, sound productions, event appearances, and many more obligations that limited his time with not only new but current musical talents as well. His intentions were never meant to ridicule or mock anyone, although they were often perceived that way.

Leon felt bad that Carroll was feeling so dejected. He'd never seen this side of Carroll before, as he was always outgoing and positive in his speech and mannerisms. Carroll had worked so hard to get them to where they were, yet Leon felt responsible for his voice not being good enough to meet the high standards of the Nashville sound.

On their flight back home, Leon sat quietly, as he didn't know what to say that would make things better. It is what it is, he thought to himself. There was nothing he could do or say that was going to cheer up Carroll, and that was a miserable feeling for Leon.

Then, from out of nowhere, Carroll abruptly broke the silence, "I'm sick and tired of being disrespected by those so-called professionals in Nashville. The way I do business is to treat everybody equally and with respect. Those Nashville high-class country hicks think they're above everyone else, and if you're not in their inner circle, you'll have to beg and plead to do business with them.

"To heck with them; I've observed enough and have learned enough to know that I can do this business on my own. It's not rocket science. I'm gonna purchase the right equipment and find the right people to run it; then I'm gonna create my own record label company. And when I do, those arrogant, self-centered country snobs in Nashville will be calling me!"

* * *

Just a few short months later, Carroll had indeed established his own record label company that he called "Orlando Records." After thinking it over, he realized that he didn't have to buy any expensive equipment or hire anyone to operate it after all. Instead, he decided to simply rent a local recording studio and used their employees and studio musicians to handle the production process for him. He would also use them to make copies of Leon's new record and print the Orlando Records label on them.

Now that he had his own personal recording label company established and three singles ready for production, it was time to find someone to help him distribute them to as many country music radio stations as possible.

Carroll then made some phone calls and found the top three independent recording label distributors in the country. He would have to pay a hefty price for their services, but they all agreed to distribute, promote, and support him in any way they could to get Leon's records played on as many country music radio stations across America as soon as possible.

After a few short weeks, their efforts were surprisingly yet rewardingly successful. As "Over's" popularity grew among country music radio station listeners, it continued its climb until eventually making its peak position well within the top ten on the country music charts as rated by the industry standard *Billboard Magazine*. In addition, "Over" also made history as the first time a single by an independent recording label made the top ten without the circulation of any major label distributors.

Carroll Fulmer had successfully beaten the so-called Nashville elite at their own game.

However, Carroll was smart enough to know when to celebrate and when to get back to business. He was also the kind of businessman who appreciated people who promoted his product and would make an honest effort to reward them for their hard work and support in any way he could.

He called his independent distributors and got a list of names, phone numbers, and addresses of all the one hundred twenty Billboard-affiliated radio stations used for gathering data that controlled the Billboard Magazine rating charts. Carroll and Leon then began a campaign of making phone calls to every individual country music radio station program director in the United States, inviting them to breakfast, lunch, or dinner at their discretion.

They then flew across the country to every single station, introducing themselves face-to-face with each program director, showing their appreciation for playing Leon's records. Carroll wined and dined them all at the very best local restaurants and bars in each city. Their "get to know us" campaign was a huge success. The talk among radio program directors was that Carroll Fulmer was the real thing. This was a man of his word and a man who believed in and stood behind his product. Carroll Fulmer had made a commendable name for himself. He soon became known as the most popular and successful independent recording label owner of his time.

But there was a problem. Well, sort of. It was the responsibility of the so-called Nashville legends to review the country music Billboard charts daily. As "Over" made its historic climb up the charts, the Nashville bigwigs began calling around and asking each other, "Who's behind this 'Orlando' independent recording label that has a song in the top ten of the country music charts?"

To them, it was absurd that an independent recording label had a song that was doing so well. To make matters worse, it was not only the very first song by this independent label, but it was also out-charting most of the major label songs. How is it possible that an unknown independent label is doing so well, they would ask themselves.

It didn't take long for the tables to turn. The Nashville music executives soon found out that Carroll Fulmer was the man behind the name Orlando Records. The problem was that they had never heard of him before, and if they had, they didn't remember him because they didn't think he was worth wasting their time on.

Nevertheless, as Leon's single got more and more playtime, and as Leon's name kept coming up in conversations, the Nashville music executives did their research and found the contact information for Carroll Fulmer. It wasn't long before it was them who were beginning to call Carroll's office for an appointment to discuss him doing business with them to format his songs using their label.

Meanwhile, back in Orlando, Carroll and Leon were busy making plans to organize a group of musicians to prepare for an inaugural tour to jump-start Leon's music career when the phone rang.

"Mr. Fulmer," said Carroll's receptionist, "there's a Mr. Jim Foglesong on line one. He says he's calling from Capitol Records in Nashville and requests to speak with you."

Carroll paused for a second, and with a cunning, mischievous smile, looked at Leon then pressed a button on the intercom to answer his receptionist saying, "Tell him I can't take his call right now, but leave a message and a phone number and I'll return his call."

"Yes, sir," Mr. Fulmer answered the receptionist.

Leon sat momentarily dazed and confused, freaking out over Carroll's reply.

"What are you doing, Carroll?" a very perplexed Leon asked. "That's the same man we visited with a few months ago. Carroll, he's the president of Capitol Records, one of the top country music labels in the world. When people like him call, they expect you to hear what he has to say."

Carroll couldn't help but chuckle out loud. He'd pranked Leon out of having a little fun and at the same time, avoided a call from Jim Foglesong out of spite and retribution.

"I know," Carroll laughed. "I'm not ignoring him; I'm just temporarily avoiding him. I'm giving him a dose of his own medicine. I don't appreciate anyone disrespecting me the way that man did on our last trip to Nashville. I'm sure he's calling because he's upset that an unknown independent label is outperforming most of the songs that his label has on the charts right now. And since 'Over' is doing so well on the charts, he's probably more concerned about the effect it's having on his greedy pocketbook."

Well, that was just one of many calls from the Nashville elite. Other label representatives in the same position as Foglesong would also call and would receive the same response from Carroll's office. Then, after a while, the calls from Nashville became few and far between. However, that was about to change as Carroll and Leon began working on their next music strategy.

As "Over" had reached its peak on the Billboard charts, it was time to introduce their next single called "Giving Up Easy." This time when they would call the one hundred twenty radio station program directors, they would know them by name, as having already established a good rapport with them during "Over's" premier into the country music scene.

When the independent label distributors began sending out copies of "Giving Up Easy," the station program directors were eager to play it. And play it they did. "Giving Up Easy" was so well received that it entered the top one hundred on the Billboard charts at number forty-five.

That was unheard of at the time for any record produced by a major label. What made "Giving Up Easy" stand out among all the other songs in the top one hundred was the fact that it was produced and distributed by a little-known independent label called "Orlando Records". It was the first time that an independent label had a song that premiered in the top one hundred at the time. To make matters even more intriguing, the name Leon Everette was beginning to become well known, not only among the station program directors but more importantly, by their numerous listening fans.

As with "Over," "Giving Up Easy" began its climb up the country music charts, and with that climb began yet another barrage of phone calls from the Nashville elite to Carroll Fulmer's office in Orlando. This time, however, Carroll would take their calls one by one just to listen to the pleas and requests to visit them in Nashville to discuss doing business with them. Some of their words were so sweetly spoken that you'd think they were surely talking with a piece of candy in their mouth. My, my, my, how the tables had surely turned.

Finally, Carroll spoke with someone whom he felt had a tone of genuine sincerity and not of greed or self-importance. It was Jerry Bradley, the president of RCA Records in Nashville. After a friendly but convincing discussion of the potential success of Leon Everette's music being distributed by RCA Records, Carroll agreed to meet with him in Nashville the following week.

So, once again, Carroll and Leon flew back to Nashville, this time with a *personal invitation* and a confirmed appointment time. As they walked along the sidewalk in front of the RCA headquarters in Nashville, Carroll turned to Leon to say, "Leon, when we go in, just follow my lead. We're about to find out just how important we are to these people."

Leon didn't have a clue as to what Carroll was talking about but neither was he going to question him. As they entered the doorway of the elaborate lobby of the RCA headquarters building, Carroll saw a sign that had employee information written on it. As soon as he saw "Jerry Bradley Suite 1A", he never broke his stride as he walked right by the receptionist's desk and straight into Jerry Bradley's office unannounced.

Sitting behind a beautiful, dark-cherry wood business desk decorated with small country music figurines and a lamp topped with a cowboy hat for a shade was none other than RCA Records President Jerry Bradley.

Without hesitation, Carroll abruptly interjected, "Mr. Bradley, Carroll Fulmer, and this is my client, Leon Everette. It's a pleasure to finally meet you, sir!"

A shaken receptionist quickly approached Mr. Bradley's doorway, exclaiming, "I'm sorry, Mr. Bradley, but..."

"It's alright, Melody. I was expecting these two gentlemen. Gentlemen, may I offer you a cup of coffee or something else to drink?"

"No, but thank you, Mr. Bradley," Carroll replied.

"That'll be all Melody. Please close the door as you leave. Thank you," requested Mr. Bradley.

Mr. Bradley then extended his hand out to shake hands with his two visitors, and with a soft-spoken, congenial southern drawl accent began speaking, "Gentlemen, please have a seat, and welcome to RCA Records. Believe me when I say the pleasure of meeting you is all mine."

Right away, Carroll and Leon were put at ease. Carroll's little "get to know you" test had worked to perfection. This man was the real thing, and he wasn't annoyed in the slightest by their abrupt, unannounced introduction.

"The feeling is quite mutual," Carroll said. "We've been looking forward to this moment for some time now."

"Carroll, Leon," Mr. Bradley began, "please allow me to get straight to the point of my asking you to take time out of your busy schedule to meet with me here today. First of all, Leon, you have an amazing talent, and your voice is unique in the way that it draws a listener in, so to speak, as they hear it from a radio or any other playback device. That, my friend, is what people in my position are looking for in quality country music entertainment.

"And Carroll, I've done my homework on you, as well. I am beyond impressed with how you've established such a successful independent record label with absolutely no prior experience whatsoever. It took RCA years to establish itself as a player in the music business. On the other hand, it only took you less than a year to establish your label. That is truly amazing!

"Speaking of labels and music, I've invited you here to consider signing Leon under the RCA label. I realize that 'Over' continues to do well and that 'Giving Up Easy' is making a climb on the charts, but what I propose won't stop any of that momentum.

"I come from the 'old school' where a man's word and a handshake are as good as a signed legal document. If you join me at RCA, I promise you that I will do all I can to make 'Over' and 'Giving Up Easy' a continued success, as well as the future of Leon's singing career.

"If we wait for a signed contract to become a legal document, we'll have lost as many as five to six weeks of the momentum of 'Over' and 'Giving Up Easy' playtime and sales, whereas if we do it as I'm proposing, Leon will get more exposure and the songs will get more playing time because we have many, many more stations than the independent labels have access to."

Carroll looked at Leon, and Leon shrugged his shoulders and nodded his head as if to say, "It's okay with me if it's okay with you."

Carroll and Leon then extended their hand to Mr. Bradley, and as Mr. Bradley shook each one's hand, said, "Gentlemen, as of this moment, you're the newest member of the family of RCA Records, and I'm proud to have the privilege of being the first to welcome you aboard."

Mr. Bradley then reached for his intercom system on his

desk and made a call to Melody, "Melody, please have all of the department heads meet with me in the boardroom immediately."

"Yes, sir," Mr. Bradley, "Melody replied."

"Gentlemen, please follow me," Mr. Bradley requested, "I want to introduce you to our staff."

Carroll and Leon followed Mr. Bradley a short distance down a hallway to the executive boardroom. Upon entering, they saw a long, oblong, shining wood table surrounded by about twelve or so posh chairs.

One by one, staff department heads, including marketing, sales, public relations, promotions, and others, began entering the room and filling the empty chairs.

After everyone was accounted for and seated, Mr. Bradley proudly announced, "Ladies and Gentlemen, please join me in welcoming our newest brothers to the family of RCA Records— Mr. Carroll Fulmer, and Mr. Leon Everette."

After a short round of applause, Mr. Bradley continued by describing their recent agreement and then said, "Even though 'Over' and 'Giving Up Easy' still have an Orlando Records label, as of this time, they are, in fact, now covered under the auspices and rights of RCA.

"In due time, we will re-service the Orlando Records label with an official RCA label. But in the meantime, I want you to continue to publicize, promote, and push for even more playing time for both records. Right now, their momentum is at a good pace, and I want to see it continue, or if possible, increase in popularity."

* * *

Carroll and Leon then flew back home and announced the good news to their family and friends. To say the least, everyone was overjoyed. All their hard work and personal sacrifices had finally been recognized and rewarded. The next time Leon would go to Nashville, most of those of authority and influence would now know who he was without an introduction. From here on out, Leon Everette was not only known as simply the new singer in town but also as potentially becoming the "next big thing," adding to a long, quality line of Nashville performers.

After about a month or so, Mr. Bradley called for Carroll and Leon to come back to Nashville to sign the official legal binding contract. In so doing, Orlando Records would be no more. However, from that moment forward, wherever Carroll Fulmer went in Nashville, he would be greeted with open arms and pleasantry and some would even roll out the red carpet, so to speak, as if he was a part of country music royalty. But through all the praise and adoration, Carroll Fulmer never, in the least, lost his mild-mannered composure and genuine respect for his present and future fellow business partners.

Through all the difficulties and hardships, high expectations, and disappointing results, Carroll and Leon's dreams finally came to fruition. Although all the legal jargon had finally been completed, there was still a lot of work to be done. They would have to buy a tour bus, assemble a band of musicians, and plan a tour. There was no time to waste—it was now time to get this show on the road!

Chapter 16

## Midnight Maroon

**In the days** and weeks that followed their signing of a contract with RCA, Carroll and Leon limited their celebratory occasion to a joyous, but bare minimum. They now had an unwavering, self-imposed momentum compelling them to achieve their next desired goals—to continue finding musicians and organize a band, purchase a tour bus, and plan their first official road tour.

Finding band musicians in the country music industry was usually not a hard task to accomplish, as there was an overwhelming resource to choose from. The hard part would be to find the right people to fit their respective positions for Leon's style of music. It's kind of like finding the right piece to fit an exact spot when putting a jigsaw puzzle together. You either have the right piece or you don't, and Leon was very selective when it came to making the right choice for his musicians.

Leon had been an admirer of Norvel Felts his entire life and he was very familiar with the type of musical instruments that supported his style of music. Now, Leon's intention was not to copy Norvel Felts' brand of music but to use it as an example to help him find his own specifically talented, quality musicians.

After all, people like Hank Williams, Jr. did the same thing. He used his father, Hank Williams, Sr., as an example to follow and learn from, only to establish his distinct style of country music.

Leon meticulously searched far and wide to find the perfect choices for putting his band together, and after filling all the positions, the original "Hurricane" band would include the following members:

| | |
|---|---|
| *Mike Hanson* | *Drummer* |
| *Buzz Murphey* | *Keyboard* |
| *Ronnie Myers* | *Bass* |
| *Randy Wagner* | *Lead guitar* |
| *Ira Johnson* | *Steel guitar* |
| *Tony Stevens* | *Fiddle, harmonica, banjo* |
| *Terry Smith* | *Acoustic guitar, frontman, backup vocals* |

In the meantime, in Orlando, FL., Carroll was busy trying to find a tour bus to accommodate the band and all their traveling needs. After a thorough search, he found a classic. It was a used but very well-preserved GMC 4104 that was originally made for the Greyhound Bus Lines. Although it had a lot of miles on the odometer, Carroll had an expert mechanic thoroughly inspect it for mechanical longevity and road-worthy durability. Several upgrades were performed on the engine, brakes, and transmission, but all in all, it ended up being the perfect fit for the new band's needs.

The interior of the bus was immaculate, but Carroll had a local body shop make major changes by removing all the seats and converting it into an actual traveling home by adding basic and specific amenities to fit the band's needs while away on the road.

The last thing the bus needed was a visual identity that

passersby would be able to recognize and would immediately know that it was the bus that carried the band and its lead singer, Leon Everette. For that decision, Carroll would need Leon to come to Florida to make the color choices and any other modifications that he wanted to complete the bus's final details.

* * *

Carroll and Leon met with a local body shop owner who presented Leon with a paint sample booklet along with a variety of individual paint sample templates that were about one inch square. Leon scanned the booklet and templates and finally decided on a signature color— "Midnight Maroon."

To Leon, just the sound of the name "Midnight Maroon" sounded poetic. *How could you possibly go wrong by choosing this gorgeous color*, he convinced himself.

"You know, you can't always go by these color samples, right?" said the body shop painter.

"What do you mean?" asked Leon.

"Well, some of these samples can be quite deceiving, and I've used this one in the past, and the final results didn't exactly match what the customer expected," replied the painter.

Leon studied the paint sample once again and did a quick scan through the booklet and other samples but couldn't see how he could go wrong by choosing that particular one.

"Midnight Maroon—this one stands out more to me than any of the others," said a confident Leon.

"Are you sure?" asked the painter.

"Yeah, I'm sure," answered Leon.

"Okay, then, 'Midnight Maroon' it is. Give me a couple of weeks, and I'll give you a call when it's ready to be picked up," said the painter.

Over the next couple of weeks, Leon and the band practiced learning a selection of songs in Leon's hometown of Ward, SC. In the meantime, Carroll remained in Orlando, telephone consulting with a booking agency in Nashville, working on scheduling tour dates and events for the band's first road tour.

As predicted, after two weeks, the body shop painter called Carroll to let him know that the bus was ready to be picked up. Carroll notified Leon, and Leon made immediate plans to return to Florida, as he was excited to see the results of the newly painted "Midnight Maroon" colored tour bus.

After arriving at the body shop, Carroll and Leon were asked to wait outside in the shop's parking lot. The shop owner then came out and joined them and held his hands as if holding a megaphone around his mouth and shouted, "Robbie, bring out that gorgeous 'Midnight Maroon' tour bus for Mr. Fulmer and Mr. Everette to see."

As the huge, oversized roll-up door began to rise along the side of the paint shop, the name "Leon Everette" could be seen in the small window above the windshield at the top of the bus. Standing erect with his feet slightly spread and both hands on his hips, Leon proudly smiled with anxious anticipation as the bus began to roll out onto the parking lot.

The manly sound of the powerful diesel engine and the low-changing gears added to his anxiety. Then, suddenly, his smiling face turned to shock and disbelief, as the "Midnight Maroon" paint job looked more like a "Cirrhosis of the Liver" color.

The painter was right all along. As forewarned, the color on the paint sample didn't match the results as painted on the bus. Leon had, once again, learned a valuable lesson the hard way. If you want to know about playing guitar, ask a professional guitarist. If you want an opinion about painting a bus, listen to what an expert body shop painter advises.

As Leon stood looking dazed and confused, Carroll was beside himself, laughing uncontrollably. The paint job was impeccable, but the color was "horse-liver" ugly.

"You didn't need to put your name on the front after all," Carroll uncontrollably laughed. "After a while, when folks see this bus coming, they're gonna automatically know that this ugly thing belongs to none other than Leon Everette."

It took a minute, but Leon finally joined in the fun with Carroll as they walked around checking out the bus, hysterically laughing out loud and totally out of control. The joke was on Leon, but he no longer cared. He had made his choice, although it turned out to be a minor disappointment.

To find something positive about the color he had chosen, Leon convinced himself by saying, "In the long run it will bring a lot of laughter and pointed jokes wherever it goes, to all who will see it in the days to come. Besides, if this will bring smiles and laughter to my fans and people along the way, then so be it. The world can always use more laughter, even if the joke will always be on me."

That afternoon, Leon drove the bus back home to Ward, SC, to show it to the members of the band. Upon his arrival, the laughter and joking started all over, as Carroll had phoned ahead letting them in on the joke about the newly painted bus.

As Leon parked and exited the bus, the band members gathered around to greet him on his return home.

"What the heck is this, Leon?" one of the band members asked. "That is one ugly bus right there!"

"I know," replied another band member. "It's Leon Everette's mobile chopped liver express! We didn't realize you were advertising chopped liver on the side, Leon," they all laughed.

Yet another band member chimed in, "Don't have anything to go with your grilled onions and gravy? Don't worry, call 1-800-My-Liver, and Leon Everette will bring his Chopped Liver Express right to your door. It's a real crowd-pleaser!"

"Well, at least you won't have a hard time finding a parking space in this thing," said yet another band member.

"Why not?" asked Leon.

"Because this thing is so ugly nobody would want to park anywhere near it!" he laughed.

"Hey, Leon, what do you call a nightmare on Elm Street?" asked another.

"I don't know," answered Leon. "What do you call a nightmare on Elm Street?"

"Leon Everette driving his ugly, liver-colored tour bus!" he answered.

And that was just the beginning of the many "liver and ugly paint" jokes yet to come, but at least they now had their final piece of the organizational puzzle—their very own customized tour bus. To say they were all excited to finally start their first road tour would be an understatement.

As in most cases, when entertainers begin a concert and event tour, they give it a promotional name, such as the name of their most recently released album. While their official tour name would, after releasing their first album, be called "Hurricane," the name they jokingly called it among themselves in the meantime was the "Leon Everette and the Liverators" tour. And as the eloquent statesman and radio personality Paul Harvey would say, "And now you know the rest of the story."

Chapter 17

**The Maverick**

Maverick – *a person who refuses to follow the customs and rules of a group.*

**In the days** that followed, the band steadily made progress toward becoming a cohesive unit by diligently practicing their songs while Carroll and the booking agency were finalizing events and tour appearances. Once Leon was satisfied that the band had fine-tuned their instrumental and vocal skills and had a consistent sound quality that met the strict criteria for his style of music, he decided that it was time to make some serious music. And his definition of making music meant getting into a Nashville recording studio and laying down tracks.

The tour bus was full of diesel and ready to roll, sitting idly in Leon's backyard, waiting for the start of a new adventure. It was the band's first time hitting the road as a unit, and their first stop was Nashville, TN.

Up until this time, during the early 1980s, Leon had already made several top ten recordings with a variety of professional studio musicians who were members of the musician's trade union. Because of contract stipulations between the record labels and the musician's union, it was the normal business procedure for a recording studio to hire only union musicians for all in-house recording sessions. All non-union musicians, as well as other union musicians not included in the contract agreement, were, therefore, prohibited from working or recording within the confines of the recording studios.

Before organizing his official band, Leon had finished a recording of a song called "Hurricane" about which he was especially excited. The only problem with the song was that it had been recorded with the accompaniment of union studio musicians, and although he liked the song, he wasn't one hundred percent satisfied with the finished product. However, he soon realized that his newly organized band's rendition of "Hurricane" sounded better than the results from the studio musician's version.

When it came to the quality of the sound of music, Leon was meticulous. He simply would not accept a record that had a substandard sound before its release to the public, and at the time, the original studio version of "Hurricane" was one of the recordings with which he wasn't content. The studio musicians had done a very good job with their version of the song, but it just didn't satisfy the results that Leon was hoping for.

He had to find a way to somehow get his band into the recording studio and re-record "Hurricane" to achieve the sound quality that he thought the song deserved. But how? No matter what he would do, it would most certainly be unethical and possibly illegal.

While Leon respected the decision of upper management to hire only studio musicians, he didn't necessarily agree with their decision to accept an inferior sound quality of the finished products of some of their recordings. There was no doubt in his mind that his musicians were a much more cohesive unit, and their instrumental timing and precision notes were far superior to the style and sound of the RCA studio musicians.

Finally, about to run out of time and options, he decided that he would somehow sneak his band into the studio after hours when all the daytime employees had left the building. It was a good idea, but it was much easier said than done.

He would be violating a sacred code of conduct between record label executives, their studio musicians, and other personnel, but to Leon, a contract was just a piece of paper stipulating an agreement between two entities. One thing the contract didn't stipulate was the quality of the music performed by the studio musicians. And to Leon, if the musicians finished product didn't meet the standards that he expected, then they, and the record label executives, would violate unwritten obligations to their very own studio recording contract.

Having been a regular participant in the recording studios, Leon was very knowledgeable of the daily routine of the incoming and outgoing traffic of all the employees during normal business hours. If he was going to risk sneaking his band inside, after hours would be perfect, but not necessarily the wisest time. He was always up for a challenge, and if it meant getting his career off from a good to a great start, then the risks involved would be worth the reward.

For several evenings, after all the union musicians and other studio employees had clocked out on their timecards, Leon stayed behind, pretending he was going over some new tracks for his next album. When the time was right, he made his move and quickly ran to get his band, which was waiting outside in the tour bus parked in the RCA recording studio parking lot. One by one, they all stealthily sneaked into the recording studio.

Once they got inside, they somehow successfully recorded "Hurricane" and nine other songs to complete an album. Using a combined effort of their musical talents and previous studio experiences, they were able to produce and process the recordings into a professional-sounding, quality product.

Leon beamed with excitement as he replayed the new,

improved results of "Hurricane". As it turned out, all of the songs that they had re-recorded had a far superior sound quality compared to the original recordings. Leon could not have been any prouder of what this group of talented new musicians had done. He was so happy and thankful that he decided to name the band after the very song that he knew would put them all on the country music map, and that new name was "Hurricane."

After Leon had enough tracks laid down to complete the requirements of his next album, he turned in his personal band's tapes instead of the studio musician's versions. After all the songs were finished with their production mastering process, Leon's new "Hurricane" album was released to the public and became one of the top-selling albums of the time. It was also the first album featuring the original "Hurricane" band.

Surprisingly to everyone involved, several of the single records released from the album peaked well into the top ten Billboard Magazine charts. "Hurricane" topped out at number two on the Billboard charts and number one on the Record World and Cash Box Magazine charts.

However, it didn't take long for the union studio musicians to realize that the versions heard on the radio were not the versions they had recorded. It was just a matter of time before the word finally got out that Leon had sneaked his band into the recording studio and re-recorded the songs that were released to the public.

Needless to say, once it became public knowledge, Leon's disrespectful and deceptive ploy didn't go over well with the union studio musicians or the record label executives. To say the least, they were outraged that Leon had gone behind their backs and had unauthorized musicians re-record the songs that were used to make the entire "Hurricane" album. To them, that was, far and away, one of the worst forms of blasphemy that could ever be committed against the country music entertainment industry.

To make matters worse, Leon was also beginning to acquire a reputation for being a wild, out-of-control performer. Many would complain that his act was more like a rock-and-roll style rather than the laid-back, low-energy, traditional country style. Some even called him the "Ted Nugent" of country music because of his uncharacteristic and unconventional stage presence. His performances were a high-energy style with a lot of erratic and unpredictable movements all over the stage, often extending out and interacting with the audience. Even though many traditional country artists criticized his performance style, his fans loved it, and that's all that mattered to Leon.

In retrospect, his stage presence was no more radical than that of established performers like Carl Perkins, Jerry Lee Lewis, and Jerry Reed, and some critics would even include Johnny Cash. Leon's performing style was simply a version of country music way ahead of his time, sort of like when Elvis Presley was first introduced into the world of rock-and-roll. Both Elvis and Leon were talented musicians who appeared on the music scene as being unconventional and uniquely different from the normal style that most people were accustomed to. Until their time, no one had ever seen anyone put on an act that some believed to be too provocative or over the top.

To Leon's credit, it's been said that Garth Brooks often attended his concerts and studied his attire, his movements, the way he wore his cowboy hat, and even the way he held his guitar. He also admired how Leon worked the stage and interacted with the fans in the audience, a common practice that became one of Brooks' most admired features. He supposedly used some of what he learned from observing Leon in developing his style of music and stage presence, very similar to the way Leon had learned from studying the style of his idol, Norvel Felts.

To say the least, there was a lot of back-and-forth discussion between Leon, the musician's union, and the record label executives. When all the debates were said and done, his songs did so well on the charts that it was decided that the studio musicians would still be paid for their time in the recording sessions, and Leon would be allowed to have his musicians accompany him in future recording sessions.

It's still a mystery as to how the recording label was able to get around their violating their agreement with the musician's union contract by letting Leon's unauthorized musicians record in the studio. The only viable answer is that having heard both versions of the songs, it appears that the record label executives realized that in some cases they had been settling for a lesser quality sound all along. Because of Leon's ear for music, everyone agreed that the "Hurricane" band versions of all the songs on the "Hurricane" album were noticeably better than the studio musician's version.

To their credit, the recording label probably sought legal counsel to amend the contract to allow preferred musicians to record in situations agreed to by amicable parties. Nevertheless, Leon's convincing view on the matter was that successful recording outcomes always trumped contract agreements. Leon was committed to making the best music possible, no matter what was written or stipulated by any form or legal document.

The country music tabloids had a field day with the controversy. In his very first attempt to make a successful album with RCA Records, he had violated the trust of the very people who were sticking their necks out to make him succeed. The record labels had a long, proud history of making successful recordings and launching numerous successful careers for unproven talents, using a system of trust and responsibility expected by both parties. In addition, they were investing a lot of time and money in an unproven product, yet this is how he earns their trust, by doing things his way and not the well-established and proven contract-binding way.

In a move to sell more copies, the tabloids labeled Leon with the moniker "The Maverick" because he went against the grain of the standard Nashville recording process. Their story was that he was a man on a mission, and if the record labels couldn't give him the sound that he wanted, then he would do whatever it took to get the quality recordings that the fans deserved, even if it meant going behind their backs to get it.

He'd just released his first professional studio album, and the quality of the songs and the controversy of how it was produced was so prevalent that his popularity and notoriety from the sales of magazines, albums, and single records gave him the identity of being an outlaw hero. The fans loved the songs, and they loved the tabloid story behind them. In addition, many of the other musicians had a lot of respect for him, as well, as he had gone against traditional industry standards and had stood up for what he thought was best for his music, and most importantly, for his fans.

The TV and radio stations and other media outlets swarmed to get an interview with Leon. Surprisingly, Leon's side of the story, as well as his ruggedly handsome good looks, polite mannerisms, and likeability, increased his fan base exponentially across the country. Magazines with his picture on the cover or with his given name or his moniker, *"The Maverick,"* mentioned in a story inside the pages would sell out almost as quickly as they were stocked on the shelves of magazine outlets or displays on each side of a grocery store check-out aisle.

As it turned out, the clandestine maneuver also resulted in a big win for the RCA recording label, as well. To their surprise and delight, "Hurricane" sales exceeded far beyond their expectations, which meant the company made a lot more money than they had expected, which, in the end, is all that mattered to the corporate bottom line.

In addition, the media world of country music now had a new subject for conversational fodder, although a controversial one, which they could use to potentially increase their sales and marketing techniques. *The Maverick* had violated the trust of the very people supporting him, yet in so doing, he also made the record label richer by using unethical methods to ensure that his album would be a better one. As it turned out, his album surpassed everyone's expectations. The record label executives would eventually get over their embarrassment and frustrations, as their pride and self-esteem were, over time, restored to normalcy by the addition of more than expected money in their bank accounts resulting from their very first business experience with their new client.

To say the least, Leon's start in the country music industry was a rocky but interesting one. Although he'd defied the music business laws of physics, he would go on to have eleven albums to top out in the top ten on the Billboard charts, nine of which would be honored as having the status of being gold by industry standards. Equally important was the fact that he stood by his high standards and principles, resulting in establishing a fan base that had an appetite for a style of country music with a different variety and flair from the traditional style that had long past become stale and predictable.

"The Maverick" had indeed gone against the grain of country music industry standards, and in so doing, became an outlaw to some and a hero to others. He was also a rebel on a mission, and that mission was to provide the best music and entertainment possible to satisfy the needs of country music lovers all over the world.

Instead of being depicted as an outlaw on a poster inside a post office to appease bounty hunters, this desperado was the kind that would be portrayed on entertainment venue posters as "Wanted—Live and In-Person" at any country music fan base arena both near and far—anywhere and anytime.

Chapter 18

**The Maverick and the Mafia**

**At the ACM** (Academy of Country Music) awards presentation in Los Angeles, CA, "Hurricane" was voted "Most Popular Tour Band" of 1983. Even before being honored with the prestigious award, Leon and the band were already in high demand and were received like country music elite wherever they performed. One of those stops was during a western United States tour at a venue called "The Frontier Social Club" in El Paso, Texas.

El Paso is a border town located at the westernmost point of the state of Texas. In most U.S. bordering states, when you crossed a border, it was to enter a new county and state. In El Paso, when you crossed the border, you would be entering not only a new county and state but also an entirely new country—Mexico.

Booking a concert in a border town such as El Paso was often risky, as it limits the odds of having a good patronage turnout for a show. Although the metropolitan population of El Paso at this time was just over five hundred thousand, the income level was one of the lowest in the state of Texas. In all probability, adding to the risk involved, most concert-goers were more than likely living from paycheck to paycheck. Attending a popular country music artist concert was a luxury for most, to say the least. Furthermore, since potential patrons on the Mexican side of the border had limited access to the United States, Leon and "Hurricane" were taking an unprecedented gamble of having to earn enough revenue to cover their wages and expenses.

During most weather seasons, this part of the country was usually considered a dry climate, but when the "Hurricane" tour bus pulled up in front of the Frontier Social Club, an unexpected but welcomed light rain had begun to fall. The local farmers were overjoyed, as their fields had become dry, crusty, and famished from thirst. Almost equally excited were the local concertgoers, as they weren't about to let a little rain put a damper on their plans for the evening. They had been waiting for months to see Leon Everette and "Hurricane," and the end of the day couldn't come quick enough, rain or shine.

The Frontier Social Club of El Paso was one of five combination nightclub and concert venues belonging to a franchise conglomerate located west of the Mississippi River. The rumors were that the clubs were mafia-owned and operated, and in addition to selling alcohol and offering concert performances and other social events, laundering money was a key function of the enterprise.

Leon and the band had been given a "heads up" warning of who they were doing business with long before the contract was signed for them to perform. Several country music performers, including Johnny Rodriquez (Down on the Rio Grande), Bobby Bare (Detroit City), and John Anderson (Just a Swingin'), had all forewarned Leon about the corrupt, egotistical manager at the social club named Gino Stellina.

Stellina had a reputation for wanting people to believe that he was a corporate big shot and someone who you didn't want to cross, both personally and in business. He was most well-known among country music performers as being a cocky, two-faced snob who treated everyone around him as "little people".

One of his most famous ploys was annoyingly holding back payments from country music performers after their show. He seemed to get a kick out of watching them squirm, beg, and plead for their entitled payment at the end of their respective performances. Eventually, he would pay them off, but not without being petty and mean-spirited. In extreme cases, it would take days for some to receive their payment.

Leon and the band were pleasantly surprised as they entered the lobby of the Frontier Social Club for the first time. The name of the venue didn't come close to matching the eloquence of the establishment. The lobby floors were made of pristine, white marble accented with streaks of gray throughout. Overhead, vaulted ceilings were accented with an arrangement of wooden "dental work" trim fabricated by artisan craftsmen. Hanging from above was a series of enormous crystal chandeliers reflecting their gorgeous lighting throughout the entire concourse walkway. Lavish crown molding adorned the outer ceiling walls, and eloquent, decorative ornamental molding and wood etching framed each of the six-swinging double-door entryways leading into the main auditorium. To say the least, the Frontier Social Club looked more like a small aristocratic palace than a southwestern nightclub or concert hall.

Inside the elaborate swinging doorways, the concert hall floor was strategically equipped with small, stylish tables, some for seating only two and others large enough to seat up to four patrons. Bright white linen tablecloths adorned the tabletops with a decorative candle located in the center, obviously designed for intimate lighting.

Posh seating could accommodate as many as five to six hundred patrons, and there was not a bad seat in the house. Stylishly upholstered, red-padded seats were the main attraction of the private booths located alongside two of the four arena walls. They too were decorated with linen tablecloths and a candle centerpiece. At the junction of the two aligning walls was a large corner booth that could sit up to six people comfortably.

Just off to each side of the stage area were two well-equipped minibars. Two more mini-bars were located just inside the arena on either side of the entrance doorways. Last but not least, a glossy, over-size oak parquet dance floor separated the stage from a lush, low-pile, designer-carpeted seating area.

The stage area was very user-friendly for all the musicians with plenty of space to move around after having set up their equipment. The lighting and sound equipment dynamics were of the highest caliber and precisely positioned and calibrated, not only for the stage performers but for the audience, as well.

The entire event staff was easily recognizable, as they were all dressed in vivid red French-cut blazers and black formal trousers. Some of the ladies wore formal trousers, as well, as others opted to wear a slightly below-the-knee semi-formal black gown. The men wore sparkling white, starched dress shirts with black ties and patent leather shoes. The ladies wore a similar white blouse with either black low-cut or high heel shoes.

Leon and the band members were unified in their suspicion of the stylishly dressed men in their fancy red blazers. By their rugged looks and bulky size, they were more than likely to have been security guards and more specifically, mafia soldiers disguised as event staff.

As the band and road crew unloaded the bus and set up their equipment, one of the "Redcoats", as the band members secretly called them, escorted Leon to one end of the long lobby hallway to the club manager's office.

"Mr. Everette, or should I say Maverick," the club manager said teasingly, "my name is Gino Stellina. Welcome to El Paso. We've been looking forward to having you for quite some time.

I have really good news for you. Both of your performances for this evening have been sold out."

"Please, call me Leon, that other name is just a tabloid moniker," replied an excited Leon. Thank you for letting me know. That is good news! The band will be excited to hear that, as well."

"If there's anything I can do to assist you and your band, please don't hesitate to ask," continued Stellina. "We want to make your visit with us as pleasant as possible. If you'll excuse me, I have an important phone call to make, and if you don't mind, I'll have one of my staff members show you around to get you acclimated to our facility."

As Leon and the staff member left his office, Stellina returned to his managerial duties. In his sinister, spiteful mind, he couldn't help but think that Leon was just another backroads country hick trying to make a dollar off his establishment. Although Leon and the band had proven to be a viable resource for concert revenue, he wasn't fond of what he'd read in the tabloids about how Leon had gone behind the backs of the executives in Nashville and skirted around ethical company policy. Before the night was over, he would show this Leon fellow what a "real" Maverick is like.

Leon and his "Redcoat" escort toured the entire facility, and everything Leon saw either met or exceeded his standards and expectations. Up until that time, it was one of the nicest venues of its kind that he and the band had ever had the opportunity to perform. To say the least, it was far more superior to a much smaller nightclub, an all-day drive down I-10 in San Antonio, where they recently had to perform behind a protective barrier made of chicken wire. Fortunately, their performance must have gone over well, as they were not met with a hostile audience, throwing anything they could get their hands on against the shielding chicken wire fencing.

After touring the building and concert hall, Leon went inside the arena to help the road crew set up their equipment on the stage. As he began assembling the speaker wiring and microphones, he couldn't help but think about his earlier experience of meeting Stellina for the first time. The introduction didn't go anywhere near what he had expected. Stellina came across as being professional and on the up and up and not the belligerent snob that he had been warned about. But the evening was far from over, and he could only hope that his opinion of him wouldn't change by the time they boarded the bus and were on their way to their next destination.

Leon and the band gave two performances that evening, one at six o'clock, then another at nine o'clock. Each performance was about an hour and a half long and both audiences were formidable and graciously loud, but to the band, that meant they were all having a good time.

After the last performance, Leon signed autographs in the lobby while the band and road crew loaded the equipment on the bus. After signing his last autograph, Leon joined the band on the bus and they all waited for Bobby Martin, the road manager, who had gone to the manager's office to get their payment for their long night's work. After a short while, Bobby returned to the bus and walked toward the back, straight to Leon.

"We got a problem," said Bobby.

"What do you mean, we got a problem?" asked Leon.

"Well, Stellina says he ain't paying us," replied Bobby.

"Why not?" asked Leon, "did we do something he didn't approve of?"

"No, not at all. He even made a compliment about what a good job y'all did," Bobby continued. "All he said was 'good job, but I ain't paying y'all tonight. I told him that you weren't going to like that answer."

"Is that all he said?" asked Leon.

"No," replied Bobby, "he said he didn't give a damn what that hillbilly likes! Y'all aren't getting paid tonight! But, before I left, I saw an envelope on his desk with your name on it, and I assume it was your payment for tonight's performances."

"That ain't right," said a frustrated Leon. "We had a deal, and I'm gonna get our money one way or another."

Leon went to the back of the bus where his sleeping quarters were located, and took off all of his clothes except for his Jockey undershorts. After undressing, he headed straight for the bus door.

All the band members were shocked by the way he was dressed as he passed by each one along the way.

"Where are you going?" one asked.

"I'm going to get our money!" said an emphatic Leon.

"Like that?" asked another.

"Yes, like this," Leon firmly answered.

"Ronnie," Leon said to the bus driver, "I want you to keep the bus door open, the engine running, and all systems ready to go, just in case you see me running back here after I go inside to get our money. And I want all of y'all to stay seated and if I'm not back in ten minutes, come looking for me."

The entire band had a look of bewilderment. What is Leon up to and why is he all but butt-naked, about to leave the bus in a slow, drizzling rain? Sure they wanted their money, but not to this extreme.

Leon stepped off the bus, his bare feet splashing against the wet asphalt parking lot, and quickly walked toward the club's entrance. Although he didn't have to walk very far, by the time he approached the door to the club, his entire body and Jockey shorts were soaking wet. Upon entering the lobby, he paced himself as if on a mission, looking straight ahead down the long hallway leading up to the manager's office.

Just inside, a couple of "Redcoats" were finishing their nightly duties straightening up the lobby when they were taken aback upon seeing an almost naked, rain-drenched Leon enter the building. They stood statuesque as they watched Leon's footprints leave their wet markings along the marbled floor leading to Stellina's office. One of the "Redcoats" remained by the exit door and motioned for the other to go get help, as, by Leon's bizarre dress and callous body language, they assumed all hell was about to break loose.

As Leon stormed into the manager's office the first thing he saw was Stellina sitting in a high-back, executive-style chair on rollers, behind a massive wooden desk. To say the least, Stellina was shocked by his impromptu entrance and unexpected appearance.

"Who the hell do you think you are coming into my office dressed like that? What the hell do you want?" asked a furious Stellina.

"I want my money!" exclaimed Leon.

Leon looked down, scanning the top of the desk, where he saw an envelope with his name on it. Stellina quickly grabbed the envelope and threw it into the top left-hand desk drawer, then slammed the drawer shut.

"You'll get your money when I say it's time, and now ain't the time. Now get out of my office!" Stellina shouted.

Leon moved slightly closer and pounded the desktop with a loud thud with his fist.

"I want my money, and I want it now!" Leon firmly replied.

Then Stellina stood and lunged his upper body forward as to get into Leon's face. Leon's first reflex was to grab his necktie and pull it tight against his throat, slamming his head on the hard wooden surface of the desk.

"Just give me my money, and I'll be on my way!" Leon exclaimed.

But Stellina wasn't giving up so easily, as he tried to wiggle loose from Leon's grip, only to feel the tension around his neck getting tighter and tighter. Leon pulled on the long, skinny satin material choking Stellina into temporary submission. Every time Stellina would resist his hold, Leon would slam his head against the hard desktop.

By now, Leon had enough length of the tie and Stellina's

body in a position across the desk that he could put one foot on the tie to hold Stellina's head down, as he reached for the envelope in the top desk drawer.

Then, in one quick motion, Leon slammed the drawer open and retrieved the envelope, released his hold on the tie, and pushed Stellina backward. Stellina fell into the chair and began to quickly roll away from the desk, pounding his head on a brick wall behind him. Stellina's limp body slipped out of the chair, falling uncontrollably to the floor, leaving a splatter of blood on the brick-and-mortar wall.

All this commotion had happened in a mere few minutes. Leon then took off down the hallway toward the lobby, crashing through oncoming "Redcoats" like a bowling ball smashing through pins, then bolted toward the exit door.

Leon's bare feet were mostly dry by now and were making good traction with the marble floor, but the slick-bottomed dress shoes of the "Redcoats" would only slip and slide across the damp pathway following Leon's trail. In addition, the frustrated "Redcoats" couldn't get a hold of Leon, as he didn't have anything on for them to grasp and his wet body was too slippery to grab onto.

Leon crashed through the lobby exit doorway and sped toward the bus in an all-out sprint fleeing his angry pursuers, his feet splashing against the wet pavement with each pounding thrust along the way.

"Ronnie, take off!" shouted Leon as he sped across the wet pavement toward the waiting bus.

"The 'Redcoats' are coming! The 'Redcoats' are coming!" the members of the band shouted and laughed. But Leon was too fast for them to catch up, as he caught up with the rolling bus, grabbed the handrail just inside the folding double door, and swung himself safely on board.

As Leon made his way to a nearby seat, he held up one hand with the envelope in it and shouted, "It wasn't pretty, but I got y'all's money!"

The whole band erupted in laughter and jubilation, high-fiving and popping the tops of cold cans of beer. Someone handed Leon a towel and he made his way to the back of the bus and changed into some dry clothing, then joined in on the celebration.

There was some murmuring among some of the band members, as they were afraid that they may now be wanted by the mob. Leon tried to reassure them that he would do everything in his power to protect them, but he didn't have any other recourse to getting their money. Nevertheless, it was an uncomfortable feeling thinking that the mafia may be drawing up contracts and that the ink was about to dry.

In the meantime, Ronnie floored the gas pedal and the bus quickly sped away. Soon they were on I-25 North with a four-plus hour drive to their next destination.

Along the way, after having a few drinks, they all reveled in the satisfaction of the crowd's response to their successful performances at the El Paso Frontier Social Club, as well as their exciting escape from potential harm and hostility. But they were all having too much fun at the time to even think about what the consequences might be upon their arrival in Albuquerque, New Mexico, as their Saturday night's performance would be at none other than Albuquerque's own *Frontier Social Club.*

Chapter 19




**The Maverick Meets the Don**




**After a short celebration,** the band slept throughout their long drive from El Paso to Albuquerque. After arriving around six o'clock that morning, Ronnie pulled the bus into a motel parking lot adjacent to the Albuquerque Frontier Social Club property. The tired, hungover band checked in with the motel desk clerk and then went to their respective rooms. It was early and the club was not open, so the road crew would have to wait a few more hours before they could unload the band's equipment and begin setting up.

Around three o'clock that afternoon, after getting some well-deserved rest, Leon and the band began their normal routine of getting ready for their next performance. There was an uncomfortable, worrisome feeling among everyone, as they still weren't sure if there was going to be any trouble from the club's staff, as their previous experience at the last affiliated social club was challenging and unpredictable, to say the least. However, at least they were all awake and up and walking around, so they took that as a good sign.

As they walked across the parking lot toward the social club, Leon and the band saw four muscular-built men dressed in none other than vivid red blazers waiting just inside the glass-enclosed wall of the club's entrance. Some of the band members began whispering as they meticulously made their way across the parking lot, wondering if they should be saying their last goodbye or to turn and run, as this moment had the potential of surely being their last time together.

"Just be cool," said a calm Leon. "Act normal, as if nothing ever happened. We don't know what they know, and they may not know what we know. All we can do is take it one step at a time. If there is any pushback, let me do all the talking."

As they got closer and closer, the featureless, staring gaze of the four men never changed. Not a smile. Not a smirk. Just straight-faced and unreadable. Then, as Leon reached for the handle to open the door, two of the men swung each of the double doors open and with a warm, courteous smile, gave them all a robust welcome to their social club.

"Mr. Everette and members of the band," one of the staff members said, "welcome to the Albuquerque Frontier Social Club. If there is anything you need or if there is anything we can do to accommodate you or make your visit with us a more pleasant one, please don't hesitate to ask any of our staff members."

It could be a trap, the band members thought. They could just be setting them up. Needless to say, they were all inexperienced on what to expect from mafia personnel and had no idea of how to correctly respond to their actions. But, for now, they would play it safe and just go with the flow and hope for the best.

Fortunately, the rest of the afternoon went without a hitch. While Leon met with the club manager, the band began setting up their equipment on stage and going over some final details to work out a couple of new songs.

The Albuquerque Frontier Social Club was much like the one in El Paso, except for a few structural and aesthetic changes.

Like the one in El Paso, the staff was exceptionally nice, politely helpful, and easily recognizable.

It was almost surreal as to how well the rest of the evening transpired for Leon and the band. As in El Paso, they performed two sold-out shows at six and nine o'clock to both enthusiastically, appreciative audiences. After the concert, Leon signed autographs while the band and road crew loaded up the equipment on the bus.

As Leon finished talking with his last group of fans, he joined the band on the bus, and they all anxiously waited for Bobby to return from the manager's office with their payment for their evening performances.

From their position on the bus, everyone could see the entire lobby through the glass wall of the front of the concert arena. By now fifteen long minutes had passed, but it must have seemed like hours, as Bobby was gone much longer than expected. All they could see, for the time being, were two "Redcoats" standing just inside as if guarding the double-door entryway.

"Why is he taking so long?" one of the band members nervously asked.

"I'm not sure, but this doesn't look good or feel right," said another.

"I'll give him a couple more minutes," Leon spoke up, "and if he's not back by then, then I guess I'll have to go in and check on him."

"You're not going to strip down butt-naked again, are you?" asked another.

Everyone on the bus uneasily laughed. It wasn't ordinarily funny, but in an unnerving way, it was funny, nevertheless.

"Give me a little credit. I wasn't butt-naked—I still had my Jockey shorts on," Leon smiled, as he humored them. "No, I'm not going in like I did last time, but if I do have to go in and I'm not back in five minutes, y'all need to come to find me."

Then, about five minutes later, Bobby was seen walking inside the long walkway of the lobby, appearing to be escorted by two "Redcoats", one on either side. It was hard to tell if Bobby was nervous or not, but to the members of the band, his present situation was suspicious, to say the least.

"This is it!" exclaimed one of the band members. "Those goons are coming for us!"

"Settle down! Nothing's happened yet," said a reassuring Leon. "We don't know what's going to happen until it happens, ok?"

As Bobby approached the double-door exit, the two men inside swung the doors open and Bobby walked out alone toward the bus, looking back as if thanking them for their courteous gesture.

Once again, Bobby boarded the bus and walked straight to Leon, and handed Leon the envelope with their night's wages.

"Any problem?" asked Leon.

"No, not at all. The manager was on a phone call when I got to his office, and I waited until he finished before going inside. I'm sorry it took so long. You guys weren't worried about me were you?" Bobby teased.

The bus erupted with laughter and everyone's anxious emotions turned to calm and serenity.

Then, just as Ronnie was about to put the bus in gear and pull away, a masculine-looking, well-dressed man in a black executive business suit approached the bus, extending his hand with a motion as if to signal for Ronnie to hold the bus. Suddenly, there was an uneasy look on everyone's face. The man approaching the bus looked as if he was of Italian descent, subliminally indicating that he might be a representative of the local mafia. If that was true, then they probably did need to be concerned. The brief calm and serenity had immediately turned to anxious emotions once again for everyone on board.

The man stepped onto the bus, stopping just short of landing on the top step and looked around, scanning everyone on board. In a low, seriously confident voice said, "I'm looking for Mr. Leon Everette."

No one said a word, but every band member, in unison, quickly turned their heads and looked straight at Leon. It was then obvious to the man at that point, who Leon Everette was. All the band members breathed a sigh of relief but remained concerned about the man's motive.

Then, unexpectedly, he said, "Mr. Everette, I'd like to commend you and your band on both of your outstanding performances tonight. From the positive reaction of your audiences as well as compliments from our staff, you guys put on an impressive show. Mr. Everette, there's someone inside that would like to meet you and have a word with you. Would you mind coming with me?"

"Who is it?" asked a curious Leon.

"It's my boss," replied the man. "He's come from our social club headquarters in Pueblo, Colorado just to have a conversation with you."

There was a short pause, as Leon tried to understand what this "conversation" was all about. The "boss" had traveled over five hours to have a conversation. There were so many variables as to what the "boss'" intentions were. Whatever the reason, he didn't have a choice but to comply.

"Well, it must be important, if it's your boss and he's come so far," answered Leon. "Please, lead the way."

Leon reluctantly stepped off the bus, and as he approached the building lobby, he was thinking that this must be it; my game of life is over. He was sure he was about to meet his maker. And there was no need for him to run 'cause he's too easy to find.

The well-dressed man escorted Leon inside the social club to the main lobby lounge. It was the largest of all the other lounges and was distinctively decorated with a theme of the Albuquerque Native American heritage paraphernalia and cultural art. The locals were especially proud of their Native American heritages which primarily included the Pueblo, Apache, and Navajo nations.

Mounted on each wall were examples of brightly colored blankets and shawls, artistically designed handmade pottery and woven baskets, turquoise and amethyst jewelry, and photographs and paintings of various people of some of the proud, foregone tribes.

One large oil painting, mounted in the center of the wall behind the bar, caught Leon's eye. It was an old, long-haired, war-torn-looking Indian man with a bright red bandana tied around his forehead, with a look as if he was ready to lead his brave warriors into battle. The description at the bottom of the painting simply read "Geronimo". Not having his name would not have mattered to the locals who frequented the bar, as this was Apache territory, and every native here was well aware of who Geronimo was.

The old man had strong-looking, deep eyes, a sun-dried, crusty face, and the look of someone wrestling with the emotion of being both sad and proud at the same time.

As Leon approached the bar, he couldn't resist temporarily staring back into the soulful eyes of one of the greatest Indian warrior chiefs this territory had ever known. And now he was about to meet yet another local chief of a tribe of a different heritage, sitting at the bar just a few steps away.

"Boss, this is Mr. Leon Everette," said the well-dressed man.

As Leon began to extend his hand to the "boss" for a handshake, the "boss" continued his forward-looking pose, staring straight ahead, never turning toward Leon and never attempting to receive his hand, and with a deep, soft tone spoke, "Please, have a seat, Mr. Everette."

The well-dressed man pointed to a bar stool two seats to the right, away from the man waiting at the bar. Leon didn't know why he was directed to sit on that particular seat, but neither did he ask. He just supposed it was some kind of mafia technique giving the "boss" a little room for protection in case the conversation between them got out of hand.

The "boss" made a nod with his head indicating to his

assistant that it was time for him to leave. Without saying a word, the well-dressed man walked across the barroom floor and stood statuesque as if guarding the doorway.

The "boss" was a sixty-something-year-old man with well-kempt silver hair combed straight back and groomed to perfection, leaving no hair out of place. He was dressed in a bright white tuxedo or formal evening jacket with an elegant-looking black bow tie and matching trousers. A gorgeous, oval-shaped turquoise stone encased in a solid silver band accented the cuff links protruding from his jacket sleeve. Leon's first impression of him was that he resembled an Italian version of Ricardo Montalbán of the Fantasy Island TV series, but that was a thought that he would most certainly keep to himself.

The "boss" was drinking Jack Daniels Black Label liquor on the rocks, as the bottle was positioned on the bar and to his right. His glass was partially full, but it was hard to tell how many drinks he'd already had, but the bottle measured about three-quarters full.

A slow-burning Marlboro Gold 100's cigarette was smoldering in an ashtray to his left. Marlboro Gold 100's was considered to be a "manly gentleman's" choice of quality tobacco products. The white, sleek cardboard, "flip-top" box with gold accenting was one of the signature features of its masculinity. Another masculine signature of the cigarette was that it was 100mm long, compared to a normal cigarette, which was typically just 70mm.

After making all these observations, the "boss" still had not made one move to look toward Leon. He maintained a continuous gaze straight ahead as if he was trying to win a staring contest with Geronimo to see which one would be the first to blink.

With a nod of his head, the "boss" motioned for the bartender standing at one end of the bar to come forward.

Then, the "boss" once again broke his silence.

"What'd you have to drink, Mr. Everette?" he asked.

Leon didn't want a drink, but out of courtesy and goodwill, he certainly wasn't going to turn down the invitation from the "boss".

"I'll have a vodka with grapefruit juice, thank you," replied Leon.

The bartender reached beneath the bar top and grabbed a crystal-clear cocktail glass with a colorful print of a Navajo "dream catcher" on one side and the pride of the western frontier, the American bison, on the other.

As the bartender prepared Leon's drink, the "boss" reached for his cigarette and took a long drag, then slowly exhaled the smoke to his left, away from Leon.

After preparing Leon's drink, the "boss" made a nod with his head as if to motion for the bartender to leave.

The "boss" placed the cigarette back into the ashtray, as Leon patiently waited for his next move. The "boss" then began his seemingly long-awaited conversation, continuing to look straight ahead at the wall behind the bar.

"Now, Mr. Everette," began the "boss," "I want you to be completely honest with me. Tell me one thing. 'Exactly' what happened in El Paso last night?"

Leon was sure this was the end. He maybe had time to finish his drink but after that, it was anyone's guess as to what was to come next.

"Well, nothing 'happened'. But just like we did here in Albuquerque, we performed two shows to sell-out crowds, who we think thoroughly enjoyed themselves," answered Leon.

"I ain't talkin' about that. What happened in El Paso last night!" the "boss" said in a stern tone.

"Are you talkin' about how we got paid?" asked a hesitant Leon.

"Exactly, and I want to hear every single detail," replied the "boss". "I've heard one side, now I want to hear your side of the story, so be very careful with your words and be very specific as you describe 'exactly' what happened."

Leon reached for his glass of vodka and grapefruit juice and took a larger-than-usual swallow of his freshly poured drink, then landed the glass with a low, but firm-sounding thud on the varnished surface of the hard wooden bar top. He then paused momentarily, as the drink made its way down and his head became clear from the rush of the alcohol.

"Ok, you want the truth. I'll tell you exactly what happened," said a confident Leon.

"After our performances, I sent my road manager to get our pay, but my manager came back and said that 'your' manager, Mr. Stellina, refused to pay us for our two performances, even though he complimented what a good job we did.

"So, I went to see Mr. Stellina myself. I don't have any idea as to what his reasons were, but he was very disrespectful and assured me that we weren't getting paid last night and that we'd get paid whenever he decided that it was time for us to get paid."

The "boss", still looking straight ahead, listened closely and tuned out everything except Leon's voice.

"Sir," continued Leon, "I don't mean no disrespect to your organization, but I'm responsible for making sure that my crew is paid on time. When we get paid, most of their money is sent back home to their families to make sure their bills are paid, and their children are fed. Besides, we've learned that it's not safe to carry a large sum of cash on our persons while on the road.

"The crew only keeps enough money to themselves to meet expenses while on the road. The last time we were paid was after a show in San Antonio last Saturday night. Last Monday, one of my crew members wired all of his money back home to his wife except for what he would need for the rest of the week while on the road.

"Before Friday night's performance, he spent his last quarter making a phone call to his wife to see how she was doing with her cancer treatments, with the expectation that he'd be paid after the show. He assured her that he'd find a Western Union along the way on Monday to wire her his most recent salary—the salary we were promised for not only tonight's show but more specifically, the salary we were promised for Friday night as well."

The "boss" was becoming emotionally rapt as he intently listened to every crucial detail of Leon's voice. In addition, he still hadn't made the slightest of a movement, sitting rigid and never surrendering from the straightforward pose he'd maintained even before Leon's arrival. The Marlboro Gold 100's cigarette in the ashtray had been reduced to about a 40mm stub but could wait for another draw, and his mostly empty glass of Jack Daniels' would have to wait for its next pour. Right now, what he was hearing from Leon was not the only the most important thing that mattered—it was the only thing that mattered.

Leon continued, "I realize that you know by now that I was dressed only in my Jockey shorts when I entered Mr. Stellina's office. I know it sounds bizarre, but I expected potential trouble and my Navy Bootcamp training taught me that technique to use in case of a fight when you're outnumbered.

"When I entered Mr. Stellina's office, he asked me why I was dressed the way I was and what did I want. I simply told him that I wanted my money.

"I looked down and saw an envelope on his desk with my name on it. Then he leaned over the desk and got in my face and told me that I wasn't getting paid tonight and that he'd pay me whenever he decided he wanted to pay me, and threw the envelope in the top desk drawer and slammed it shut."

The silver-haired "boss" continued his silence and remained in his frozen, straight-forward posture, listening carefully to every detail, mentally comparing both sides of the story that he'd been told.

"When he wouldn't comply, I banged my fist on his desk and demanded my money," Leon continued.

"When he leaned over the desk and got closer to my face, I

grabbed his necktie and began choking him. I'll tell you right now, sir, I was so mad I wanted to kill that man.

"When I finally pinned him down on his desk, I reached into the desk drawer and got my money, pushed him away from me, and he landed in his chair and the chair rolled back and hit the brick wall behind him.

"I took off running, fighting off several of the staff members along the way, then busted through the door and sprinted to the bus, and we sped away.

"I didn't like doing what I did to get my band their money, but if I had to do it all over again, I would. That's how much they mean to me.

"And that, sir, is 'exactly' what happened!"

For a moment, there was a lapse in time. The tension in the room felt thick with anxious anticipation, and the room ambiance was so quiet that you couldn't even hear the sound of a pin dropping on the tiled floor below.

The "boss" reached for his cigarette and made one slow, final draw before crushing it in the colorful Pueblo Indian-designed, porcelain ashtray. He then finished off the last of his remaining alcoholic beverage and nodded for the bartender to come to pour him another.

Still looking straightforward, the "boss" decided it was his turn to speak.

"That's about what I expected," he said in a calm, but not surprised tone.

Then, for the first time, he broke his straightforward pose. He turned his body ninety degrees on the padded bar stool, facing toward Leon, and extended his right hand out as a gesture of a handshake and said, "I want to thank you, Mr. Everette, this has been going on for a long time, and you're the first person to ever stand up to that El Paso manager."

Leon extended his right hand to complete the handshake, feeling a huge sigh of relief, yet almost choking, as his throat had been filling with saliva from his long explanation to the "boss." To his delight, the friendly handshake confirmed that he was finally able to breathe normally again.

"That manager," the "boss" continued, "is my son. As I said, this has been going on for some time now, and I appreciate you standing up to him.

"I'm glad that neither you nor anyone in your band was hurt, and I'm especially glad that you got your money.

"My son, on the other hand, is in the El Paso County Hospital. He suffered a concussion and a gash in his head. But don't worry, I don't blame you for his condition. He brought all of this on himself.

"You'd be surprised at how many times I've had to go behind him and make good on contracts with other entertainers, such as yourself. It seems like when I call Nashville that they're expecting me to ask about booking some country music entertainment, or to apologize for my son's contract indiscretions.

"I can't explain it, because I don't understand it, but for some reason, he gets a kick out of making people sweat for their money.

"Mr. Everette, I'm the general manager of all five of our Frontier Social Clubs, and neither I nor our upper management tolerates this kind of harassment. As you can see, we run a reputable establishment, and making money is our goal. And we can't continue to make money by getting a kick out of making our clients sweat for their payments.

"Sooner or later, the word will get out that our establishment can't be trusted, and it will be harder to book quality entertainment, such as yourself.

"As I said, that man over there is my son, but that doesn't mean he's exempt from a punishment of being buried six feet under, just like any other member of our proud organization, who would be so bold as to tarnish or dishonor our illustrious reputation."

Having noticed that Leon had finished his drink, the "boss" motioned for the bartender to refill his glass.

He then turned toward the well-dressed man guarding the door and motioned him over.

"Go outside to the bus and tell everyone on board to come inside. I want to buy them all a drink," he ordered.

"Mr. Everette, I know what your choice of drink is, but what does your band prefer?" asked the "boss."

"Well, like me, some of them like vodka, and most of the others prefer a cold beer," Leon responded.

"Do you have any room in your bus for some bottles of vodka and beer?" the "boss" asked.

"Yes, sir," responded Leon, "the back of the bus has some room."

"Go to the storeroom," the "boss," said to the bartender, "and tell a couple of men in there that I said to load up the back area of Mr. Everette's bus with cases of vodka, cases of beer, and cases of a variety of snack foods."

"Thank you, sir," said Leon, "that's very generous of you."

"The pleasure is all mine," replied the "boss."

The "boss" then raised his glass of Jack Daniels and said, "Here's to your safe travels, a thank you for your fine entertainment, and to a bountiful success in all of your future endeavors."

Leon returned the graciously complimentary toast and thanked the "boss" again for his generosity and hospitality. He still didn't know the "boss'" first name, but at least now he knew that instead of calling him "sir", he could address him as Mr. Stellina.

After a brief awkward celebration of drinks with the "boss," the band returned to the bus and as was their routine, drove throughout the night to their next destination. The rest of the road tour was a massive success, as shows were sold out and graciously accepted, and as fate would have it, the band was paid on time and without incident.

**LEON EVERETTE:**

Leon would make one final performance at the Frontier Social Club in El Paso during his career, but while there he noticed that Gino Stellina was no longer the manager. To this day, he's still not sure if he's still with the establishment's organization or if he'd been demoted or perhaps, reassigned to another social club. Nevertheless, it didn't matter to Leon, one way or the other. However, as much as he didn't care for Gino Stellina, Leon still hoped he didn't end up in one of the social club's notorious hiding places—that is, a place somewhere they called "six feet under."

Chapter 20

## Something's Happening Here

**Leon and the Hurricane band** were enjoying the times of their lives during the early-to-mid 1980s, yet unbeknown to them were subtle, but major decision-making changes taking place in country music executive board rooms throughout the industry landscape in Nashville. The country music format they had grown up singing and listening to, and now had become a major contributor to the industry themselves, was about to once again take on a major transition to appeal to an ever-evolving fan base demographic.

As significant were the changes that were being considered, they were far from being the first in a long line of transformations in the history of the country music industry. To understand the modifications being considered, perhaps a brief history of the ever-evolving musical format in the industry would help explain the hard business decisions being made by the record label executives during this time.

The original roots of country music were planted from songs mostly about folk tales of both real and fictional characters specific to geographical locations in the western and south-eastern parts of the United States. More commonly, the songs were ballads about heroes and villains, romance and tragedy, sprinkled occasionally with a little comedy and satire.

During the 1800s, for people living west of the Mississippi River, a "Western" style of music was introduced and often heard by cowboys singing and playing guitar and/or harmonica while sitting around a campfire at night during a cattle drive, or more intimately in a bunkhouse on a local farm or ranch. If you wanted to hear another variation of the Western style of music, you would have to visit one of the local saloons where dancing girls and crooning cowboys would entertain live audiences made up of mostly local and drifter cowboys.

Meanwhile, in the southern United States, a different style of folk song or folk music was beginning to take shape. In addition to the guitar and harmonica, drums were added as was the introduction of the banjo and fiddle. In some cases, even more, crude instruments such as rhythmic spoons, moonshine jugs, and corrugated washboards were all part of a new style of music that, when blended, would over time become known as "bluegrass."

Musicians who grew up on and studied these traditional tunes began to grow in number and eventually created fusions between the styles of the different regions. While "Western" music remained Western, and "bluegrass" music remained bluegrass, over time as the two evolved and blended, one of their new sounds became known as a new genre known as "country-western" music. Although its musical genre was well received, at the time, the ever-changing evolution of country music had already begun.

One of the first known artists to record a bonafide country music record was Jimmie C. Rogers during the 1920s. Also known as the "Father of Country Music," Rogers' music was also the inspiration for the spin-offs, or evolutions, of country music in the decades that followed that would become known as "Rock and Roll," and "The Blues," among others. His "Blue Yodel No. 9" was selected as one of *The Rock and Roll Hall of*

*Fame's 500 Songs that shaped Rock and Roll.* In addition, some of his laid-back, sultry sounds also influenced Blues legend Muddy Waters to incorporate a bluesy, soulful sound into his iconic music.

Country music had set a standard for the love of music, yet its evolution was just in the very early stages. Needless to say, every time there was a spin-off or change to the format of what was considered the standard of the music, controversy would surely follow among those who performed the music, those who were fans of the music, as well as those who were responsible for producing and promoting the music.

During the 1930s and 1940s, even Hollywood would have a huge impact on the music industry, as they introduced "singing cowboys" in many of their western-themed movies. Gene Autry and Roy Rogers, among others, were very popular at the time and highlighted this genre of country music creating a strong romanticized vision of the wild west that captured the imagination of America for decades to come.

Perhaps one of the most dynamic evolutions in the history of country music was the introduction of "Honky Tonk" music in the late 1940s and early 1950s. Now, Rock and Roll music wasn't technically introduced before Honky Tonk music, but a few seeds had been planted, so to say, that would eventually grow to become its own genre of music in the years that followed. While Rock and Roll was a major evolution from Honky Tonk music, Honky Tonk music grew from a blend of many musical genres such as "Boogie Woogie," Ragtime," "Jazz," "Rhythm and Blues," "Country-Western," and even "Gospel" music.

While all the above musical genres incorporated guitars, fiddles, pianos, drums, and in some cases horns, among other common instruments of the day, there was one instrument that differentiated Honky Tonk music from all of the rest—the *steel guitar.* Talking about controversy and evolution in music, the steel guitar was almost an entirely new genre of its own.

Believed to have been invented in Hawaii in the late 1890s,

the Hawaiian guitar made its way to the United States during the early 1900s. During this time, the sound of the Hawaiian guitar had a more "tropical" sound, and over time, was tweaked to the familiar "southern drawl" musical sound that made it a must-have in both Western swing and traditional country music formats. It was popularized in the United States by a cowboy movie star, Hoot Gibson, in the late 1920s but its popularity was kept to a small group of musicians at the time, including Jimmie C. Rogers.

During the 1930s, it was a primary instrument for the "Western Swing" style of music featuring Bob Willis and the Texas Playboys, but once again, its popularity was minimized to a small following. But, by the late 1940s, the steel guitar's popularity not only exploded among music lovers, but it became a must-have instrument for those performing in the ever-growing Honky Tonks around the southeastern United States, including the well-known likes of Hank Williams, Sr., Lefty Frizzell, Ernest Tubb, Webb Pierce, and the "Queen of Country Music," Kitty Wells.

By the early 1950s, the Honky Tonk sound was being challenged in a competition for fans' support for an up-and-coming new musical genre—Rock and Roll. Among the fan base was an ever-growing number of young music lovers who were attracted to the "electric" sound of the guitar and more rhythmic drums. To them, the Honky Tonk sound was nice, but it was becoming an identity more appealing to an older audience. That shouldn't be surprising, as Honky Tonk music, at its inception, was favored by a younger audience leaving the music formats before it to the older audiences.

Whereas Honky Tonk music had an identity with the steel guitar, Rock and Roll music's identity became the sound of the electric guitar. Although the electric guitar had been invented decades ago, it was not until the first mass production of the all-new Fender Esquire that the electric guitar would explode onto the music scene. At the time, the Rock and Roll audience was growing stronger and stronger, and it looked as if it were here to stay. For the first time, country music had some serious competition and with competition comes the responsibility of business decision-makers to tweak the industry.

Despite the difficulties country music faced during this time, some saw it as an opportunity to reinvent the genre. A collection of producers and record companies out of Nashville, including Columbia Records, RCA Records, and Decca Records, ended up taking America by storm with a new style of country music that focused on smoothness and polish. The performers that these companies paired up with, such as Chet Atkins, Patsy Cline, Jim Reeves, Eddie Arnold, and Loretta Lynn, among others, excelled in helping create this new, more mellow sound. In time, this new sound would become known as "Traditional" country music. Instead of trying to compete with Rock and Roll at its own game as Honky Tonk tried, the sophisticated sound coming out of the Nashville labels was unique and stood out on its own.

Throughout the 1950s and 1960s, country-western music flourished adding the likes of George Jones, Tammy Wynette, Faren Young, Dolly Parton, and many others. Over time, the term country-western title became simply Country Music. It also kept its "Traditional" moniker, but that term began being used as an "umbrella" category to cover all previous evolutions of country music, including Western-Swing, Bluegrass, Honky Tonk, and even Rockabilly.

During the 60s, while many artists and fans were taken with the stylishly refined songs coming out of Nashville, it had also gathered its fair share of detractors who felt the style was too commercialized and didn't have enough artistic range. With what some would call a quiet rebellion against the Nashville sound, Buck Owens introduced the "Bakersfield Sound" as an attempt to bring more humanity and passion back into the country music format. Ordinary guys facing ordinary problems were the focus of many of these songs making them much more relatable and down to earth. Another well-known artist for this style of country music was Bakersfield, California's own Merle Haggard.

And just when it seemed as if all was well and that country music had finally reached a sense of calm and serenity in the industry, with the new decade of the 70s came yet another change and rebellion. This time it was caused by a group of musicians that were opposed to the commercial control of the Nashville recording labels. If they were going to record their music in Nashville, they insisted on having more control over the rights of their music that the Nashville record labels had monopolized using what they considered unfair business practices.

In addition, these rebel musicians bucked the trend of the clean-shaven and well-kempt hair of their predecessors, to a more unconventional style by having long hair, beards, and often overtly smoking marijuana. However, as did their predecessors, they too, generously indulged themselves in the consumption of alcohol. The "Outlaws," as they were labeled by the industry, included Waylen Jennings, Willie Nelson, Kris Kristofferson, Hank Williams, Jr., and David Allen Coe, among a few others. These good ol' boys proudly stood their ground against the stalwarts of the country music industry and through it all, with the help of propaganda initiated by the record label executives, gained a reputation of "being good at being bad."

In reality, they weren't as bad as the record labels tried to make them out to be and the fan base saw right through the smoke screen the record labels were trying to expose. In the end, fans saw them as good ol' boys who were true to their principles and through their success and devotion to their music, became a symbol of pride throughout the country music industry. It took a while, but the two sides finally put aside their differences, and once again, all was seemingly well in Nashville.

By now, the decade of the 80s had just begun, and just as sure as the sun would rise over the Great Smoky Mountains, everyone knew that in due time a day was coming for yet another series of events that would lead to change in country music, and with change, would come more controversy. Unfortunately for Leon and the Hurricane band, some of those changes and controversies would have the potential to have a negative impact on their careers as well.

Chapter 21

## The Beginning of the End

**To the dismay** and disbelief of many country music fans as well as their iconic country music legends, the decade of the 80s continued with a subtle, but substantial transition within the country music industry that had its origins during the 1970s. The once "pure" Country sound was being relegated to being a lesser-used format in favor of a more modern genre of a less than traditional country music style in country music stations all over the United States. The pre-1980 country music format, which was once considered as being the pride of conventional country music, would eventually have a sub-category of its own and become known as simply "Classic Country" or "Country Gold."

The aging, heart and soul of the country music fan base were being discussed at board meetings all across Nashville. "We have to make changes to Country Music," they said, "or we'll lose our fan base. The older generation is shrinking and that, among commercial and other issues, is causing a downturn in our investments. We need to adapt to the times and incorporate a sound with a less southern drawl and tweak the abrasive musical twang in a way that will appeal to the up-and-coming youthful generation. If we don't change our format now, the Country Music industry will surely die." Well, to the joy of the aging country music fans, the Country Music industry did not and has not died, but adding to their frustrations, it did lose its most prominent characteristic—its soul.

The carefully executed business transition was to slowly phase out the traditional country music format to make way for a more inclusive youthful country music style, all to satisfy the needs of profit-driven industry leadership. The die-hard, deep-rooted industry leaders and stalwarts like Jerry Bradley and Jim Foglesong were strategically being replaced by new, less-experienced record label executives with unproven, fresh ideas to entice the ever-growing younger audience. To the ire of Leon, Carroll Fulmer, along with other artists' business managers, was also designated to be replaced and relieved of his managerial duties.

The music once inspired by country music legends from the 50s, 60s, and 70s was being isolated like an old horse put out to pasture. While they were still somewhere roaming the musical landscape, their usefulness was becoming less and less important to the industry leaders. The country music establishment was beginning to realize that their loyal base of followers was growing older and with that finite demographic, their listening audience was becoming smaller and smaller due to the realization of their longevity in life.

To sustain the business, they would have to make some difficult decisions and personal sacrifices. For country music to survive, they felt that they had no choice except to begin a trend of music that would attract the attention of a more youthful audience. They needed a new breed of talent that would not only appeal to the youth, but would also help stabilize the industry and, at the same time, compensate for their potentially shrinking payday. It was quite simple but a clever ploy—"entice, capture, then own the youthful fan base, then keep them for a lifetime." If successful, the country music industry would once again be stable for decades to come.

In making that decision, they assured themselves that there was no way they could teach their so-called "old horses" their new tricks. However, they decided that it would be better to keep their "old horses" around for special weekend airtime using a pre-recorded program format to satisfy the listening needs of their aging audience. To their credit, while the "old horses" were to be categorized as a lesser useful part of the industry landscape, at least the new leadership had the dignity of not shutting their barn door completely closed.

While shock waves traveled throughout the music industry in Nashville with the dramatic change in organizational leadership and program format transformations, over time, when the dust had settled and everything was back to a more amicable atmosphere, the new breed of country music executives put their plans in motion. To their credit, although controversial at the time, their business moves were skilfully and artfully ingenious. In fact, their leadership in the industry was so successful that in the years to come, some of them would be inducted into the Country Music Hall of Fame for their contributions to the industry.

The theory behind their success is debatable, but one of the more probable reasons is their ability to acknowledge the decline in popularity of Rock and Roll music during the decades of the late 70s and throughout the 80s. As was the case of a once-aging fan base for traditional country music, so was the fan base of Rock and Roll during these decades.

In addition, as was once again the case for Country Music, so did Rock and Roll began to get "watered" down by spin-offs such as "Punk Rock," "Heavy Metal," "Gothic Rock," "Disco," and other alternative genres. Although these variations still categorically remained under the umbrella of "Rock and Roll," their cohesiveness never lived up in comparison to the standard that had been established by those labeled under the "Traditional" Country Music format.

Slowly but surely, the avid fans of Elvis Presley, The Beach Boys, The Beatles, The Rolling Stones, Mowtown, and so many others were sadly losing their once-exclusive Rock and Roll radio stations. As the hardcore Rock of the 50s, 60s, and 70s began to phase out into almost obscurity as far as its presence on any dial on a radio, sadly, so did its fan base wane in the listening audience. What seemed like an overnight conversion was, in reality, a slow, methodical transition of a Rock and Roll fan base yearning to find their music on the radio only to find the next closest thing—the *New Country* format.

The new Nashville executives had achieved their goals. While covertly observing the aging Rock and Roll audience decline in numbers and watching many of their once-loyal Rock and Roll music stations being converted to a less diverse format called "Classic Rock," they purposefully aimed their focus on capturing the disenfranchised fan base demographic. During this time, the Rock and Roll faithful felt as if they were "wandering in the wilderness." As traditional country music was relegated to a format of limited play time under the category of "Classic Country," so did rock become less used on the radio except for "Variety Music" and "Classic Rock" formats. The structure of their once beloved music was losing its once highly esteemed presence as the stations that once played their music were fading from having been one of the options that were once a prominent presence on the radio dial. Perhaps the most bitter pill for the rock fan base to swallow, and as the old saying goes, "as if to pour salt on an open wound," many of these same former Rock and Roll format stations were now converting to none other than the New Country format.

Ironically, as Rock and Roll had once evolved and became established as an independent musical genre, partially because of the influence of the Honky Tonk sound, its once-faithful following was now becoming a significant following of the New

Country sound. Somewhere in the bars and boardrooms of Nashville, the Nashville elite was covertly celebrating their victory over Rock and Roll with a new mantra—"From Honky Tonk it once came, and to Honky Tonk it has now returned."

Moreover, the beloved 45rpm vinyl record was also becoming a dinosaur in most, then eventually, all country music stations across the country. A new concept of using cassette tapes, then an electronically devised digital format was taking the place of the revered vinyl format. In addition, the feel of the DJ's hand carefully positioning a 45rpm vinyl record onto the console turntable would no longer be envisioned by the radio-listening audience. Imagining the diamond needle as it intimately touched the revolving disc for the sole purpose of following the one long, musical groove to produce a quality high-fidelity sound was becoming a mere, but a fond memory.

Sometime during the format transition, synthesizer keyboards, some accompanied by drum machines and other artificial musical instrumentations, were replacing many band instruments resulting in a less-than-realistic sound and feel to the music. In some recording studios, the warm feel, sensitivity, and soulfulness of what was once a proud component of vinyl records were being replaced by a more rigid and emotionless digital sound produced by a simple press of a software-activated button.

The country station DJs had even lost their identity to a new term called "Radio Personality". Furthermore, depending on the location, the term "Country Music" was now being called "Today's Country," "Contemporary Country," or "New Country" among other flavorless monikers.

Soon to be seldom heard were the once-revered songs of superstar legends like George Jones, Tammy Wynette, Loretta Lynn, Conway Twitty, and so many others, who were all credited for having been participants in prolonging the foundation and core of the once-prestigious country music industry. With no one to defend their proud legacy, the true roots of country music were methodically being replaced with a youthful, more rock-style entertainment format.

Sadly, a predictable rift was beginning to develop between the classic country artists and some of the up-and-coming contemporary artists. Leon was no exception. Although he was in his early 30s and was already attracting a well-balanced fan base including a youthful following, he didn't appreciate the disrespect some of the new artists and new business executives had toward some of his closet and older friends in the industry.

Many of the younger generation of artists showed very little to no reverence for the legends of the industry. To them, it was out with the old and in with the new. To make matters worse, when disagreements became heated and confrontational, the newly appointed record label executives were backing the newcomers by almost one hundred percent.

Many of the classic artists began to lose respect for the industry. Some retired or drastically cut back on performances, while others fought hard but were put in a playlist category of less importance by the industry executives. The show would go on, but my, how the dynamics and intricacies of the business had changed—and the radio listening audience was taking notice.

Legendary country artist Roy Clark became so disgruntled with the industry that he left the Nashville scene altogether. In 1983, Clark was the very first country artist to open his own country music and entertainment venue in Branson, Missouri. His venue was so successful that other legendary artists such as Ronnie Millsap, Ray Stevens, Mel Tillis, and many others also made the switch from Nashville to Branson as their entertainment headquarters.

Subsequently, even the Grand Ole Opry began adding more and more contemporary country artists to their nightly entertainment lineup. The hardcore classic country music followers were beginning to attend fewer and fewer of the Opry performances and were flocking to Branson to get their satisfactory dose of pure country gold music. Furthermore, whenever the entire cast would gather on stage and sing the country music anthem, "Will the Circle Be Unbroken" at the final call of the Grand Ole Opry performances, its inherent meaning and the pride that it stood for would not necessarily be broken, but it had, however, become spiritually bruised and morally defiled.

While all this business chicanery was going on, it was also beginning to cause emotional stress upon Leon and his band, as some of the business moves were making a direct negative impact on some of their closest friends in the industry. Industry decisions that seemed to have started as being a whimper with a low profile, were now openly being broadcast loudly and deliberately for everyone to hear and to take notice. In addition, many in and around Nashville were wondering where their careers might stand with these new changes. Leon and the Hurricane band were no exception. They all knew that it was just a matter of time before they would learn of their standing in the new corporate structure. Only time would tell, and the clock was ticking.

Chapter 22


## He Don't Know Grits


**One frosty winter's Monday** morning in 1985, Leon received a phone call from the RCA Records headquarters in Nashville. The polite, soft-spoken female voice on the other end of the line informed Leon that an executive of the RCA recording label, whose name will remain confidential out of respect for the industry, wanted to have a sit-down meeting with him at his earliest convenience. No further information was given, and the two parties compared available times and dates. Leon agreed to a meeting for the following Thursday morning at 10 o'clock.

Immediately after the phone call, Leon began to feel anxious and curious as to what was the purpose of the meeting and what was the urgency. His anxiety was for his fellow band members, as their livelihood depended on his success in the business. His curiosity was troubling, as some of his closest friends in the business had recently gotten similar phone calls and the results of their meeting were not favorable for some of them.

Unpopular decisions were being made that affected many of the older generations across the network of the country music industry. Once hard-core country artists were being relegated to a lesser-used format. In addition, for reasons that were never openly explained, many program directors, station managers, and producers across the country were being forced out and replaced by a new breed of country music administrators.

Leon didn't know what to think about the upcoming meeting. There was just so much uncertainty going on behind the scenes at the industry headquarters that it was impossible to pinpoint exactly where you and your career stood in this seemingly ever-changing administrative-guided business environment.

Not one for being shy of potential confrontation, Leon packed an overnight suitcase, got behind the wheel of his brand-new, red Corvette and headed out for Nashville early the following Wednesday morning. "Lucy", named after Leon's favorite female comedian, Lucille Ball, was a shiny red Corvette and was a real head-turner wherever she went. You might say that she was to the road what Leon was to a concert stage—hot, fast, and flashy. And whenever the two of them were alone on an open highway, it was like having a love affair on wheels.

Leon stayed overnight at a Nashville hotel and early the next morning, arrived at the RCA Records parking lot about fifteen minutes early for his appointment. He approached the reception area and was greeted by a pleasant young lady who politely asked him to have a seat in the waiting area.

"Would you like a bottle of water or a cup of coffee while you wait?" asked the receptionist.

"No, I'm fine," said Leon, "but thank you just the same."

"Hopefully, he'll be with you shortly," said the less-than-assuring receptionist.

"Hopefully, he'll be with you shortly." Leon thought. She makes it sound as if he has a problem with time management.

While waiting for his appointment time to arrive, he could hear loud talking and spirited laughter coming from the executives' office. He couldn't tell what was being said or how many were in the room, but they all seemed to be having a very lively conversation.

Leon looked at his watch, and after thirty minutes past his appointment time had elapsed, the laughter and loud talking continued off and on from the executives' office. In the meantime, two more men entered the waiting area. One was about twenty years old and the other looked as if he was in his forties. Another newcomer trying to get an interview for an audition, Leon thought. And the older gentleman is probably his manager.

After forty-five minutes had passed, the executive's door finally opened, and four young men and one older man left the office.

Another new group and their manager, Leon thought. The executive then looked directly at Leon as if he was acknowledging him. But as Leon began to rise from his sitting position, the executive made an unexpected move.

"Leon, I'll be with you shortly," he said as his eyes turned toward the other two men in the room and with a hand gesture, invited them into his office. "This won't take long, Leon," said the executive. "We just have to finalize some business details, sign a recording contract, and then I'll be right with you. I appreciate your understanding."

But Leon was far from being understanding. He was emotionally caught up between having been disrespected and becoming outright livid! It was all that he could do to hold back his anger. He had driven all day the day before, purposely stayed overnight, and was earlier than expected for his appointment, and now he's being cast aside like an old, unworthy relic. He was beginning to understand and now experience the resentment that some of his older friends in the business had and the anguish they were going through. It became very clear that he was on the wrong side of the familiar phrase going around Nashville— "out with the old, and in with the new."

Finally, after about a half-hour had passed, the door to the executive's office opened. The two men left, both smiling from ear to ear, and the executive motioned to Leon, "Leon, I'll see you now." Looking at his watch, he said, "I'm sorry about the delay. I guess I let time slip up on me. Come on in."

That's about the pitiful and insincere apology that I've ever heard, Leon thought. Holding back his anger and his tongue, Leon entered the office and sat down across from the desk of the executive.

"How have you been, Leon?" asked the executive, "It's been a while since we've had an opportunity to have a one-on-one conversation."

"I'm doing fine," replied Leon getting straight to the point. "So, what is this all about?"

"Okay, Leon, I'll cut to the chase. As you may know by now, the industry is going through some growing pains right now. The older generation is getting older, and unfortunately, we're losing some very beloved members of the family along the way. Business discussions have been made and now the execution of putting unpopular decisions into action has begun. To be blunt, we're in the process of revamping our entire industry, from the administrative leadership to production managers, to the broadcasting and recording equipment. In addition, unfortunately, were also meticulously having to phase out or retire the older generation of performers across the board from our standard playlist and performance venues."

Leon sat rigid and unmoving. It was all that he could do to hold back his anger, but before he could utter a word, the executive continued his explanation. As Leon listened to the executive, he soon realized that the executive's words rolled off his tongue effortlessly and to the point, as if they had been rehearsed prior to this moment, as an actor would rehearse a scene before the actual performance. Then it dawned on Leon that this was indeed just a repeat of many other conversations the executive had had with previous performers. The oration was part of a process, and it would take many appointments and a scheduled time to complete. Leon was just the next star to fall and unfortunately, he wouldn't be the last.

"Leon, all things having been considered, we've thought long and hard about how to proceed as to what is the best business plan for the betterment of the industry. The final decisions were not made overnight but were discussed and dissected, often with highly tempered conversations among the top executives in the business throughout the past few years.

"As for you, the news is not all bad, but some things have been decided that, at first, you may not understand and agree with. Hopefully, over time, you will understand why we made those decisions and will come to accept them as you continue your career.

"First of all, the bad news. Carroll Fulmer is being relieved of his responsibilities as for you and your band's managerial duties."

"Wait a minute!" interrupted an irate Leon. "You can't fire Carroll. He's been with me all these years. If it weren't for Carroll Fulmer, I wouldn't have made it on my own in Nashville."

"I'm sorry, Leon, but Carroll's usefulness to us has run its course," continued the executive.

"What do you mean his usefulness has run its course?" blurted Leon. "Carroll Fulmer is the hardest working, most dedicated, and most trustworthy friend that I've had in my career. You can't just throw him out like dirty bath water!"

"I know this is all a jolt to your consciousness," continued the executive, "but we've already hired a manager for you to take over his responsibilities. I think you'll like him. He was supposed to be here today so I could introduce you to him, but he had a family emergency at the last minute back home that he had to take care of. I'll make arrangements to have you meet him as soon as we're all conveniently available.

"Trust me, his music management background is impeccable and his relationship with executives and performers in the music business is highly commendable. He's been very successful in the pop music industry in New York City and wants to expand his expertise into the country music industry."

"A New York Yankee?" Shouted Leon, "You've hired a New York Yankee pop music manager to guide my country music career? Heck, I'll bet he don't even know what grits are, much less know how to run a southern boy's country music career. You want me to be a guinea pig for a pop music pansy to learn country music from? That's the worst idea I've ever heard of in all my years as a country music performer!"

"Believe me," said the executive, "I understand your frustration. But in time, you'll see that this could be a potential new start or even a boost to your career. You're right, Carroll Fulmer is one of the most sincere and hard-working managers in the industry. It's just that with our new business plan, and don't take this the wrong way, but his usefulness has run its course. He's taken you as far as his expertise in the business is capable of in these competitive times."

Leon's posture grew limp and lifeless like air leaving a deflating balloon. His head bowed lowly, momentarily staring incoherently at the lushly carpeted floor. His best friend in the business, Carroll Fulmer, was gone. His safety net, his guidance counselor, his "go-to" friend and ally for all things—both personal and business, had been written off like a dead hero in a Western novel. And to add insult to injury, Leon had no opportunity for input in the decision whatsoever, and apparently, the decision was now final and without any further discussion.

As Leon continued his motionless pose and trance-like stare, the executive continued with his conversation. "Leon, I do have some good news for you. Your new manager has been working hard making phone calls and booking dates for your next tour. As of today, he's already confirmed at least ten public appearances including commercials, nightclub gigs, and full-blown concert dates. In addition, he's arranged a new country music group to join you in the concert appearances. You've probably never heard of them, but with your notoriety and fan base, they're sure to make it big time in no time."

"What do you mean they will be joining me during the concert appearances?" asked a perplexed Leon.

"Well, as I said, with your success in the business and with your following of fans, we're going to have you open for them on the tour," replied the executive. "Your name and picture will be on all the posters and marquees announcing your introduction of the new act in town. This new group has just what Nashville needs right now—a country vibe with a rock and roll groove. As a matter of fact, I have a sample poster that we're considering to help get this promotional campaign off to a good start. Check this out."

Leon reached out for the poster as the executive offered it to him. What he saw made him want to not only sink lower in the chair but to crawl under that expensive carpet beneath his feet. The poster showed large lettering headlining Nashville's newest act at the top followed by the time, date, and location, and at the bottom third of the page was a small picture of Leon with the phrase, "With Special Guests Leon Everette and the Hurricane Band."

"So, you want me, someone who's been loyal to the business all these years, to take second fiddle behind a group that no one's ever heard of? And you want my fans to be the draw to help jump-start the career for the new boys in town?" replied Leon. "That's just downright insulting and disrespectful! There's no way that Leon Everette and the Hurricane band are going to use our fan base for a publicity stunt, such as this!"

"Well, before you say any more, Leon," said the executive, "take a deep breath and go home and discuss it with the band and get their opinion. Your career is going through a bit of a "rough patch" as of late, and we're hoping that this might be just the thing to get you back on track."

For once in his life, Leon was speechless. The executive was right, he was going through a rough patch. Due to his belligerent attitude brought on by alcohol consumption problems, his career was somewhat in jeopardy. He'd just completed his second alcohol-related rehab program in hopes of sobering up, but with conversations like this one, that might be hard to achieve.

Besides, what could he say that would change anything? He could cuss him out and tell him how he really felt, but that would make an already bad situation even worse. There was no sense in digging the hole any deeper, as he was already in a situation over his head and out of his control. What was said and done had been said and now was done. The lot had been cast and he drew the short straw. Without Carroll Fulmer, his negotiating skills were less than desirable and certainly less professional and effective than those of Carroll Fulmer.

Begrudgingly, Leon left the executive's office, taking the sample concert poster with him. He also took a cassette tape that the executive gave him with demos of songs that were chosen by his new manager for him to consider recording for a potential new album to be released before the summer concert series was scheduled to begin.

He'd struggled with staying sober and purposely avoided getting drunk the night before, as he wanted to have all his senses fully alert to deal with anything thrown his way during the meeting with the executive. Forget the two successful sobriety rehabs; this was a new day, and after what he'd just gone through, he was sure to tie one on before the sun would lose its place in the darkening sky over the South Carolina horizon.

Nevertheless, as angry and disappointed as he was, he knew that before he made any rash decisions about his career that he would discuss all the new details from the meeting with the band and get their thoughts and opinions. There was a lot to process in considering the pros versus the cons, plus it was going to be hard to continue doing what he loved under the guidance of someone he didn't trust and with ideas of which he didn't approve.

No matter what his final decision would be, he still had the integrity to allow the group to make their final paychecks as members of the Hurricane band and would finish this potential one-last tour with them. Sadly, the thought that haunted him the most was when the band had performed its last encore of the summer concert tour, and the tour bus had made its final stop at the end of the line, so it would also be the end of the line for his once illustrious country music career.

Chapter 23

## The End of an Era

**Desperate and disillusioned,** it was time to leave Nashville, and get back home and announce the disheartening news. Leon hastily climbed into his red Corvette and he and Lucy hit the interstate back to South Carolina. Needless to say, the trip back home would be much quicker than the trip to Nashville.

As he approached the outskirts of Nashville, his curiosity got the better of him. The concert poster was sitting on the passenger's seat with the cassette tape sitting on top of it. He reluctantly, but curiously inserted the tape into the dashboard cassette player. There were a total of ten songs on the cassette, and as he listened to each one about halfway through, he would hit the next track selection button, as each one sounded similar to all of the rest. There was no steel guitar, no fiddle, no harmonica, and the drums had a crisp, but annoyingly hardened sound. Most disappointing of all were the vocals, as they sounded as if they were coming from someone who was desperately trying to imitate a warm, but artificial southern dialect.

So, this is the new country sound, he thought. It was more like rock and roll with an imitation sound of country music blended in. Whatever it was, it wasn't the country music that he'd grown up listening to and it surely wasn't the country music that he enjoyed performing during his career in the industry.

He quickly ejected the tape, threw it back on top of the poster and drove in silence the rest of the way back home. The quiet rhythm of the tires strumming along the cracks in the roadway was the only sound he heard for miles. After a while, he began recalling the early days of his career and how he'd achieved awards and commendations for numerous categories in country, as well as rockabilly music. Most of his album sales were above average and his fan base was one of the most popular in the industry. In just a few short years he'd accomplished almost everything, and then some, that he'd dreamed to achieve. So, what was there to hope for now? At this stage of his career, the few goals he'd not achieved were, for various reasons, unapproachable, especially with the new alignment of the music industry and more especially without the assistance and guidance of Carroll Fulmer.

At one point, he became emotionally distraught as he began to understand that with the new, reorganized playlist format, his music would be played less, as the program managers were being instructed to give the new, country-rock talent the majority of the radio airways. Less exposure to the airways would mean fewer album sales, resulting in less compensation for him and the Hurricane band.

Not long into the trip, he recalled what the executive said about him going through a rough patch. It was indeed a difficult time. The stress and responsibilities of being a successful artist and making sure the band was adequately financially supported was a burden he hadn't considered when he first began his career. The demands of the road while on tour and the demands of the record label between appearances were difficult tasks for any up-and-coming performer. Unfortunately, it was a common practice for others in his profession, many of whom also met the same fate, resulting in alcohol and/or drug rehabilitation.

However, there was no one to blame but himself. He was the one with a condescending attitude and arrogant disposition. He was beginning to realize that it was no wonder that his songs didn't receive the on-air play time throughout his career as compared to some of his peers. Were the record label executives purposely and intentionally holding him back from the success that he thought he deserved? Was this a form of punishment for his despicable attitude? In retrospect, it sure seemed that way, yet he would now unselfishly take full responsibility for his actions. But it was no time for self-pity. Serious decisions were to be made and their outcome would affect not only him and his family but the Hurricane band and their families as well.

As he crossed the state line into South Carolina, Leon recalled another discouraging moment of the meeting with the executive. He loved the country music life, but the management was proposing tweaking his style of music to a more modern sound—a sound with a less country feel and influence. It was a style and sound that he knew he wouldn't be comfortable with. Not only was it disingenuous, but it was also an outright fraud on country music. Furthermore, it would be something that he would have to fake on stage and there was no way he was going to put on an act just to satisfy the needs of a group of money-hungry industry executives.

After arriving home from the meeting in Nashville, Leon told Kathy the details of his trip to Nashville and why he was considering ending his career. Her first reaction was met with understandable disappointment, as she knew how much Leon enjoyed performing. In an effort to console him, she advised him to reconsider all the intricate details and not to make a hasty decision. In her mind, it would be better for everyone involved if he would just take a step back and process everything that had taken place up until this point, as well as the potential for unforeseen things that might take place in the weeks and months to come. But after considering all the negative factors being imposed on him without his consent or for an opportunity for a fair rebuttal, and the stress that he carried as the most responsible person for the band, she began to understand the burden that he was carrying. More importantly, she began to understand the reason for his disheartening attitude toward the industry administrators as they wanted him to change his style of music and perform under the guise of phony, insincere pretenses.

After wrapping her mind around all the details of Leon's meeting, seeing the disappointment in his eyes and hearing the frustration in his voice, she became determined on doing whatever it took to make Leon somehow feel less depressed and somehow find something positive about his unfortunate, negative situation.

After Leon's health and state of mind, her concerns turned toward what the future would hold, not only for Leon but also for the family as well. She knew that money wasn't a problem, as Leon had made and saved enough over the years to make them financially stable for the rest of their lives. They would still be able to afford a nice home, the kids would have financial support for potentially going to college, and as far as the family's health, Leon had made sure that they were all in good hands as he had made sure that they had the best healthcare coverage on the market.

Nevertheless, her immediate concern was for Leon. What was he going to do now? His once steady, mostly glamorous career was potentially coming to an unexpected screeching halt and there were no immediate plans as to how he would move forward with his life and his new career, whatever that might entail. Leon was a mover and a shaker. There was no idleness in his lifestyle whatsoever. All he knew was how to run wide open with whatever his daily activity included. He had to be doing something productive or he would possibly go insane, not to mention everyone else around him.

The following day, Leon called for the band to meet with him on the tour bus to discuss his recent visit to Nashville. As the band members assembled, they could all see the uncertainty and vagueness in Leon's eyes, as they assumed the news was more than likely not favorable. After everyone was accounted for, Leon began discussing his reason for the unscheduled, hastily-called assembly.

"Thank you all for coming on such short notice," he began. "As you know, I was called to Nashville yesterday to meet with the top executive of RCA Recording which ended up being a discussion of your and my future career in the industry. First of all, I was literally blindsided by the executive, as I had absolutely no knowledge whatsoever as to what the meeting was about."

Leon went on to describe in detail all the business aspects of the meeting. The news of the firing of Carroll Fulmer seemed to be the most disappointing of all. In addition, the description of the new manager wasn't very encouraging as well.

Then, Leon displayed the sample concert poster. Not surprisingly, they all nodded in disapproval and began murmuring among themselves about how upsetting and disrespectful this was, not only to them but especially to Leon. When it came to putting on a show, they knew that Leon was a devoted, no-nonsense, hard act to follow on any stage. They also knew that his country groove with a rock-style flair was exactly what the new industry standard was looking for in new talent. Although his style was often controversial among "traditional" country music followers, looking back and to his credit, he was a talent way ahead of his time. The style of music and the stage presence that Leon demonstrated in the early to mid-80s is what eventually would be duplicated by future performers beginning in the decade of the 90s up to the present day.

And to make matters worse, and of all the gall, the new management wanted Leon to change his style of music to resemble a less-than-country sound with an emphasis on a new rock-style vibe, as demonstrated by the tracks on the cassette tape that Leon played for them.

"This is what they want us to sound like," said a disheartened Leon. "I don't know about y'all, but I can't see myself faking this kind of music. I have to play the music that comes from my soul and not music that comes from my head. If I tried to entertain people with this style of music, my career would be over in no time."

Leon was pleased to see that everyone agreed with him. But now it was time to tell them something that none of them ever thought they would hear, especially at this stage of his career.

"Now I want y'all to know that I love you all with the deepest of sincerity," Leon began, "but I've talked it over with Kathy, and I have decided to call it quits after the summer tour is over."

"You can't quit, Leon," replied one member. "What about your fans? This will certainly leave a void in their love for your music. To them, this will be like an addict quitting their music cold turkey. The only way they can get their fix will be to listen to their old albums."

"You can't be serious, Leon," said another. "Are you sure this is what is best for you, your family, and your fans?"

The murmuring and talking over one another went on momentarily when Leon finally interrupted them, saying, "Y'all listen up! I am very serious about the decisions that I've made. The only reason that I haven't quit already is that I want to finish this last tour with you all so that you can have time to get your future careers and financial affairs in order. All of you are very talented musicians and singers, and there are plenty of quality acts available that will take any of you on in a heartbeat. My only advice is that you follow your heart and find the right individual act or group that meets your quality and style of music. So, from this point forward, start getting your affairs in order. If I hear anything new from

Nashville, I'll let you know. In the meantime, I wish you all the best."

Not being one for idleness, and to help keep their minds from worrying as well as to keep their musical talents well-tuned, Leon continued to have the band practice daily. Then, about a week later, Leon got a call from the RCA Recording headquarters in Nashville, asking him to return to meet his new manager and to finalize details of his and the band's immediate future.

Once again, Leon and Lucy hit the road to Nashville. This time, it was an afternoon meeting, and Leon didn't have to spend the night to be on time. But this time was also different because before he arrived, Leon had more than a few drinks of vodka to supposedly help calm his nerves and demeanor. Needless to say, his nerves were never tested, but his demeanor was less than admirable.

First of all, he purposely made himself an hour and a half late for the meeting, to the dismay of the waiting executives, including his new manager from New York. Then, without going into the fragile details that occurred behind closed doors, when the executives began discussing something that Leon didn't agree with, he would interrupt them, often by talking over them and using malicious expletives to argue his point.

It goes without saying that the meeting did not go as planned by the executives. The only thing Leon agreed on was to finish the summer road tour. He also pretty much told them where they could stick the concert poster and cassette tapes and refused to record any of the songs selected by his so-called new manager. And as for "Nipper," the RCA dog mascot that represented the recording label's image, well he could kiss his anatomy where "the sun don't shine".

As he was leaving the meeting, Leon informed them that this would be his last business dealings with them and that when the tour was over, so would be their business relationship. The RCA executive and Leon's new manager were beyond furious and threatened to blackball him from the industry if he followed through on his threat to refuse to honor the final year of his contract. It didn't take a psychic to predict that, like a good song sung out of key, this business relationship was certain to end on an inevitable bad note.

Once again, and for the last time, Leon left Nashville for home. The next day, he met with all of the band members and told them the results of the meeting. They were all heartbroken and disappointed but agreed to honor the dates and venues of the summer event series.

Without going into all of the details about the summer tour, all of the scheduled events were sold-out performances. The new country artist group that headlined the tour was met with mixed reviews, and in less than two years and without the support of Leon's fan base, dissolved their business relationship with RCA Records due to poor record sales and poor venue attendance.

But that didn't faze the industry management, as they had many others waiting in the wings. Their philosophy was that if you have enough baited hooks in the water, eventually, you're bound to catch the big fish. And unfortunately for them, as for Leon and the Hurricane band, they were the big fish that got away.

As promised, when the tour bus was parked at his home in Ward, SC, for the last time, Leon shook hands and hugged all the band members and thanked them for their dedication to helping make his and their careers successful.

And, as the bus had come to the end of the line, so had Leon's career. Leon swore that he'd never take another step, much less another ride on that bus, and would never return to Nashville as a country music entertainer. He'd had his last bus ride, he'd sung his last country song, and he'd performed his last stage appearance.

The final phase of a once-promising career had sadly come to a dramatically disappointing end. Although the country music industry had lost a rising icon, Leon's frustrations and stress from the business were finally over. Nashville had once again squandered a worthy and popular talent. Leon, on the other hand, had gained peace of mind and personal freedom, while at the same time, restoring his dignity by proudly standing by his personal standards and his musician's code of ethics.

From humble beginnings, Leon's successful career as a country music artist started with a top-ten song called "Over." Ironically, now at the end of his illustrious career, his love for country music entertainment was now "Over," as well.

Chapter 24

## New Beginnings

**In the days** that followed the end of the final road tour with the Hurricane band, Leon spent some quality time with family and friends, mostly relaxing and reacquainting himself with being a stay-at-home husband and father. During this time, Kathy had answered the phone on many occasions with calls from the RCA Recording Group in Nashville but told them that Leon was unavailable to take their calls. After several unsuccessful attempts and having never received any calls back from Leon, the calls from Music City stopped and so did Leon's music stopped being played on the radio airways. Just as management had promised, Leon had been officially blackballed from the industry.

Many friends and fans across the country weren't sure what had happened to Leon, as he was here one minute and gone the next without any explanation. Oddly, there wasn't an official announcement of his retirement, nor were there any magazine articles explaining his absence from the music scene. And that was especially odd to the fans, as the country music tabloids loved to cover both the good and the not-so-good activities of their beloved "Maverick." Was he back in alcohol rehab? Was he overseas on an extended tour? Speculations were rampant, and with no concrete information to go on, some people even thought that he had died and that the music industry, for whatever reason, had quietly allowed him to fade away without any fanfare whatsoever. Nevertheless, Leon moved on with his life and purposely avoided the quiet noise of uncertainty coming out of Nashville.

His official last business transaction in closing out his career was selling both of his tour buses—one to an up-and-coming group called the Forester Sisters and the other to a popular artist and fellow musician, Eddie Rabbit. Having finally divested himself from all duties and responsibilities of his career, it was time to look forward and see what the future had to offer.

From this point on, he would never look back and wonder, "What if?" As far as he was concerned, he'd accomplished almost everything he'd set out to achieve during his brief but memorable career. Sure, there were some unforeseen and unfortunate bumps in the road, but most, if not all, artists had experienced similar or worse fates throughout their careers as well.

Although he couldn't change the personal mistakes and poor business decisions he'd made in the past, he would, however, use his former ill-fated experiences to learn from and hopefully help him make better, more mature decisions in the future. He was in complete control now of his present and future and the decisions he would make from this point forward would be, for better or for worse, his responsibility and his alone.

After spending several weeks painting and making interior and exterior improvements to their home, including a major overhaul of the landscaping, Kathy suggested they take a break and recommended visiting a flea market one weekend in a neighboring South Carolina county. Leon was not one for retail shopping, but he did enjoy the relaxed atmosphere and genuine low pressure to buy from a huge selection of quality goods at less than normal retail outlet prices routinely offered at flea markets.

The flea market experience was so enjoyable that they made it a regular Fall weekend get-away routine by visiting various flea markets across South and North Carolina. While Leon was not much of a buyer, he was, however, a curious observer. At some point, he began to notice that the people doing the most purchasing of goods seemed to be the ladies in the crowd. The men in the crowd seemed to be more for browsing the wares and goods and less active in their purchasing, yet they appeared to be there for moral support and having their wallets and credit cards available when the ladies decided on a purchase of their own.

After several visits to a variety of flea markets, Leon noticed a trend in the ladies' purchasing choices. One of the more popular items was both handmade and factory-made crafts, whatnots, and curios, including wicker products and furniture. Leon soon learned that many of the best-selling items were made by an Asian company out of Hong Kong. In private covert conversations with the owner or manager of the booths, he would gather as much information as he could about the manufacturing company and how and where the goods were purchased. In just a few short weeks, he had gathered enough information that he could start an import-export company of his own by purchasing quality wicker furniture and other popular crafts and accessories at substantially low wholesale prices.

By the time the following Spring arrived, Leon and Kathy were well-stocked and organized with their new merchandise and in time became one of the most popular and successful flea market booth destinations in all of South and North Carolina. Their business also became one of Michael's Arts and Crafts' most popular suppliers of wicker furniture and accessories. In just a few short years, during the late 1980s, their company would be among the most successful import-export suppliers of their kind in all of the southeastern United States.

Then, one day in 1989, from out of nowhere, a local businessman and entrepreneur named Curtis Carlisle approached Leon about a potential business opportunity. Carlisle happened to own twelve acres of land that included a former flea market with long, twin outdoor covered and paved vendor booth spacing, plus a large covered and partially enclosed spacious structure for housing more delicate vendor wares and goods.

The location of the former flea market was an excellent commercial and professional tract of land in an area convenient to the intersection of Interstate 20 and major South Carolina Highway 1. He also happened to be a local fan of the former Leon Everette and the Hurricane band notoriety, and after finding out Leon's contact information, decided to give him a call.

"Hello, Leon," this is Curt Carlisle, "how are you?"

Like Leon, Carlisle was a well-known name in the area, yet Leon knew his name but had not met or spoken with him up until this time.

"I'm fine, and I hope you are, as well," Leon replied.

"I'm great, Leon," Carlisle responded. "Just so you know, I've followed your music career over the years and was disappointed to learn that you had left the business, as I have always appreciated and enjoyed your style of music. Your fans, including myself, really miss your music being heard over the radio nowadays, but I've noticed that you've rebounded and have been successful in your import-export business since those days in Nashville. I'm really glad that all worked out in your favor in the end.

"As a matter of fact, the reason I'm calling is that I have a business proposal that I'd like to discuss with you sometime in case you may be interested in expanding your entrepreneurial portfolio."

"What kind of business do you have in mind?" asked a curious Leon.

"Well, it would be easier if I could show you rather than try to explain it to you over the phone," said Carlisle. "Would it be possible to meet with you at the old Aiken Flea Market location at I-20 and Highway 1 sometime?"

"Yeah, I'm free this afternoon. What about one o'clock?" asked Leon.

"One o'clock. That's perfect! Thanks, Leon, I'll see you there," replied an excited Carlisle.

While Leon didn't know Carlisle personally, he'd heard of him from his support of community development projects and other personal business interests and investments. He was especially known for his leadership and sponsorship in the development and completion of the gateway entrance to the city of North Augusta. As you crossed the bridge over the Savannah River coming from Augusta, GA, into North Augusta, SC, the first thing you'd see was a beautiful fountain and flower garden in the middle of the roadway rotunda honoring the veterans of all United States wars.

From all that he'd heard, Carlisle was on the up-and-up, and he'd never heard anything negative about him whatsoever. So, perhaps it wouldn't hurt to hear what one of the pillows of the community had to say. Besides, a short trip to the old Aiken Flea Market could be a time to recall fond memories of its former days of glory as a once local favorite destination before its unfortunate hardship and decline in recent years.

Upon Leon's arrival, Carlisle was waiting in front of what was once called the old flea market pavilion.

"Hey, Leon, I'm glad you could make it. It's nice to meet you," said a grateful Carlisle.

"Nice to meet you as well, Curt," replied Leon.

"Leon, I'll get right to my reason for asking you to meet with me," Carlisle said as he began his business proposal. "As you can see, the old flea market's foundational features are still very structurally sound, and with a little good old-fashioned hard work, could be upgraded to become not only a local but a regional nightclub. And with your name and star quality, I think we, as partners, could turn this location into one of the most popular nightclub destinations for miles around."

As Carlisle walked Leon around the property showing him how all the existing structures could be renovated to become a potential five-star entertainment venue, Leon listened optimistically with caution. Everything he heard from Carlisle sounded positive, and he could envision good results from every detail that Carlisle proposed.

The location was ideal for potential patrons from nearby Augusta, GA, as well as for others living about an hour's drive away coming from Columbia, SC, straight down I-20. Most of the layout of the existing structure was already in place, needing mostly upgrades to meet local codes and ordinances specifications. The parking lot still had a good layer of asphalt and most of the electrical and plumbing infrastructure was already intact. The main object of monetary investment would be the pavilion area where outer walls, an entertainment stage, a beverage bar, patron tables, chairs, etc., had to be accounted for. The metal roof and concrete floor were of minimal concern at the time.

Carlisle was one of those smooth-talking, silver-tongue types. As the old saying goes, "He could sell ice cubes to an Eskimo." However, as he continued to paint the picture of how that location and the potential for a nightclub could be a success for Leon, everything that he said made sense. Before long, Leon was not only picturing neon lights and men and women dressed in cowboy attire having the time of their lives, but he was also beginning to see dollar signs teasing his imagination.

"Okay, Curt, this all sounds good, but exactly how do I fit into your plans," asked an inquisitive Leon.

"Well," replied Carlisle, "I've already invested the majority of the risks by purchasing the property. I just need another investor or two to help with renovations and marketing to get it up and going."

"Well, don't take this the wrong way, Kurt, but I'm not using my money to invest in anything that involves such a risk as this. Don't get me wrong, I think it's a good idea. I just don't think it's worth my taking a chance on putting up such a substantial sum of money only to potentially get a return, at the very least, in the long run."

Carlisle was disappointed in Leon's answer, but having been placed in similar business deals in the past, he had to think fast so that Leon would not leave without at least some form of commitment to the project.

"Very well," said Carlisle, "I understand your reasoning, and I don't blame you, but I do believe you're passing up a once-in-a-lifetime opportunity. I thought you might not agree to my first proposal, so I've prepared a second option."

"Oh, there's a second option?" Leon smiled with hesitation.

"In business proposals as significant as this one, I always have a second option," smiled Carlisle. "It's like a plan 'B'. So, here's my final proposal. You can take it or leave it, and I won't bother or pressure you, whatsoever, with whatever you decide. It's not my intention to talk you into something that you're not completely comfortable with. I've made business deals and investments all of my life, some having far more financial risks than this one, and everyone that I decided to take a gamble on, or better yet—past business ventures that were decided only after having been considerably evaluated by thorough study and research of all of the pros and cons, all of which turned out very profitable for me and my fellow business partners."

As Leon listened to Carlisle's pitch, he was trying hard to discern if it was too good to be true or if everything was just as Carlisle had described. There was no doubt that he was indeed a smooth talker, yet overwhelmingly convincing at the same time.

"So, here's option number 2. As I suggested before, would you be interested in my using your name as an appeal to draw public interest on behalf of the venue?" Carlisle continued. "If so, we could advertise it as Leon Everette's 'Hurricane Central' as a reference to the notoriety of your country music career as well as one of your more popular hit songs, 'Hurricane.' And with your direct connections to your friends and contacts in the country music industry, we could even hold periodic country music concerts with other notable artists including yourself.

"If we can find another partner to help with the initial investment, your monetary investment would be minimal, depending on what the other partner has to offer. It's a good business practice that all investors have at least a little "skin" in the business to hold them personally responsible for the deal. As I said, your name and notoriety go a long way, and with that being taken into consideration, you won't have to have anywhere near the monetary investment as the other partner and myself.

"In addition, your responsibility would be to function as a project manager overseeing all construction improvements, and when the club opens, you will take on the role of the club manager, handling all responsibilities of running the club as a viable business providing quality entertainment and informal hospitality in a safe, secure environment. How do you like the sound of that?"

Having heard all the details of "option number 2," Leon was cautiously tempted to agree to all of the terms of the deal. Minimal financial investment? Oversee construction projects? Manage a nightclub? It was like having a job of a lifetime being offered on a silver platter. This was a no-brainer. What could possibly go wrong?

"It all sounds good, but to be honest, it's a lot to take in and I need to take time to consider all that you've proposed before I make a decision," answered Leon. "Besides, I think that it's only fair that I discuss it with my wife and family before I give you my final answer."

"I agree," responded Carlisle, as he extended his right hand to Leon. "Take all the time you need, and in the meantime, let me know if you know anyone else who you think might be interested in coming in with us to meet the other monetary goals to get this project up and going. I've extended my financial resources about as far as I can go. Without another investor, this venture is dead in the water, and I'll have to reconsider my options on what else I can do to make this property profitable."

"Okay, I understand," said Leon.

"Thanks again for meeting with me," said an appreciative Carlisle. "I look forward to seeing you again soon."

"Thank you, as well," said Leon.

As Leon was driving across the paved parking lot toward the exit for the main roadway, he looked into his rearview mirror and imagined the old, faded, wooden sign that read "Aiken Flea Market" as being a huge, neon-lit signage with large lettering advertising, "Hurricane Central," that could be seen by passing vehicles along I-20 and SC Highway 1. The thought of performing once again intrigued him, but if anyone ever wanted to see Leon Everette perform again, this would be the place where they'd have to go.

Chapter 25

## The Proposal

**Leon waited until suppertime** to tell Kathy about his business proposal with Carlisle earlier that day so that he would have her undivided attention. After hearing all the details of the meeting, for the most part, she agreed that it all sounded like a good idea. And like Leon, she also had concerning thoughts telling her that it almost sounded too good to be true. Then, the third-degree questioning began.

"What about the import-export business?" she asked. "We've got a good thing going, and I can't see just throwing all that money, time, and effort we've invested away on something we're both prematurity interested in and skeptical about at the same time."

"Well, to be honest," Leon replied, "I'm getting a little tired of it. I know we're doing well, and we have some really good business contacts and regular paying customers, but it's just getting to be more of a hassle and too monotonous. I'm not complaining; it's just gotten to be boring and too repetitious for me."

"Well, you never said anything about being bored with it before now," continued Kathy.

"I know. I know. I've kept it to myself because I see how much you enjoy it," said Leon.

"Yes, I do enjoy it. I enjoy going to different flea markets across the two-state area and meeting with people, some whom I know and others I've never met. It gives me something of a social life that I wouldn't have if we didn't have the business. It also takes my mind off things and allows me to get out of this house on a regular basis. Besides, I enjoy the money we're making as well," said Kathy.

"Well, I have an idea," Leon responded. "Now that we've established a comfortable business infrastructure, I don't see why you can't take full responsibility for running it on your own. You've pretty much done that already, as I've only been involved lately in the heavy lifting of loading and unloading goods and wares. You've been in more control of the business aspect than I have.

"Don't worry; I won't leave you totally on your own until you feel you're one hundred percent confident that you can run the business without my help or input. Besides, even if I do decide to join with Carlisle, it's not like I'll be another county or state away; I'll be right down the road in Aiken if you ever need me to help you with anything."

"So, what is this 'nightclub' going to cost us?" Kathy asked with slight sarcasm.

"According to what Carlisle and I have agreed to, it depends on what one more investor has to offer," Leon quickly responded. "I told Carlisle that I wasn't comfortable investing any of my money on an investment that involved a level of risks as this one. If we can find one more investor to make the deal fair for all, then my investment will be minimal, at the most."

"Well, exactly how will you be involved, and are you going to be paid for your involvement?" asked Kathy.

"Okay, here's the deal," Leon explained, "Carlisle says that using my name, based on my country music career and popularity, would be an immediate draw for country music fans for miles away."

"So, your investment will be using your name as a claim to fame, so to speak," asked Kathy.

"Yep, for the most part," replied Leon, "and when construction begins, I'll be the project manager overseeing construction; then, after it's completed, I'll be the manager of the nightclub."

"Exactly when will you begin making money on this and just how much will it be?" asked a curious Kathy. "It sounds like you're going to be away from home an awful lot. At the very least you might as well get paid for your time."

Well, there's the bottom line—money, Leon thought. It's always about the money with her. The next thing she'll want to know is what's in it for her. Leon had to take back control of the conversation before she could make it all about her.

"Listen, Kathy," Leon explained, "we're just in the talking stage at this point. Carlisle is going to need another investor or two before any business contractual agreements or monetary transactions can be made. Right now, we just need to decide if we're going to keep the import-export business and if you're going to continue to run it."

"Hump!" Kathy sighed, with her lips squeezed tightly and her bottom jaw forced to one side of her face as if she'd taken a bite out of a ripe lemon. She wanted to say more but soon realized that it wasn't worth an argument at this point since, all in all, everything was just in the talking stage at this point.

"Okay. Okay," mumbled Kathy, "we'll see."

There was a lot more she wanted to say, and Leon could see it in her eyes, but to avoid any negativity he quickly changed the subject for something more relatable and more favorable for her.

"Okay, I have an idea," Leon suggested, "since we have a big event in Charlotte this weekend, let's do a trial run of you taking complete control of the business, and I'll be there to advise you in case you need any assistance. If all goes well, we can continue to operate this way until you're completely comfortable with it and in the meantime, we can decide on the other issue as more details become available."

There was a short hesitation, but Kathy finally ended the conversation with a simple, "Okay, that sounds good."

At first, Kathy was somewhat reluctant, but she tried not to show it. The self-centered wheels in her mind were spinning. If she was going to own and operate the import-export business without Leon's involvement at some point, then why should he be involved when it came to the profits being made? At the time, she received thirty-five percent, Leon received thirty-five percent, and thirty percent went back into supporting the business infrastructure. As the wheels continued to spin, she could see herself one day in full control of the business, taking on all of the physical and administrative duties. Without Leon in the picture, why shouldn't she be allowed a seventy percent cut of the profits? And even better, why not be in control of all the profits? The conversation was technically over, but the crafty wheels in her mind continued to spin.

Shortly after mentioning the event in Charlotte, Leon remembered an old friend who lived there that he thought might make a good investment partner for Carlisle's project. A couple of years after Leon retired from his country music career, a friend of a friend suggested Leon as a reference to a man named Jason Altman, who needed someone to produce an album for one of his clients.

Jason Altman was a well-known businessman, not only in the Charlotte area but nationwide. In addition to other businesses, he owned eleven A&P Grocery stores across the country. During its earlier days, the A&P corporation was one of the top sellers in not only food services and goods but at the top of all retail enterprises. Later, when corporate conglomerates made massive business merges, many of the A&P enterprises were united with other businesses under one major corporate structure. Among those included in the merger were Altman A&P

stores. Nevertheless, although Altman may have lost control of his A&P stores, he'd gained a lot more revenue and stock options with the business merger. To say the least, Jason Altman was a very, very rich man.

* * *

As the story goes, Altman and his friend were having trouble making a successful studio album. They had ten quality songs, but they just weren't satisfied with the production results for one reason or another. As a last resort and as suggested by a mutual friend, Altman reached out to Leon for help.

"Hello, may I speak with Mr. Leon Everette, please?" Altman politely asked.

"This is Leon, how may I help you," answered Leon.

"Mr. Everette," continued Altman, "you don't know me, but my name is Jason Altman. A mutual friend of ours recommended you as a possible source to help me with a project I'm working on."

"Please, call me Leon," Leon interjected.

"Okay, thank you," Altman said. "Leon, I'm in the process of helping a friend of mine record his first studio album, and to be quite frank, the results so far are not what we initially expected. We have ten good songs, but the arrangements and other production issues are a mess. Would you be interested in coming to Charlotte and producing this album for me? I'll gladly pay you for your time and all expenses, even if we're still not satisfied with the results."

"How soon do you need this to be done," asked Leon.

"Well, obviously I don't know what your schedule is, but we need it done as soon as possible. This project should have been finished and on the record store shelves months ago," answered Altman.

"Mr. Altman," Leon began before he was interrupted.

"Jason. Please," said Altman.

227

"Jason," Leon began, "It just so happens that I'm both very fond and forever grateful toward our mutual friend. There was a time when I was in dire need, and he came to my aid with no questions asked and no return favors to be promised. I'd be delighted to help you with your project, but there is one thing that I must correct you on."

"What's that, Leon?" asked a nervous Altman.

"When I produce a studio album, I guarantee you you'll be pleased with the results. I am my most nitpicking critic, and if I'm not satisfied, then no one will be satisfied. Trust me, when I get through with your project, that album will be ready for distribution as fast as the production machine can spin the discs."

Leon wasn't necessarily bragging—well, maybe a little, but everything he said was true. In the prime of his career, when it came to studio musical compositions and vocal sound arrangements, even the best studio sound engineers in the business would often ask him for advice when it came to finalizing a quality production project.

Sure enough, Leon went on to produce the album for Altman and his friend, and the result of the album was eventually a top-ten hit. The young performer's very first album, as well as his country music career, was an instant success.

Leon had left the studio in Charlotte with complete confidence in his work, yet refused to accept any compensation, whatsoever. Besides, he wasn't doing it as much for Altman as he was secretly, but thankfully repaying a long-ago mutual friend who had once helped him in an even more difficult personal situation.

* * *

As a man of his word, Leon reached out to Altman, fulfilling his promise to Carlisle in his search for another potential investor for his property. There was no doubt that Altman had money and since their last successful joint business venture, he had not only become a fan of country music but had also become an investor in country music, although from a discrete perspective. Leon's only concern was that he wanted to make sure that he was approaching Altman in his support of Carlisle and not as a form of payback or asking for a favor in return for their prior business arrangement.

"Hello, Jason?" asked Leon as he initiated the phone call.

"Hey, Leon! How are you?" answered an excited Altman. "It's good to hear from you. How've you been?"

"I'm doing good, and I hope that you are as well," replied Leon. "I've got an idea that I'd like to run by you."

"Go ahead. Shoot," said Altman.

"I'm calling as a favor to a friend of mine from Aiken, SC. His name is Curt Carlisle. He's a very successful local business-man, and he's making inquiries for people with business skills, such as yours for investing in a potential country music night-club to be located between Augusta and Columbia, just off I-20 and SC Highway1. The property in question is the old Aiken Flea Market.

"Would you be interested in coming down and meeting with us at the location of the property he has in mind so that he can show you around and explain all the pertinent details of the project? Trust me, there's no obligation whatsoever. He just wants to talk with other investors and see if his idea could potentially be a profitable one. No one's going to twist your arm or try to talk you into anything that you're uncomfortable with. He's sincerely merely seeking an outside point of view of his vision to turn this property into a successful watering hole and entertainment venue.

"I've met with him and he's shown me the property and explained his vision and has asked me if he could use my name as a sort of 'calling card' regarding my former country music career. As a matter of fact, he wants to advertise the club as

'Leon Everette's Hurricane Central, a reference to me and my most popular hit song, 'Hurricane'."

"Leon, I have to admit," replied Altman, "it sounds intriguing. As you suggested, I won't make any promises, but I'd be willing to meet with him. I'm familiar with the intersection, and I think I know where the property is. So, if you'll set up a time and date, I'll see you then and there."

Leon contacted Carlisle, and he and Altman agreed to meet at noon on Thursday of the following week, as Leon wasn't ready to leave Kathy on her own for the upcoming scheduled weekend flea market event in Myrtle Beach, SC. Their business was doing so well that they had every weekend from May 1st to October 31st scheduled at flea markets somewhere in either South or North Carolina. Any other personal or business activities would have to be done between Monday and Thursday.

Just as planned, the three men met at the old flea market in Aiken, and Carlisle made his best-ever business spiel to Altman. Carlisle meticulously explained every positive and every negative concerning the project, and when all was said and done, the positives highly outweighed the negatives.

To everyone's delight, Altman came away from the meeting being more than just a little impressed. His first impression of Carlisle was that he reminded him of himself—a man, who when he had a heartfelt vision of potential prosperity, could face the challenge head-on without the fear of risk and void of self-doubt and the possibility of failure.

As the three men walked away that day, going their separate ways, each one had a lighter step in their walk. Carlisle had been even more convincing in his approach, and this time, Leon was less skeptical and more practical in his sharing of Carlisle's vision for the property. It seemed like a win-win situation for him, as he would have minimal capital to invest. At the very least, he would only lose the time he'd spent on the project, and whatever the outcome, good or bad, he certainly wouldn't lose any sleep over it.

Altman left in a state of intrigue. There were a lot of pieces to the puzzle, but when completed, it had a high potential to be a puzzle that everyone would enjoy, having been a partner in putting it all together. Sure, there were challenging risks, but he wasn't one for shying away from a challenge—especially if there was a potential fortune to be made as the final result.

Carlisle was the last one to leave the property. He sat alone just outside the old pavilion for a while and then walked the property envisioning the many possibilities the structures had to offer. As the sun slowly descended on the western horizon, he couldn't help but think that the next time he would see it, another day would be born, illuminating a new dawn that would bring him one day closer to achieving the most ambitious dream and vision of his long, successful business career. One day, in the foreseeable future, this would not be just the skeletal remains of a failed foregone business venture, nor an elusive nightclub and entertainment venue, but would be the place that many joyful friends and patrons would someday call "the house that Curt Carlisle built;" a place he was adamantly determined to call, "Leon Everette's Hurricane Central."

Chapter 26

## Rock and Roll Woman Meets Country Music Man

**By this stage** of their long, tumultuous marriage, Kathy and Leon had reached a phase of bitterness toward one another that only the love for their children was holding them together. Kathy was feeling the financial pressure and future uncertainty of running the import-export business on her own. Adding to her stress was the fact that Leon was drinking more than ever and being away from home more, dealing with Carlisle and Altman in their goal of establishing the nightclub. The hostility between Kathy and Leon became so vile that it had gotten to the point of loud shouting and unmerciful cussing one another, almost to the point of throwing blows at each other. Thankfully, no physical altercations took place, but it was inevitable that the marriage was all but over—and that was just a matter of time.

After having met with Carlisle and Altman on several occasions in the months that followed their first official business meeting, the three men met at Carlisle's lawyer's office in Aiken to finalize the business agreement concerning the renovation and operation of their new venture to be called "Hurricane Central." Altman and Leon had their lawyers there as well. The final agreement was that Carlisle's investment would be the property he had purchased for the project; Altman agreed to make the necessary monies available to pay for all renovations, including furniture, fixtures, etc., to complete the entire infrastructure; Leon agreed to invest whatever money was needed to install theatrical stage lighting and sound equipment, but with a stipulation not to exceed two hundred thousand dollars. In addition, the lawyers made sure that, as per their agreement, he would put it in writing to agree to allow the other two investors to use his name and notoriety as a major part of his investment. Furthermore, he was to oversee the construction of the renovations and manage the club upon its opening. His payment for managing the club would be worked out with Carlisle and Altman at a point in time before the club's opening.

For the most part, the construction of the club went as well as could be expected. Leon helped with procuring the various city and county building and general construction permits, as well as helping with the overall interior design of the bar and stage portion of the facility. After all of the renovations were finally completed, Hurricane Central opened in the latter part of 1990 to standing-room-only crowds. The first-weekend opening featured a concert by none other than their favorite local artist, Leon Everette. The nightclub was so successful that it became one of the most desired adult entertainment destinations for country music lovers in all of western South Carolina and eastern Georgia.

Over the next few years, Leon was able to arrange concerts for other well-known country music performers including Waylon Jennings, John Anderson, and Confederate Railroad, to name a few. After becoming well-established, the club became "the place" to go for meeting friends, dancing, and enjoying quality country music entertainment. Like any other nightclub serving alcohol to high-spirited patrons, occasional fights weren't uncommon, but for the most part, it was a safe, friendly, fun environment.

By the mid-1990s, Leon and Kathy had reached their final stage of discontent with one another. Two of the three children were older now and had moved out and were enjoying their new lifestyle of being independent, leaving the younger teenage son as the only child living at home. By this time, Leon had moved out of the house and had taken up residence at the club. His drinking addiction continued, and his demeanor around Kathy was beyond being harsh and, to say the least, very unloving. The bitterness between the couple had evolved into the despising of one other such that neither one could stand to be in the presence of the other. The relationship between them was not only broken—it was shattered beyond the slightest possibility of reconciliation.

* * *

Sometime during the mid-1990s, Kathy's niece, Barbie, and her best friend, Diane, visited the club. Diane was a hardcore rock n' roller with no knowledge of country music whatsoever. She could tell you the names of all her favorite rock and roll groups and knew the words to most of their hit songs, but she didn't have any clue as to what the difference was between Hank Williams, Jr. and Charlie Pride. She did, however, know that there was a song called "Your Cheatin' Heart" but had no idea who wrote or sang it. Recently, she and Barbie, who was a country music fanatic, were riding in Barbie's car listening to a country music station when the song came on. Diane was in the process of going through a contested divorce at the time, and she mentioned that the song reminded her of her soon-to-be second ex-husband. And at the time, that was about the extent of her country music experience.

Barbie had tried on several occasions to talk Diane into going to Hurricane Central with her, but Diane always came up with an excuse not to go. Rock and roll was her thing and she had no common interest in country music at all. Even though

Barbie tried telling her that her uncle Leon was once a famous country music artist and had an interest in the club, Diane refused to be swayed into going with her.

Then, one Thursday night, the club advertised "Ladies Night," which meant that all ladies' drinks were at a reduced price, including buy one and get your girlfriend one for free. Besides, free drinks and lots of mostly single women would surely mean lots of available men to share their favorite beverages with. And what woman doesn't like having a drink and conversation with a friendly male companion? Well, for whatever reason, Diane finally decided to go with Barbie and have a fun girls' night out on the town. Barbie immediately found her Uncle Leon and introduced him to Diane. The introduction was not meant for potential romantic reasons but just to put a face to the name she'd been telling Diane about for the past few months.

After the introduction, Diane and Leon parted as new acquaintances, and Leon made his way to the stage to sing a few songs for his next session. Up until this time, Diane's only knowledge of Leon was what Barbie had told her. As a matter of fact, up until this time, all that she knew about country music was what Barbie had told her, but after hearing Leon's performance, she not only became a new fan of country music but also became the newest member of the Leon Everette fan club. His smooth, velvety voice and the emotion that he put into playing his music made her feel the passion of the songs as she could understand every lyric and feel every emotion being sung.

For a moment, she had a flashback of her riding in Barbie's car, listening to the country music station on the radio just a short time ago and recalled the lyrics to the song being played. She had no idea that the woman singing the song was country music legend Patsy Cline, singing a song written by another country music legend, Hank Williams, Sr.:

*"Your cheatin' heart will make you weep*

*You'll cry and cry and try to sleep*
*But sleep won't come the whole night through*
*Your cheatin' heart will tell on you."*

Right then, she realized that that country music song was about the life of a real-life person—a person who had been dealing with issues similar to, or possibly the same as she was going through leading up to her soon-to-be divorce. She had been a loyal wife and supported her husband throughout their marriage, but in time, for whatever reasons, they both had a loss of love in their once-promising relationship. There had been no cheating involved, but just like the song lyrics suggested, both surely lost a lot of sleep, as well as crying and walking the floor for many a night, leading up to the weeks and months before their final separation.

The feelings she was having and the emotions that she felt were like some sort of premonition or out-of-body experience. In real-time, she had been "living" the message of the song in her head for months but had no idea that the song existed. Amazingly, the woman singing the song was singing about what was going on, not only in her life but in both of their lives. She had an unexpected feeling of euphoria, but she'd not even finished her first drink nor had she taken any pills, so it couldn't possibly be the liquor or any form of medication. She didn't realize it at the time, but she had been smitten by the lure, intrigue, and authenticity of traditional country music.

She and Leon didn't have any further conversations that evening, only nodding and saying hello in passing. She had wanted to compliment him on his singing, but he was always surrounded by other people or was too busy helping the club wait-staff with their duties.

As she and Barbie got in the car to leave the club that night, Barbie was taken aback, as the first thing Diane did was turn on the radio, turn up the sound, and tune in to a local country music station. Diane immediately noticed the call numbers indicating the station's identity. Over and over in her head, she repeated the numbers, and as soon as she arrived at her car, she promptly set the dial on her radio to her first-ever country music radio station. Rock and roll was mostly about having fun and partying, but she had now learned that country music was all of that, plus the true-to-life experiences just like hers but played out with a heartfelt passion for everyone to hear and share. From that night forward, in her mind, she became country music's newest fan, and more importantly, Leon Everette's number-one fan.

Chapter 27

**Who Ya Gone Call?**

**The club continued** to operate with success in the following months, and Diane became a regular visitor. Her relationship with Leon had grown from a friendly one to a romantic one. Ironically, both of their divorces were finalized during the same year, and shortly thereafter, they both found a house and moved in together.

Then, one Saturday evening, in early 1996, there was an unannounced visit by the local fire marshal. It's believed that a concerned patron had reported that there were not enough fire exits to accommodate the large crowds routinely hosted by the club owners. The fire marshal asked one of the waitresses where the manager was and when he found Leon, he informed him of his formidable but disappointing news.

"Mr. Everette, my name is Captain Turner with the Aiken Fire Department," the marshal introduced himself. "How are you this evening?"

"I'm fine," Leon replied, not knowing what to expect.

"Is there someplace quiet that we can talk?" asked the captain.

"Sure, follow me," answered Leon.

Upon entering a room away from all of the noise and commotion inside the bar area, the captain began to explain his purpose for his visit.

"Mr. Everette," he began, "I'm sorry to inform you, but your establishment is violating a serious fire code by not having enough fire exits to accommodate a crowd such as you have here tonight."

"Not enough fire exits?" Leon exclaimed. "We've been open and operating for almost seven years and were told from the very beginning that everything was up to code. I don't understand why we're all of a sudden not in compliance."

"I know, and it's not your fault," the marshal said, trying to put Leon at ease. "I'm not sure how you were allowed to operate without having enough fire exits for as long as you have, but as you can surely see, the two doors that you do have are not adequate to accommodate the safe exit of such a large capacity of people, many who may happen to be inebriated, trying to escape during an actual full-blown fire event. I'm sorry, but I'm going to have to ask you to shut down your operation when you close for the night and not to reopen until we have had an opportunity to inspect the installation of a new fire door exit. I'm not going to write you up for a violation, but I am obligated to write you a courtesy warning indicating that I have informed you of a potential fire safety hazard by not having adequate numbers of fire exits. Upon having the door installed, including a lighted exit sign above the doorway, please give me a call, and someone will come out as soon as possible so that you don't have to be shut down any longer than you have to be."

By this time in the evening, Leon had had several drinks of a mixture of vodka and grapefruit juice. After hearing the fire marshal's warning, his intellect dictated that he'd have a few more drinks before the night would be over. Upon closing the club, he assembled all the staff and told them the news. The bar would be shut down immediately and there was no reason to report to work the following Monday evening, as the building would not be within compliance with the fire marshal's orders by then. While he had everyone there, he asked if anyone knew of anyone who could install the door for him. One of the staff spoke up and suggested he contact Lester Herron, a local builder and contractor.

"That's a great idea!" Leon replied. "I've known Lester for a long time. He's a man with a good heart and one who takes pride in his craftsmanship. I'll give him a call tomorrow afternoon because I know he'll be at church most of the day."

The next day, after overcoming a Saturday night hangover, Leon called Lester Herron and told him his situation. Mr. Herron met with Leon the following Monday morning and after reviewing all of the job requirements, told him that he could install the doorway for him, but it would be Wednesday before it would be completed. Leon was excited to hear that the installation could be completed by mid-week, and if he could coordinate an inspection with the fire marshal, the club could potentially be reopened by the weekend.

Mr. Herron already had a full day of work planned for Monday, but before he left, he gave Leon a list of materials needed to install the doorway.

"Leon," said Mr. Herron, "if you'll take this list of materials to the building supply store in Aiken and pick them up for me, that will save a lot of time. In the meantime, I'll have an electrician come by tomorrow and install the electrical service for the exit sign over the doorway. I'll also have a crew of men ready to get started installing the doorway early Wednesday morning. If everything goes as planned, you should be able to have it inspected by the fire marshal, if he's available, on Thursday."

"Can you get me an estimate for what it'll cost for the installation so I can notify the owners?" asked Leon.

"Don't worry about that right now," replied Mr. Herron. "You know, even though we haven't seen each other for a good while now, we have been friends for a long time. I don't have time to stop what I'm doing and quote you a price right now, but I think you know that I'll be fair and that I'll make sure you're satisfied with the results. So for now, go get the materials and pay for them, and I'll make sure everything else is taken care of."

After Mr. Herron left, Leon went straight to the building supply store and purchased all of the necessary materials. As promised, Mr. Herron and his crew finished installing the new doorway and exit sign by late Wednesday afternoon. To say the least, Leon was overjoyed at having the work performed so quickly and professionally. He'd already notified the fire marshal and had an appointment to meet with him the next day. His next job was to call all the staff and inform them to report to work Thursday evening, as he didn't see any reason why the fire marshal would fail the inspection.

As he was about to make his phone calls, Mr. Herron walked by.

"Lester," said Leon, "Let me know how much I owe you, and I'll write you a check."

"Oh, that won't be necessary, Leon," replied Mr. Herron.

"What do you mean that won't be necessary?" asked a perplexed Leon.

"Well," answered Mr. Herron, "a check won't be necessary, but as payment, I would like for you to visit my church this Sunday morning as a type of repayment."

"Oh, no!" exclaimed Leon. "I ain't goin' to no church. Give me a number, and let me make out this check for you."

"Trust me, Leon," replied Mr. Herron, "this would mean more than all the money in the world to me if you'd come to church on Sunday. Besides, there's a chance that you'll get something more valuable than money if you'll come."

"I don't know what you mean," said a curious Leon. "I don't know of anything that at the right price, money can't buy."

"Ok, Leon," said Mr. Herron in a serious tone, "I didn't want to get into a conversation about religion and salvation because I imagined that it would turn you away. All that I'm simply asking is that you come to the Holiness Church on Highway 1 at eleven o'clock Sunday morning. No one will embarrass you or try to make you do anything that you're not comfortable with."

"Lester, I appreciate the offer. I do," responded Leon, "but I don't think that church is a place for a drunken sinner like me."

"Well, I disagree, Leon," answered Mr. Herron. "Church is exactly the place you need to be. That's where all sinners go to get their redemption for salvation. I'd like to stay and continue this conversation, but I'm late for another appointment. Make your phone calls and think about it and let me know what you decide."

Leon didn't have time to respond as the phone in the kitchen rang. In the meantime, Mr. Herron gathered his tools and headed for his truck parked just outside the front door.

When Leon had contacted all of his employees, he looked around to thank Mr. Herron and offer to pay him once again before he left, but Mr. Herron was nowhere to be seen. One of Mr. Herron's employees was still cleaning up debris from the doorway installation and Leon asked him about Mr. Herron's whereabouts.

"I just saw him go out the front door, Mr. Everette," replied the worker. "He left me to clean the rest of this mess up before I leave. Is there anything I can do for you?"

Without answering, Leon rushed toward the front door to catch Mr. Herron before he left, hoping he could pay him by check, as he definitely didn't want to go to church on Sunday.

As Leon burst through the front door, Mr. Herron was starting up his truck and was about to pull away.

"Lester, stop!" shouted Leon. "Let me pay you. How much do I owe you?"

"You don't owe me anything, Leon," smiled Mr. Herron, "but you owe it to yourself to go to church on Sunday."

"That's not fair!" exclaimed Leon. "Please, let me pay you!"

"Life's not fair, Leon," laughed Mr. Herron. "All that I ask as my only payment is that I see you in church Sunday morning. Remember, the Holiness Church on Highway 1. The service starts at eleven o'clock. I look forward to seeing you there."

And with that final awkward goodbye, Mr. Herron drove away. With a checkbook in one hand and a pen in the other, Leon stood like a statue as he watched Mr. Herron's truck leave the parking lot. His heart grew heavy, and his body felt hollow. Mr. Herron had stopped what he was doing in his life to help him get out of a bind so that he could go forward with his. It was more than just a friendly favor—it was an act of pure human kindness and impassioned brotherly love.

He looked down at the checkbook and pen and slowly put them away as he recalled what Mr. Herron had said as he was leaving— "You don't owe me anything, but you owe it to yourself to go to church on Sunday." I don't owe him anything, but I do owe myself, Leon thought. How is that possible? Maybe he'd had one drink too many and was having a hard time understanding what Mr. Herron meant. Whatever he meant, he certainly wasn't going to write a check out to himself, and more importantly, there was no way he was going to church on Sunday.

He'd known Lester for most of his life, and he knew Lester's heart and Christian lifestyle. He soon recalled that every time he'd see Lester that he would always have a feeling of jealousy toward him, but not for spiteful purposes, but more of being envious. Lester had a demeanor of being "Christ-like" but never made anyone around him feel like he was better than them. He just always seemed to have a good spirit about him, no matter where or what the situation may have been. It was an infectious spirit—one that seemed to draw him to Jesus as Leon was drawn to alcohol.

Perhaps there was something special about being a disciple of Jesus, as Lester wasn't always a church-going follower of Jesus himself. At one time, he was living a life as bad, if not worse of a sinner as Leon—and that was hard for Leon to understand. How can someone who was once as bad a sinner as me end up being so pleasant and joyful all the time? he thought. The only way he would know would be to find out for himself and that involved a few things he wasn't comfortable with— mainly having to go to church.

As Mr. Herron's truck slowly faded into the sunset, the last thing Leon recalled from their conversation was that the church service would begin at eleven o'clock Sunday morning at the Holiness Church on Highway 1. Would he honor Mr. Herron's request, return the favor, and pay his debt in full? He was a lot of things, but he wasn't one to owe a friendly debt to anyone. At the same time, he also wasn't one to have to be persuaded to go to church on a Sunday morning.

As he turned to go back into the nightclub, the thought of not being able to pay Mr. Herron played heavily on Leon's mind. Mr. Herron's laborer had finished cleaning up the construction debris and was on his way out, leaving Leon alone in the club. Leon poured himself a drink and sat alone in the darkened bar, thinking about the chaotic events that had happened in the past few short days. The club that he was responsible for had been shut down, and neither he nor anyone else was personally responsible for the fire safety infraction. Sure, he was concerned about the safety of his patrons, but his immediate concern had been for the financial welfare of his employees. What if Mr. Herron and his crew hadn't gotten the club back in business as quickly as they did? How long would his employees have gone without employment? Would he have had to find new employees? All the potentially dire consequences were, at the very least, unnerving to think about. And if any of them had come to fruition, it would surely take more than a shot of whiskey to keep his calm composure and more importantly, his sanity.

Mr. Herron had come through as a good friend, seemingly from out of nowhere. Sure, his name was mentioned by one of

Leon's employees as someone who could help with the fire door issue. But for reasons he couldn't explain, Leon couldn't help but think that it may not have been just a coincidence that of all the people that he knew, Lester Herron, a self-professed "man of God," was the one who ended up, not only getting the job but getting the job done quickly and efficiently. Was it possible that he had been made available by a covertly strategic plan and the result of some kind of other-worldly influence? Leon had seen a lot of strange and unusual events in his life, and this was just another one to add to that list.

Leon continued to sip his drink. He held the glass up and looked at the remaining swallow of liquid inside. Perhaps, he thought, the questionable logic of trying to make sense of it all may have been the result of the alcohol playing tricks on his mind. Regardless, the seemingly miraculous turn of events involving the fire door issue was at the very least, a stroke of luck or just a downright bizarre series of events. But, then again, this was Lester Herron, and Lester Herron had a strong and faithful relationship with his "God and Savior." Could every-thing that had taken place this week that involved Lester Herron have been the result of an almighty, invisible God? Lester Herron would surely think so.

Chapter 28

**Prelude to Salvation**

**Leon continued to** sit quietly alone, the only sounds being the low moaning noises of refrigerant appliances behind the bar and the occasional thump of the ice machine discharging a fresh load of crushed ice. He took a good look around at the interior of the club making himself fully aware of where he was, not only physically, but where he was at this point in the time of his life as well. For the last seven years, he'd lived, worked, and entertained guests in a building with a dimly lit environment, the faint smell of sour beer and human vomit, and obnoxious patrons whose petty arguments and bar room brawls always seemed to be someone else's fought.

He turned around on the bar stool and saw his reflection in the mirror on the wall behind the bar. What he saw made him sad. It was the face of a tired, aging, unhappy man. A man that he thought surely deserved to be in a better place than this. What was he thinking? What kind of life was this for a man with his vocal talents and with an ambition to always be the very best in whatever he was doing? He'd been doing this same thing for the past seven years. If this is where he was now, where would he be seven years from now? Still a low-life bar manager? Still subservient to alcohol? Still looking in a mirror and wondering who that loser was? Really?

He slowly turned back around and began to stare at the floor below in deep, concerning thought. There was something about Lester Herron that he just couldn't let go of. Then he recalled one of the last things Lester had said the last time he saw him leaving Hurricane Central: "Leon, you don't owe me anything, but you owe it to yourself to be in church Sunday morning." Ironically, at that same moment, he recalled his mama often saying that "God works in mysterious ways. He has a way of making the impossible possible." Had Mr. Herron's "God" placed him in Leon's life at this time to give him some kind of "wake-up" call? Is this a part of the process of how someone "being saved" happens? If so, was this his potential *prelude to salvation*?

Leon downed the last swallow of his drink landing the empty glass with a loud thud on top of the hard oak bar top. As the final rush of the whiskey faded, he began having unsettling thoughts competing with his body's physical reaction to the alcohol. Once it seemed as if all physical and mental senses had stabilized, he found himself overcome with unsavory sensations of insecurity. Then, he began feeling an unusual tug of something powerful pulling on his heartstrings—it was like a battle between the emotions of guilt versus the emotions of unworthiness. Whether the results of the tug of war ended in a tie or a winner, the outcome for Leon would surely be traumatic. And equally bothersome, in the back of his mind, a haunting voice that sounded like a faraway Lester Herron kept reminding him over and over and over that "church starts at eleven o'clock Sunday morning."

The tug of war continued, torturing him with humiliation and shame, daring him to cry out for help. A guilty voice began demeaning him, "You're a no-good, low-down, self-centered sinner." On the other side of his head, a voice of unworthiness began belittling him, "You're a pathetic, useless, hopeless piece of crap. You'll never amount to anything on your own. Who's gonna help you now, Leon, your alcohol? Well, how has that been working for you? Go ahead, treat yourself to a bottle of that all-in-one "self-help" elixir behind the bar. And don't you dare listen to that self-righteous Lester Herron. He wants you to think that all of your troubles will disappear if you just go to church Sunday morning. But Leon, they don't serve alcohol at church, and regardless of what Lester Herron says, you won't see anyone there named Jesus to save you from all of your sinful, wicked ways."

After a short pause, everything went dark and quiet. Then, in a calm, solemn voice as if spoken by an angel, Lester Herron could be heard saying, "Leon, don't listen to him. That's the voice of Satan, and he's a liar and a deceiver and will say and do anything to prevent you from going to church. No, you won't see Jesus if you go to church, but I can assure you that His Spirit will be there in His stead. Jesus once said, 'For where two or three are gathered together in My name, I am there in the midst of them.' Rest assured, Leon, that there will be many Christians gathered there, and they will be more than happy to pray for you in asking their Lord and Savior, Jesus Christ, to forgive you of your sins and help you overcome these feelings of guilt and unworthiness."

"There is one more thing that I think will help you with your decision to go or not go to church. There is a verse of scripture in the Old Testament of the Bible that brings comfort and peace of mind to all Christians. It's a promise from God, that if you'll put your faith in Him and follow His commandments, He will be with you and guide you all the days of your life. Repeat the following over and over until it overcomes that wicked voice of negativity and self-doubt you're hearing from Satan:

> *"Trust in the LORD with all your heart,*
> *and lean not on your own understanding;*
> *in all your ways acknowledge Him,*

*and He shall direct your paths."*
*"Trust in the LORD with all your heart,*
*and lean not on your own understanding;*
*in all your ways acknowledge Him,*
*and He shall direct your paths."*
*"Trust in the LORD with all your heart,*
*and lean not on your own understanding;*
*in all your ways acknowledge Him,*
*and He shall direct your paths."*

Then, all of a sudden, he was startled out of his deep, trance-like thought by the sound of the phone ringing in the kitchen. The phone rang and rang, as Leon sat unmoving from his unwavering position at the bar. When the phone stopped ringing, Leon took a moment and was finally able to compose himself and restore his cognitive ability. Having made himself aware of his well-being and immediate surroundings, he left the bar and went to his office to prepare the night's work schedule for his employees. Everything appeared to be fine and in order as he checked the work schedule on the monthly calendar. He double-checked the day and date on the calendar and took notice of how many and of which employees were expected to report to work that evening.

After completing his work, he left his office and turned off the light on his way out. The bar was quiet and dimly lit, just as he'd left it. He took a long look around and surveyed the whole inside of the club. There was no one there but him, but for some reason, he didn't feel alone. He then recalled that the day on the calendar read "Thursday." He took a deep breath and slowly exhaled it. His mind was completely clear now, and he finally had a positive outlook going into the evening.

He recalled the Bible verse that Lester Herron's voice had spoken to him and quietly repeated it over and over until he had remembered it word for word. Then, as he was about to leave to go run an errand, he spoke the words out loud, this time with conviction:

> *"Trust in the LORD with all your heart,*
> *and lean not on your own understanding.*
> *in all your ways acknowledge Him, and*
> *He shall direct your paths."*

Having felt a peace of mind that he had not felt in some time, he got in his truck and as he was leaving Hurricane Central, he realized that he was following the same path that Lester Herron had followed the last time he saw him leave Hurricane Central. Lester Herron was a good, wholesome, Christian man and a good example to follow. He had insisted that "Leon owed it to himself" to be in church on Sunday morning.

Leon felt as if he was caught in an uncomfortable but self-imposed dilemma. He wanted desperately to honor his debt to Lester Herron, yet he had no desire whatsoever to attend a church service. Then, it dawned on him that today was Thursday, meaning Sunday morning was just a few short days away. Equally important was the fact that like every Sunday morning, the Holiness Church on Highway 1 would start at eleven o'clock. A haunting reminder kept echoing in the darkness of his mind, asking him over and over...*What are you going to do?*

Chapter 29


**The Rocky Road to Salvation**


**Weekends at Hurricane Central** usually seemed to go by a lot quicker than the weekday business hours, probably due to having a higher volume of patrons and a higher level of activity. But this Thursday through Saturday seemed to fly by faster than normal to Leon, and he knew exactly why—Sunday morning was now less than two hours away, and that meant he'd have to follow through on his promise to Lester Herron of attending church service the following morning.

It was now ten o'clock, and the club would have to close the bar at midnight due to South Carolina state Blue Laws, which prohibited the sale of alcohol on Sunday. It was a law that every bar owner despised because they would have to send paying customers away or either face a stiff fine and/or jail time.

Blue Laws are as old as the thirteenth century and were common in England whose early colonists continued their tradition upon their arrival to America. Blue laws also originally included the prohibition of regular work on Sundays, plus any buying, selling, traveling, public entertainment, or sports. It's not officially known where the term "Blue" comes from, but among bar owners, it was an inside joke that if you don't obey them, then the men in "blue" will come and arrest you. As far as the customer, if you're not allowed to purchase alcohol after midnight on Saturday, that would surely make you have a feeling of being "blue." Some customers even argued that they should be called "Red Laws," as not having to be able to buy alcohol after a certain time would make one "red in the face" from being so mad.

Not being able to purchase alcohol after midnight on Saturday was one thing, but consuming it was another. The mere act of drinking alcohol was not illegal, and that's exactly what Leon and a small group of friends did between Saturday midnight and Sunday morning. They would have a private party of their own, listen to the music on the jukebox, play pool, or just sit around joking and having fun and fellowship.

Just before closing time, Leon was feeling pretty good about himself, as he'd consumed the regular dose of his favorite choice of liquid courage and was now feeling invincible and ready to take on any reasonable challenge—including going to church in just a few short hours. He approached the bar and called for his bartender, known by everyone as "Hank," to join him in conversation. Now, Hank's real name was Bailey Long, but he had all of the physical characteristics of Hank Williams, Jr., and if you'd put a cowboy hat and a pair of dark sunglasses on him, it would be hard to tell one from the other.

"Hank, are you planning on staying after we close, or are you going home?" Leon asked.

"Oh, I plan on staying and shootin' some pool to see if I can win a few bucks from them two loudmouth drunks over there before I leave," answered Hank. "They look like they've had more than enough to drink, and I don't think they're sure which end of the pool cue to use to strike a ball."

"Yeah, I see what you mean. That looks like easy money. Hank, I was wondering if you'd do me a favor after we close up," Leon said.

"Sure, Leon." Hank replied, "What do you need?"

"Well, you remember the contractor, Lester Herron, who installed the fire door for me?" Leon asked.

"Yeah, I remember him," replied Hank.

"Well, he wouldn't let me pay him for the work that he did for me," continued Leon. "As his form of payment, he tricked me into attending his church service at 11:00 this morning, and I need a ride because I'll be too drunk to drive by then."

"I don't mind driving you to church, Leon, but I ain't goin' inside," demanded Hank.

"No, no, no!" responded Leon. "Just drive me to the church. I'll go inside and make sure Lester sees me; then I'll leave. I won't be gone any longer than five minutes."

"Okay, then," replied Hank, "I can do that for you. Just give me a heads-up before we're to leave."

"Will do, and thanks Hank," replied Leon.

By the time daybreak came around, most everyone had either left the bar, was still shootin' pool, or were passed out with their head resting on a table or the bar top, including Hank.

Leon never went to sleep that night, as he knew that once he did, he'd never wake up in time to make it to the church. Nevertheless, he was feeling tired from the lack of sleep and was so drunk that he couldn't hit the floor with his cowboy hat if he had to. But, when he looked at his wristwatch and saw that it was 11:05 am, he was startled from his drunken state and became somewhat semi-sober for just long enough to wake Hank and walk him out to his truck.

"Come on, Hank, it's time to go," said a nervous Leon. "As a matter of fact, we're already late."

"Ok, ok, I'm comin'," replied Hank. "So, where's this church we're goin' to anyway?"

"Take the exit road to the red light and turn left," replied Leon. "The Holiness Church will be on the right about eight miles down Highway 1."

LEON EVERETTE:

While waiting for the light to turn green, Leon pulled out a couple of cigarettes and lit them both—one for him and one for Hank. It was still cool outside, and the windows to the truck were up, and the heater was on. Leon hadn't had a shower since Thursday night, and he still had the same clothes on that he changed into after the shower. Leon didn't know any better at the time, but by now, his clothes were so wrinkled that they looked as if he'd slept in them, and they smelled like stale beer and cigarette smoke from the toxic environment of the bar. But that was the least of his concerns; besides he was too drunk to know any better.

As they pulled into the parking lot of the church, they noticed that it was about three-quarters full. Straight ahead, they saw a "First Time Visitors" sign reserving a courtesy parking space.

"Looks like Lester was expecting me after all," Leon said. "He went as far as to have them reserve a parking spot for me. Park right there, Hank."

After bringing the truck to a stop, they each lowered their windows, allowing the smoke to dissipate.

"Ok, Hank," Leon said, "stay here. I'll be right back."

"Don't be long, Leon," Hank demanded.

"Oh, I won't," responded Leon. "As I said, I'm going in, and when I see Lester, and he sees me, then I'm coming right back out. I won't be gone but for five minutes tops."

Leon swung open the truck door and turned his body sideways in the seat as he sat momentarily, getting his physical and mental faculties in order. He slowly extended his left foot, but the pavement below seemed too far away to make a stand. Finally, he grabbed the top of the truck door with both hands and pulled himself up and out of the seat and onto the pavement below. He slowly maintained his balance and, with one quick thrust, slammed the door shut as his body landed against the side of the truck to keep from falling.

From all appearances, there didn't seem to be anyone else around, but he could hear music coming from the small, wood-framed, white church just a few yards away. From his estimate, the church seemed too small to manage the number of people compared to the number of cars in the parking lot. It didn't matter, though. He wouldn't need a seat anyway. He was just going to show up and then leave.

As he approached the church, he noticed that there were just two steps leading up to the doorway. What he didn't notice was that once the door was opened, there was a threshold transitioning piece about three-quarters of an inch high, extending the width of the doorway. As you entered the doorway, there was no foyer whatsoever. Once the door was opened you were immediately inside the sanctuary of the church. And when Leon opened the door and stepped inside, he tripped over the threshold and landed flat on his face.

The music kept playing and didn't miss a beat. Leon used all of his strength to gather himself and was about to force his way upright when he noticed someone from his right side approach him.

"Are you alright, young man?" an older gentleman asked, coming to his aid. He carefully cradled Leon's arm, helping him to his feet, and assisted him unscathed to a nearby chair. "The Lord sure has a funny way of bringing people to their knees, he laughed. Thank goodness we have a God with a sense of humor!"

Leon smiled with a look of appreciation as he was aware that the man, who he'd never seen before, was sincere in his effort not only to assist him but to lessen the discomfort of embarrassment.

It took Leon a moment to maintain his composure, but when he did, the first thing he remembered seeing was the joyful look of none other than Lester Herron playing guitar in a band on a small stage at the front of the congregation. Lester was smiling so big that the corners of his mouth were raised nearly to his eyeballs. Leon wasn't sure if he was smiling so big because he was glad to see him or because of how he made his entrance into the sanctuary. Probably a little of both, Leon thought, as he managed to return a friendly smile.

Well, that's it, Leon thought. Lester's acknowledged that I'm here and that's all I came for. Then the song ended, and another song with a high-energy tempo began. By the time the banjo and violin were highly strummed, everyone who wasn't already on their feet, surely was by now. The loud, fast-paced music had the room full of electric energy and the whole congregation clapping and stopping to the rhythm of the beat— including Leon.

The music was very entertaining and right up Leon's alley— gospel music with a country music flair. The band and the vocalists had the whole place singing and swaying to the sound of joyful, what he imagined to be Christian soul music. As the band continued to play, Leon soon learned that this music and the lyrics weren't just for entertainment; it was what they called praise and worship music—all in dedication to their Lord and Savior, Jesus Christ, as stated by the bandleader.

After one of the songs, one man got up and said a prayer and before you knew it, the band struck up another song, this one a slower, soul-searching song. As the song played, a couple of men passed around offering plates. At first, Leon was taken aback, as he hadn't prepared for a cover charge. Then he recalled the man saying, "Brothers and sisters, don't burden yourselves, but give from your heart by giving what you can."

When the plate finally reached Leon, he made a hand motion as if he was donating, then passed the offering plate on as if it were a hot potato. He was embarrassed that he didn't have any money to contribute, and he didn't want anyone to see that he might have seemed disrespectful.

By now, fifteen minutes or so had passed by. But Ol' Hank

didn't mind, as he'd passed out in the truck, assuming Leon would awaken him when it was time to go.

Leon was enjoying the music so much that he lost all track of time. After the offering song ended, a man approached the stage, said a prayer, then began a sermon.

"Where in the world are you today?" asked the preacher. "More importantly, where in the world will you be tomorrow? That is the topic of today's sermon."

The preacher had a calm, captivating voice—one that would hold your attention, eagerly awaiting the message yet to come.

With the opening of the first few spoken words, Leon was spellbound and slightly sobered from his inebriation. "Where in the world am I, and where in the world will I be tomorrow?" he thought. That was a good question and one that he didn't feel comfortable answering, as he knew where he was in the world at the time, and he wasn't happy about his current lifestyle or his potential future. The bigger and more troubling question was if he continued doing as he'd been doing for the past seven years, where would he be in the years to come? If he didn't change his ways, he'd possibly either be dead or at the very least, still feeling unhappy, unworthy, and miserable.

As the preacher continued to speak, Leon became more and more alert. He was eager to hear every word coming from his mouth, as he imagined the preacher was aiming the sermon directly toward him.

"Are you presently, or have you recently, felt yourself being burdened by the sin in your life? Do you feel that your lifestyle is stuck in a rut, and you don't have the power to overcome the invisible force of temptation, greed, uselessness, or whatever it is that's overpowering your ability to control your life? Then, you're not alone, my brothers and sisters. We all have these times of troubles and woes, but there is hope for all of us. Listen to what the Bible says in Isaiah 40:30-31:

*Even those who are young grow weak;*
*young people can fall exhausted.*
*But those who trust in the Lord for help*
*will find their strength renewed.*
*They will rise on wings like eagles;*
*they will run and not get weary;*
*they will walk and not grow weak.*

"Yes, you heard that right. Those who trust in the Lord for help will find their strength renewed. If you're feeling down and out and feel as if you're being held hostage to sin, then have faith in Jesus, my friends, and place your trust in the Lord, and he will give you strength to overcome your transgressions, your heartache, and anything else that may be troubling you. I've told you this many times before, but I think someone here needs to hear it again, Proverbs 3:5-6:

*"Trust in the Lord..."*

As Leon heard those first few words, he immediately recognized the scripture and began saying the words quietly out loud:

*"Trust in the* LORD *with all your heart,*
*and lean not on your own understanding.*
*in all your ways acknowledge Him,*
*and He shall direct your paths."*

As the preacher continued to speak, Leon's heart began to flutter. He imagined that there was no one else in the room and that the preacher was speaking specifically to him. Everything he said was spot on about his unworthy, sinful lifestyle. He looked down and noticed the nicotine-stained fingers from smoking cigarettes. He felt the harshness in his throat from the effects of alcohol and tobacco. His clothes looked as if he'd slept in them for days, and he could only imagine the reeking, nause-ating smell he was carrying everywhere he went. Then, he began to have feelings of guilt and unworthiness. If there ever was an example of how sin looked, smelled, and presented itself, then he would be the perfect example.

But now, for once, he had a glimmer of hope. Trust in the Lord, he thought. I want to know more about this and how I can use it in my life. In the back of his mind, he was already plan-ning to be at this exact place the following Sunday.

After the sermon ended, Lester made his way toward Leon and thanked him for coming.

"I appreciate you coming, Leon. I knew you would because I know you're a man of your word," said a grateful Lester. "I hope you enjoyed your visit. Remember, the doors are always open, and you're welcome anytime. I hope to see you again soon."

"Thank you for inviting me, Lester," said Leon. "I must admit, I didn't want to come, but I knew I had to in return for what you did for me. But although we're even now, I might just surprise you one day and visit again soon. I got a good taste of the gospel today, and I feel like I'm hungry for more."

"You don't know how glad I am to hear you say that, Leon," Lester continued. "If you keep the faith and follow His commandments, Jesus will bless you beyond your expectations. He will not only fill your cup, so to speak, but he'll fill your cup until it runs over. There's still a whole lot left for you to learn about the gospel, Leon, but remember this: there's power in prayer, and the results of prayer are from faith in the Lord. For the Bible says, 'Ask, and it will be given unto you'."

Lester then embraced Leon for a brotherly hug as they said their goodbyes. Leon left the church with his head lifted much higher than when he had first entered. To his surprise, many of the church members had waited outside to greet him as he left. Some shook hands while others gave gratuitous hugs with seemingly no concern for how he looked or smelled. Not only did they make him feel welcome—they made him feel as if he was one of their own. This wasn't just a group of individual Christians, he thought. This is what a Christian family looks and feels like. The love and passion that they had for one another, as well as toward him, were self-evident. He hadn't expected anything like this, but he knew it was something that he not only wanted more of but something that he needed more of.

God truly works in mysterious ways, he thought. Perhaps his assumption was correct—Lester's God had put him in Leon's life at this time. Leon's lifestyle had caused him to slowly start digging himself deeper and deeper into a hole of misery, and the hole seemed to grow wider and deeper by the day. But now he knew there was a way to get out of that deep, seemingly bottomless pit—have faith and put your trust in the Lord. From what he'd learned today, there was no hole so deep that Jesus couldn't help saving someone from being buried by their bad habits and sinful ways.

Leon said his final goodbyes and slowly staggered to the truck where Hank had been patiently waiting. He opened the truck door and awakened a deep-sleeping Hank. Now, as far as Hank knew, he had no idea as to how long Leon had been gone. Startled from his deep, tiring sleep, Hank had an immediate knee-jerk reaction as he quickly snapped to an upright position. "You back already? How'd it go? Did you see Lester?"

"It went well, and yes, I saw Lester," Leon answered. "It wasn't what I had expected, though—it was much better than what I had expected. The music was good, the sermon was very inspiring, and the people were some of the most friendly and pleasant I've ever met."

"Wow!" Hank exclaimed. "I must have really been passed out. I thought you were gone for just a few minutes. I didn't realize you had stayed for the whole service."

"Well, I'm glad you slept well," replied Leon. "Now, let's get back home so we can both get some much-needed rest and sleep."

As they were on their way back to the club, Leon reached into his shirt pocket and pulled out a pack of cigarettes. As he pulled one from the pack, he studied it for a moment and thought to himself that one day, but not today, he would be strong enough to overcome that disgusting, unhealthy, bad habit. Although he wasn't strong enough to overcome it by himself at the time, one day soon, after learning more about having faith and trusting in the Lord, that day would surely come.

Today had been a good day. Lester Herron had been right all along. At a time when Leon thought that Lester had tricked him or had tried pressuring him into going to church, he was actually encouraging him to consider going for his own good. He'd once said that "Leon owed it to himself to go," and he was right about that, too. Leon was stubborn, reluctant, and hard-headed, but after going, he began to see some things in a new light. He thought about how most of the people that he associated with daily were much like himself—sinful, bitter, and miserable. On the other hand, the people at the church seemed happy, carefree and comforted knowing they had a friend in Jesus.

Today, for the first time in a long time, after leaving the church, he felt a slight relief from the burdens he'd been shouldering. He had left with a spirit of hope, self-importance, and blessed assurance of salvation to all who call on the name of the Lord. He realized that for people like himself, the road to salvation would be a rocky one. There would be many hills and valleys and twists and turns and even bumps and potholes along the way, but once he was able to find that long, straight, and narrow road, he knew it would lead to his final destination of choice.

He wouldn't travel that road today. He probably wouldn't travel that road tomorrow. But at some point, soon he would take a detour, or perhaps a complete U-turn from the way he was going at this time, and find that road to paradise because now he had attained one of the most important pieces of that all-important road map. It was the words echoed by the preacher, Lester Herron, and his mama:

> *"Have faith and trust in the Lord with all*
> *your heart*
> *and He will guide your paths,*
> *for through Him, all things are possible."*

Chapter 30

## The Purge (Part One)

**During the week** following Leon's church service experience, Diane began to notice a slight but obvious change in Leon's demeanor and behavior. He appeared to be more cautious when he spoke, having fewer and fewer curse words as well as having a less bitter and spiteful tone in his speech. His walk seemed lighter with each step and his body posture appeared more upright, and his head seemed to be, for lack of a better description, "screwed on straight." But two things that stood out the most were Leon's change in attire and personal appearance. Oh, they were the same old cowboy shirts and blue jeans, but they were sparklingly clean and wrinkle-free. Even more striking, was that he'd taken a trip to a barber shop and had his hair and beard shaped up to a more "clean-cut," stylish look.

Up until this point, Diane's female intuition had been on autopilot, but having experienced this "new-look Leon," she would switch off the autopilot and turn on her full female instinctive operational mode. In her mind, something was going on, and Diane would make it her discrete mission to find out exactly what he'd been up to. If there was any kind of chicanery going on, she was determined to find out what it was and, if there was another person involved, who "she" was.

Throughout the week, Diane watched closely as Leon maintained his "newfound" outward appearance. It bothered her that she could only see him at night at the club, as she had a regular day job at a construction site. Throughout the workday, she couldn't help but wonder if there was a "she" involved and was somehow responsible for his new, improved outlook on life. She had never had any reason to suspect Leon of being unfaithful, but this "new" Leon was someone she would have to get to know a lot better before she would make a final judgment about his loyalty and fidelity.

Then, by the time the weekend had come and gone, Leon had resorted back to his old ways, having indulged in more than enough whiskey to drown a horse. His steps were staggered, his clothes were beer-stained, and his speech was loud and slurred. And for some oddity of nature, Diane was happy once again.

However, whether he was in a drunken state or outright sober, Leon's actions or behavior never expressed the least iota of having been unfaithful to their relationship. Sure, many pretty females visiting the club found Leon attractive, and some weren't shy about the way they expressed themselves publicly. They would go out of their way to make themselves known to him and would openly flirt, hoping to gain a spontaneous reaction of approval. To Diane's pleasure, even when he didn't know she was watching, Leon would always be his genial, honest self and would either give them a look of "thanks but no thanks," a jokingly "hands up" gesture to back off or even a warm spoken word in an appreciatively kind way, to let them know that his heart belonged to another. Diane's heart melted. This was her man. This was the Leon Everette Baughman that she was in love with and the only man in her life who mattered. However, she couldn't help but feel a sense of guilt for her lack of trust in him, but during the past week, there was just something "off" about him that caused her intuitive suspicion to work overtime.

Unfortunately for Diane, she would have that same suspicion in just a matter of a few short days to come. Adding to her dismay, she wouldn't be able to figure out the cause and reason behind his sudden change for weeks to come. The twists and turns in his life would have her feeling as if she were living out the pages of a James Patterson mystery/thriller novel. And like most Patterson novels, the ending has a surprising, unexpected outcome, and in most cases, a warm, heartfelt finale. On the other hand, this was Leon Everette we're talking about, and there was little to nothing in his life that was predictable, much less that ended on a positive note or optimistic outcome. Only time would tell, and the biological clock keeping track of his behavioral outcome was, in Diane's mind, hauntingly ticking away.

By the time Sunday morning came around, Diane had caught a ride home and had passed out for the night. Leon, on the other hand, stayed at the club drinking his favorite alcoholic beverage, vodka. He and a couple of friends played pool all night, and by 11:00 am got a ride to the Holiness Church on Highway 1. This time, he got there a little bit early and was affectionately greeted by church members as he walked from the parking lot to the church. However, due to his being a drunk going to church, he tripped over the three-quarter-inch high threshold as he entered the sanctuary and once again fell flat on his face. No one helped him up this time, and he immediately made his way to a nearby chair. And once again, no one stopped and stared or even gave him the slightest nod of being the least bit of having a "hoity-toity" attitude.

As expected, the music was outstanding. The small musical group had a way of warming up a sermon by getting the congregation in the mode for Jesus. And that was what today's sermon was about—John 3:16:

*"For God so loved the world*
*That he gave His only begotten Son*
*That whosoever believeth in Him*
*Should not perish, but have everlasting life."*

The preacher started another heartfelt sermon, this time a detailed summary of the birth and life of Jesus. He described the holy conception process of how the Holy Spirit, a third entity of the Holy Trinity, went unto a young virgin named Mary, allowing her to conceive and give birth to a sinless newborn baby that was to be called "Emanuel," or "God is with us," as foretold in the Book of Isaiah of the Old Testament.

The Archangel Gabriel was present at the birth of Jesus to comfort and console the new mother, Mary. Gabriel explained to Mary and her husband Joseph that the name "Emanuel" was the fulfillment of an Old Testament prophecy as a title bestowed upon their newborn baby to let the world know that their heavenly God was now with them here on earth in the flesh and that His earthy name was to be known as "Jesus," a second entity of the Holy Trilogy that also included "God the Father."

Leon listened intently as the preacher continued telling the story of the life of Jesus. He told about how Jesus, as a young man with little to no Jewish theological Old Testament teaching or training, could quote word for word, passages of any scripture from the Old Testament better than the leaders of the Jewish community called the Pharisees and the Sadducees. The Pharisees and the Sadducees marveled at his familiarization with the scriptures and would ask themselves, "How can this be? This young man has not been taught by our instructions!" At one point, the preacher paused and chuckled, "He knew the scriptures so well, that it almost seemed as if He'd written them all Himself."

"It's believed that when Jesus was about thirty years old," the preacher said, "He was inspired to start a new, never before taught ministry, about the 'Coming of the Kingdom of Heaven.'

He began his recruitment of followers with a man named Simon, who was a veteran fisherman. He convinced Simon that if he'd follow Him, He would make him a fisher of men. Simon was a strong, rugged, somewhat unkempt man that had a charm and charisma that made anyone around him feel safe and at peace. Jesus admired him so much that He decided to change his name to Peter, from the term 'Petra or rock' according to the Hebrew language. Peter would be the rock or foundation, upon which the forthcoming Christian following would be built. Jesus went on to find eleven more men to join him in his ministry, which He called 'disciples,' or followers of the ministry."

The preacher continued telling the stories about the many miracles Jesus performed while here on earth, including His first miracle, turning water into wine at a wedding party, followed by healing the sick and the blind, and perhaps his most influential miracle was the raising of a dead man who had been buried for four days. All totalled, Jesus performed over forty miracles, as recorded in the New Testament. "I feel confident," the preacher continued, "knowing the love that Jesus had for his fellow man, that there were surely more miracles performed that for reasons unknown, were not recorded."

Finally, the preacher closed the sermon with a prayer and an announcement that the following Sunday, he would continue his sermon on the life of Jesus. "Next Sunday," he said, "you won't want to miss the continuing story of Jesus' crucifixion and how His untimely death would become a sacrifice for the salvation of every one of you here today. That old, rugged cross wasn't just a piece of lumber hewn from a nearby forest, my friends; it is a symbol of love that Jesus has for you, the shedding of the blood of a sacrificial human Lamb, and a reminder that this would be the last place He would be publicly seen, for, after the next three days, He would rise from a cold, dark, tomb, conquering death and giving hope and salvation to all who believed in His name."

Leon had been standing along with all the others in the congregation during the preacher's final words. His drunkenness had subsided, and his mental faculties were now fully alert.

"Amen. That was awesome," he quietly spoke.

His mind was already planning his visit to the church the following Sunday. There was no way he would not be there. He now had a strong, wanting desire to hear more of the story, especially the part about salvation.

"How did all of these people get saved? More importantly, how can I be saved?"

His mind was turning cartwheels. He would soon find the answers and specifics to all his questions. His present greatest desire was to live the joyful and seemingly carefree lifestyle of his friend Lester Herron, who he knew at one time was a sinner just like himself. If someone as sinful as Lester had once been could be saved, then why couldn't he?

The details and prerequisites to salvation seemed deep and intriguing, but the preacher had made it sound simple yet exhilarating. Nevertheless, the preacher would explain all the pertinent details the following Sunday. It was up to Leon to make all the necessary arrangements to make sure he was there to hear every word he had to say.

The preacher skillfully used his words carefully and cautiously as he closed the sermon with an invitation to anyone who wanted to accept Jesus Christ as their Lord and Savior. He wasn't trying to force or put the fear of God into anyone. His motive was to make the unsaved aware of the rewards of salvation as well as the "wages" or price for sin.

As the quartet played their final instrumental song, the preacher passionately encouraged everyone to attend the next Sunday's sermon. "If you're on the fence concerning salvation, it could be the most significant message that you've ever heard," he said. "It will be a message that will include everything you need to know if you're truly seeking how to achieve the ultimate goal of every faithful Christian—how to guarantee your salvation and eternity in heaven!"

Leon was all eyes and ears by this time. He wanted more than ever to know all the necessary particulars to achieve his salvation. In just seven short days, he would have all the information that he needed. After that, it would be up to him as to what to do with it. Would he do the right thing and hold himself accountable? Would he even make an honest effort to be there next Sunday? Was there anything in his life that would prevent him from going to that "other side"? He'd used excuse after excuse throughout his life to avoid going to church. Would he use another excuse at the last minute once again?

At this specific moment, there was nothing that he could think of to prevent him from attending the next Sunday's sermon, but that was a week away, and a lot of things could happen between now and then. Leon's worst enemy at this time was himself. How would he respond to such a golden opportunity for salvation? It was the biggest decision he'd ever have to make in his long, irresponsible life. Was he now mature and confident enough to make such an important decision concerning the final destiny of his soul?

He would answer those questions another time. For now, he needed more information about how the process works. He will get those answers if he'd only show up for next Sunday's sermon. The following week will be an intensive one, as the emotional pressure of a life-changing decision would have an immediate and future impact on his way of life. The question was...was he truly ready for such a drastic change at this stage in his life? A change that meant no more alcohol, no more cigarettes, and no more wallowing in sin.

It should have been a no-brainer, but a man who had all of his life ridiculed those who chose the lifestyle of a Christian as having a "holier than thou" attitude was now struggling with the very decision to become one of their own. The answer should be quite straightforward and without hesitation. The ultimate and deciding question consisted of just two life-changing words—Salvation? Or Damnation? He, like all those who have gone on before him, would have to make that decision on his own. The forces of good and evil would certainly have colossal battles in the days leading up to his ultimate decision. He recalled somewhere along the way, having heard something about having to withstand trials and tribulations in one's daily walk with Jesus. As with every new or potentially new Christian, Leon's battle with the devil would be a devastatingly brutal one. And as was with every new Christian, unfortunately for Leon, he would have to shoulder the brunt of the apocalyptic blows yet to come his way.

Chapter 31

**The Purge (Part Two)**

**"What is going** on here?" Diane muttered. "He's starting to remind me of Dr. Jekyll and Mr. Hyde. He's his old self one day and a newer version the next. By God, something is going on here, and if it's the last thing I do, I will find out what it is!"

It was Wednesday evening, and Diane hadn't seen Leon since Saturday night. All was well and everything seemed normal then, but now here was the once again "new look" Leon with his lighter than usual step, smiling face, and pleasant disposition. The mystery was growing ever more intriguing, and whatever was going on, Leon wasn't talking about it.

Over the next few nights, Diane made it a point to ask friends and club employees if they'd noticed anything odd or different about Leon's disposition and appearance. Unfortunately, their answers weren't all that helpful. Some said that they noticed his haircut and shaped-up beard, while others noticed a change in his clothes and a slight difference in the way he talked and carried himself. But no one noticed anything so far out of the ordinary to draw suspicion or maleficence.

The rest of the week continued as usual and without any disruptions at the club or any suspicious behavior from Leon.

Then, late night Saturday came around, and Leon was his old self once again—sloppy drunk and falling over people and furniture. Having once again seen this sudden change in Leon's physical nature confirmed Diane's suspicion. What she couldn't figure out, though, was if this was Dr. Jekyll or Mr. Hyde. The two personalities were somehow overlapping, making it difficult to discern which one he was at any given time. The biggest question going through her mind was, "Who is the real Leon Everette?" Perplexed and tired of trying to understand why she had no answers to her own questions about Leon, Diane decided she'd had enough of dancing and partying for the night and went home, while Leon remained at the club and played pool with friends for the rest of the evening.

And just like clockwork, Leon had Hank drive him to church and arrive at the Holiness Church on Highway 1 Sunday morning just before the 11:00 am service started. And unfortunately, just like the two visits before, he was so drunk that he forgot about the raised threshold at the entrance, tripped and fell flat on his face for an embarrassing third Sunday in a row.

The gospel quartet had just begun their first song as Leon was acclimating himself to his seating position when he noticed that almost everyone else in the congregation was standing, swaying, and singing along with the music. He gathered his composure and joined in with them, joyfully clapping his hands and singing along.

After a couple more songs, the preacher prayed for an offering and the quartet began an offering hymn. This time, Leon was prepared. When the offering plate reached him, he deposited his alms and cordially passed along the plate to the person sitting next to him. Being able to contribute gave him a feeling of satisfaction in knowing that he gave in a gracious, voluntary manner and not because he felt he had to.

After the offering, the music stopped as did all whispering among the congregation as the preacher said a prayer, then began his sermon. "Brothers and sisters, ask yourselves these few questions. Are you saved? If not, would you like to be saved? What does it mean to be saved, some of you may ask? Well, that's the topic of today's sermon: Salvation—and the manner for which one can be assured that they are truly saved in the name of our Lord and Savior, Jesus Christ."

Leon sat up straight and focused on every word the preacher had to say. He'd waited all week for this sermon, as he was eager to hear the process that one must go through to achieve the ultimate award for legitimate access into the heavenly realm.

"In our last sermon," the preacher continued, "we discussed the birth and life of Jesus. This week, we'll discuss the death and resurrection of Jesus and why it is important to our salvation." The preacher began with a brief overview of the previous sermon and then led into the events that took place in the days leading up to Jesus' death and resurrection.

The preacher continued, "During the last week of Jesus' time here on earth, there was an annual holiday and traditional celebration taking place commemorating what is called the Jewish Passover. As recorded in the book of Exodus in the Old Testament, God commanded Moses and Aaron to have all of the Jewish families mark above the doorway to the entrance of their homes with the blood from the sacrifice of an unblemished lamb."

"For the atrocities committed against the Jews by the Pharaoh of Egypt, God made a promise to 'strike' or take the life of every firstborn in the land but would 'pass over' and spare the life of those protected by the symbolic sacrificial blood of the lamb above each Jewish doorway. God instructed Moses and Aaron to establish certain specific rites and rituals commemorating the Passover, too many to mention here, but the most important being the ritual of sacrificing the blood of an unblemished lamb as a way of showing submission and obedience to God."

"During this time, there was a plot organized by certain

Jewish leaders who were jealous and envious of how Jesus had publicly embarrassed them over the past three years by calling them out for their exploitation and misuse of the Laws of Moses, the written and often misused politically, 'religious laws of the land,' so to speak."

"Many theologians believe that the so-called straw that broke the camel's back concerning the rift between the Jewish leaders and Jesus, was when Jesus boldly proclaimed that he came not to condemn the law, but to fulfill it. According to the Old Testament prophecy, a messiah, or savior, would one day be sent by God to save the Jewish race from all present and future atrocities here on earth. Adding more fuel to the theological fire, was the fact that the Jews understood this prophecy as the messiah being a mighty warrior, or an earthly king and accused Jesus of blasphemy when He proclaimed that He was the son of God and that the Father had sent Him into the world as God in the flesh as a sacrifice for the sins of the world so that anyone who believed in Him would not perish, but have everlasting life."

"Needless to say, for all of these reasons and many other formidable actions committed by Jesus, including performing miracles and accurately quoting scripture that resulted in making a mockery of the Pharisees and the Sadducees, this enraged the Jewish leaders to the point that they wanted him crucified and put to death for his actions."

By now, Leon was sitting erect and completely sober, watching the preacher's every dramatic gesture and listening to every spoken word as the message grew more and more intense and interesting. He tried rationalizing what the preacher had said about Jesus being a man sent by God to live on earth as God in the flesh, yet the world knew Him not as who He said He was. He came not to rule the world but to save the world, and those in power wanted to not only have Him put to death but to be hung on a cross and crucified.

"At one point," the preacher continued, "the Jewish leaders

made a deal and convinced one of Jesus' very own disciples named Judas to betray Him by identifying Jesus with a brotherly kiss and embrace as a unit of Roman soldiers approached to arrest Him. He was taken and presented in a trial before the local governor representing Rome named Pontius Pilot. Pilot couldn't find anything that Jesus had done to violate Roman law and was content to let him go, but the Jewish leaders convinced him that Jesus had committed one of the most disgraceful acts of violation of Jewish law, blasphemy, which was punishable by death."

"Not wanting to be seen as being a weak, undisciplined leader to the powers to be back in Rome, Pilot washed his hands of the conviction of Jesus and allowed the Jewish leaders to spare another popular prisoner named Barabbas in His place. After the prisoner swap, Jesus received one of the most brutal physical tortures recorded in the Bible. He was crowned with a thick, sharply pointed array of thorns that were placed so hard on his head that blood ran down his face and body. He was savagely beaten with an instrument called a cat o' nine tails, which was a shortened whip with nine leather-like strands with sharp hooks on each end that when lashed against His body would pull the flesh from His violently stricken back. It's believed that he may have had as many as forty or more lashes, as was customary for the day for that form of punishment."

Leon couldn't believe what he was hearing. What a brutal, inhumane form of punishment. God sent His only son to save the world, and this is how the people of the world treated Him. Surely, there had to be a better way.

"Slandered, humiliated, beaten, and struggling for strength," the preacher continued, "Jesus' punishment had only just begun. He was made to carry a heavy, roughly hewn rugged cross across uneven, jagged terrain. As He slowly climbed the rocky, unstable incline leading to His final destination, His strength gave way, and one of His followers named

Simon of Cyrene rushed to His aid and carried the cross the rest of the way."

By this time, the preacher was in full somber mode as he prepared to continue to tell the next progression of cruel, callous forms of punishment. Every eye in the congregation was drawn toward him as if being magnetically pulled by the hypnotic attraction of the pain in his posture and facial expressions. His once crisp, sharply spoken tone was now cracking with mournful sorrow as if he was speaking at his best friend's funeral. Finally, after gathering his composure, the preacher paused, took in a deep breath, and continued his sermon. "At the top of the hill, the cross was laid about the ground. Whereas in most crucifixions, the prisoner's hands and feet were tied with rope or leather straps to support the weight of the body. But, in Jesus' case, large iron nails were driven through the sinews of the palms of each hand and into both feet as they were placed one over the other at the bottom of the cross.

"As the Roman soldiers raised the cross and violently planted it in a previously dug hole, the full weight of Jesus' body plunged downward in agony, the coarse, iron nails serving as the only means of any kind of fleshly support. And if that wasn't hideous enough, they pierced his side with a sword, all the while casting lots for the make-shift regal robe they had made for Him as a mockery of their sarcastic adaptation of Him as being the 'King of the Jews'."

Leon was immersed in deep, problematic thought, imagining the awful, inhumane sights and sounds of the scene. The outpouring of blood, the jaggedly pulled bodily flesh, the violent pounding of the piercing iron nails, His body being savagely gored with a sword of a Roman warrior, and the sinister sound of laughter and celebration as those below Him ridiculed and mocked Him as they selfishly gambled for his so-called regal robe.

Leon's eyes were swelling, as he had no control over his ability to stop them from tearing up. He nor anyone else in the room couldn't come close to imagining the pain and humiliation that Jesus had so brutally been exposed to.

Unanswerable thoughts began to crowd Leon's mind. Was this really what God had in mind as one being used as a sacrificial lamb? Leon's lungs gasped for fresh air. His head was spinning out of control, fighting for focus as his heart was rhythmically pounding blood to his brain in an attempt to neutralize the body's unprovoked reaction to the imagery of the human trauma that Jesus had experienced. He looked out across the congregation. Some of the men were caught in a stare with their mouths gaped open. Some of the ladies were frantically digging into their purses for Kleenex tissues. By now, there wasn't a dry eye in the room. Everyone was laser-focused on the preacher as he continued his heart-wrenching sermon.

The preacher hesitated and momentarily lowered his head as if in reverential awe. As he raised his head and began to speak, his voice broke with a guttural sound of sadness and humbleness. "Brothers and Sisters," lamented the preacher. "I have to pause here to remind you of something that Jesus once said about his love for others. *Greater love has no one but this than to lay down one's life for his friends.* My friends, Jesus loves every one of you. He loves you so much, that He laid down His life so that through His shedding His own precious blood as the sacrificial Lamb of God, and by His amazing, unconditional grace, your sins would be forgiven, paving the way that you may have eternal life. Yes, it goes without saying, that His sacrifice was beyond being brutal. It also meant much more than the suffering and humiliation that He went through. In addition to following through on God's plan, He did it out of love, my friends. He did it by the shedding of His blood so that you and I would not have to depend on unfulfilled, exploited religious laws to assure that we all have a guaranteed, validated pathway to salvation."

The preacher's eyes filled with tears of sorrowful human emotion. His knees became weak, pleading with his body to help maintain the downward pull of his bodily weight. He was heavy. Everything about his physicality was being challenged by the forces of gravity. He extended his arms and firmly locked his elbows, placing his hands firmly and securely on the podium before him. When he finally was able to safely stabilize himself, he finished his last solemn details about Christ's final moments on the cross.

"Although it was in the middle of the day, the sun darkened and the earth violently shook," he said. "The sky above articulated a celestial rage with the sound of excruciating thunder and violent, intense lightning. The winds blew as if coming from the wrath of the lungs of God. Then, just as quickly as it had begun, everything stopped. Jesus, in his dying breath, looked toward the sky and, in a heartfelt, solemn tone, asked God the Father to forgive them. Can you imagine that, brothers and sisters? After all the pain, humiliation, and suffering, He had the wherewithal to ask for forgiveness from his tormentors. Then, in His final words, He said, *It is finished*. His mission here on earth was complete. The symbolic veil separating the holy from the unholy was torn in two, from top to bottom. No longer would the people have to rely on the Law of Moses for salvation, for through the shedding of his sacrificial blood on the cross and by His grace, anyone can now be assured of salvation in the name of Jesus Christ."

In unison, the congregation breathed a mournful sigh. Some wept. Some swallowed, gulping deeply. But no one left. What a moment. What a story, Leon thought. What a man! More importantly, what a Savior! He'd heard bits and pieces of the story of the life of Jesus, but he'd never heard it told in such a fascinating, detailed way. As with every biblical story, there's usually a refreshing, predictable ending. This one was no different. The preacher's demeanor had changed to a more composed and poised position. The rest of the story would be much easier to communicate. You could see the eagerness in his facial expressions, and you could hear the joy returning to the sound of his voice.

"At about three o'clock in the afternoon," the preacher said, "a man named Joseph of Arimathea claimed the body of Jesus, having gotten permission from Pontius Pilot. Out of the goodness of his heart, he and his friend Nicodemus wrapped the body in a linen cloth and anointed it with burial spices and perfumed oil, then placed it in a burial tomb carved from a rocky crag for the body to be interred.

"It is suggested by some biblical scholars that three women, Mary, Jesus' mother, her friend Salome, and Mary Magdalene, may have been present and assisted with the preparation of the body. The traditional Jewish Sabbath observance would begin at nightfall, and there was to be no work performed during that time. Having completed their best preparations for the body with the amount of time for which they had to work, they rolled a huge boulder to cover the entrance to the tomb so that thieves could not plunder or steal the body.

"The next day, the chief Jewish priests asked to speak with Pilot, as they were concerned that while He was alive, they recalled that Jesus had boldly proclaimed, *After three days, I am to be raised up.* Not understanding the validity of Jesus' prophecy, the Jewish leaders asked Pilot to have Roman soldiers placed outside the tomb as guards, adding additional security to ward off any potential intruders or grave robbers.

"On the third day, after his burial and after all the celebrations of the Sabbath had officially ended, Mary and Mary Magdalene planned to go back to the tomb and complete the anointing process on the body of Jesus. Somewhere along their way, one of them asked, *Who will roll the stone away from the entrance of the tomb for us?*

"Now, brothers and sisters, I'm going to pause for a moment and ask you something that bothers me about this important scenario. Exactly where were all the men during this time? Why was it up to just a few loyal women to take on all the preparations after the burial? Anyway, I just thought that it was an interesting observation."

There was a welcomed break in the stress and anxiety of the congregation as muffled laughter was heard responding to the preacher's humorous remark.

The preacher continued, "Allow me to read to you from Matthew 28:1-8 as to what happened next.

*Now after the Sabbath, as the first day of the week began to dawn, Mary Magdalene and the other Mary came to see the tomb. And behold, there was a great earthquake; for an angel of the Lord descended from heaven and came and rolled back the stone from the door, and sat on it. His countenance was like lightning, and his clothing was as white as snow. And the guards shook for fear of him and became like dead men. But the angel answered and said to the women, "Do not be afraid, for I know that you seek Jesus who was crucified. He is not here; for He is risen, as He said. Come, see the place where the Lord lay. And go quickly and tell His disciples that He is risen from the dead, and indeed He is going before you into Galilee; there you will see Him. Behold, I have told you." So they went out quickly from the tomb with fear and great joy and ran to bring His disciple's word.*

"Jesus stayed a total of forty days on earth after His resurrection. This is authenticated by the author, Luke, in Acts 1:3:

*To whom also He shewed himself alive after His passion by many infallible proofs, being seen of them forty days, and speaking of the things pertaining to the kingdom of God.*

"Jesus did this to strengthen, teach, and confirm the faith of His disciples and to prepare them for the work before them.

"So, there you have it, my friends and fellow Christians. The question is, what will you do with having heard and learned the story and details authenticating how Jesus paved the way for your and my salvation? My brothers and sisters, Jesus has done all the hard work. It's now up to you, and you alone, to finish the process. It's your salvation that is at stake here, my friends. Now, listen to me carefully."

The preacher looked down and momentarily paused as he wanted to make sure that he had everyone's undivided attention. As he raised his head, he began speaking again, this time with a more passionate, persuasive tone. "All you have to do is believe in Jesus and acknowledge Him as the Son of God and as your redeeming Savior. Oh, you may say, but Satan believes in Jesus, and surely, he's not saved. You'd be right by saying that my friends. Satan does believe in Jesus, and he also acknowledges that He is the Son of God. However, one of the primary differences between Satan and a Christian is that as we have discussed ever so thoroughly in recent weeks, is that a Christian must believe with all his or her heart that Jesus is who He says He is, and in so doing must have irrefutable, reverential, all-knowing and all-believing faith and trust in the Lord, our God. Faith and trust, my friends. That is the cornerstone for the foundation of salvation. And that is why you may receive the joy of salvation while, on the other hand, Satan will receive the hellfire of damnation!

"So, ask yourself. Are you saved? My friends, let there be no uncertainty. Are you really and truly saved? If you doubt yourself, or if you've never had the opportunity to be saved, then be comforted in knowing that as it is written in Joel 2:32:

*And it shall come to pass that everyone who calls upon the name of the Lord shall be saved.*

"Let all those who feel beholden," he continued, "repeat after me and say this sinner's prayer quietly out loud or reverently to yourself:

*Lord Jesus, this is my simple prayer to you. I know that I am a sinner and that I fall short of the glory of God. By faith, I gratefully receive Your gift of salvation. I'm ready to trust You as my Lord and Savior. I believe You are the Son of God who died on the cross for my sins and rose from the dead on the third day. Thank You for Your forgiveness of sins and for giving me the gift of eternal life. I now invite Jesus to come into my heart and be my Savior. In Your precious name, I pray, Amen.*

If you prayed that prayer," said the preacher, "or if you want to know more about salvation before committing yourself to Jesus, we have prayer warriors and worship counselors here at the altar to pray and console you and help you with any questions and concerns about your faith and/or your salvation."

The quartet immediately struck up a slow, somber song with a heart-wrenching melody.

"Thank you all for sharing your presence with us today," said the preacher in a solemn, sincere tone. "Now, I know that I don't have to tell you this, but I think it's important for you to hear it just one more time before you leave. Ladies and gentlemen, brothers and sisters, as the line to one of my favorite childhood songs that we used to sing in Sunday School say—*Jesus loves you, this I know, for the Bible tells me so*. And if the Bible says it, then I believe it, and that settles it! Jesus loves you, my friends!

All at once, the entire congregation responded with an outburst of joyous vocal "amens", along with the clapping and raising of hands and other forms of praise in agreement with the preacher's endorsement of the validity of God's written word and for the love that Jesus has for us all.

"Now, you know the story of how and why Jesus came to earth as God in the flesh," the preacher continued. "It's all very well documented in the Bible as being a historically recorded account. That means that it has been confirmed and accurately documented by accredited witnesses of the time. Jesus paid it all, my friends. By His unconditional love and His gift of grace, you shall be free from sin and saved by the sacrificial blood shed by our Lord and Savior, the One and only Lamb of God, Jesus Christ.

"In closing, as Jesus proclaimed to those who chose to follow Him and confessed their sins before Him, He would lovingly console them by saying, *Your sins have been forgiven. Go and sin no more.* My fellow Christians, as your loving pastor and fellow Christian, I hereby relay to you those same famous consoling words that Jesus would say to His followers—*your sins have been forgiven. Now, go and sin no more.*

As the sermon closed and the congregation began to make their orderly leave from the sanctuary, Leon momentarily remained in his standing position. As one can best describe it, he was having a sort of "out of body" experience. People were coming and going and saying their pleasantries all around him, but for a short moment, he was unresponsive. His body was numb, his sight was blurred, and he couldn't find the voice mechanism to express his thoughts and courteous response to those around him. His only reply was an extension of his right hand, and the nodding of his head as a gesture of having said *thank you.*

When he finally was able to compose himself, he made his way back to the truck, where Hank was patiently waiting for him. As he opened the door to the truck, Hank saw the perplexed look on his face and excitedly asked him, "Well, how was it?"

Leon got into the truck and closed the door, never responding to Hank's question. Hank, having noticed that Leon didn't want to engage in conversation, started the truck, exited the parking lot, and headed back to Hurricane Central. Neither Hank nor Leon said another word on the quiet drive back to the club.

After arriving at the club, Hank parked the truck and started walking toward his car while Leon made his way to the entrance of the club. As Hank was about to get into his car, Leon opened the door to the club and before going in, he stopped, turned, and called out to Hank.

Surprised to hear his name called, Hank quickly turned to see what Leon had to say.

Leon was standing just inside the entrance to the club using his body to prop the door open. In a calm, convincing tone he said, "It was good, Hank. It was real good!"

Chapter 32

**The Big Reveal**

**The following Wednesday,** Diane arrived at the club around 8:30 pm. She didn't see Leon in the club, so she went to his office, but couldn't find him there either. She asked a couple of wait staff where he was, and they said that they had seen him earlier but didn't know where he was at the time. She searched the entirety of the club, then went outside and searched the parking lot and surrounding grounds. He was nowhere to be found. Finally, she ran into Hank and asked him if he'd seen Leon.

"Yeah," answered Hank, "I saw him earlier and he said that he'd be back shortly and for me to watch out for things while he was gone."

"Was everything alright with him?" Diane asked. "Is he ok? Why did he leave? Where did he go?"

"Oh," replied Hank, "he's fine. In fact, he said he wouldn't be gone long. He said he'd be back in a couple of hours, and that he was going to the Wednesday night service at the church. As I recall, I think he said the service started around seven or seven-thirty, so he should be back any time now."

"He said what?" asked a dumbfounded Diane. "Did you say he's gone to church? In the middle of the week? That man has got some serious explaining to do! Thank you, Hank; I appreciate you letting me know about this."

But why hadn't Leon told her? Was he hiding something? Was there something he didn't want her to know about?

Old Leon/new Leon. Dr. Jekyll Leon/Mr. Hyde Leon. Sunday Leon and now Wednesday Leon? Deep inside, her female intuition and personal discernment were working overtime. She had too many questions and far too few answers.

Diane took a nearby seat at the bar and sat alone, her back facing the dance floor and her front looking toward the mirrored wall behind the bar. Her limp-like posture took on a look of being frozen and unresponsive from the shock and awe she'd experienced from thinking about the many changing personalities of Leon during the past few weeks. All around, Mr. Nice Guy one day and Mr. Drunk as a Skunk the next day. She didn't have to ask, but Hank served her a stiff alcoholic beverage to calm her nerves. She didn't look up, nor did she thank Hank for the drink. She simply scooped up the shot glass and, with one long gulp, swallowed the entire drink. Having finished the drink, she slammed the glass down on the bar top with a loud thud. Hank, now at the far end of the bar, heard the same sound that he'd heard from many troubled customers before, meaning it was time for an unspoken request—a request, or more accurately, a demand for an immediate refill.

Hank slowly made his way to where Diane was seated, grabbing a bottle of whiskey along the way. He wanted to engage in conversation but knew it wasn't his place to do so at the time. Leon would be back any minute, and that was *his* job. He refilled her shot glass, turned and walked away, still imagining her sad composure in his thoughts. "The poor woman," said the *pour* man.

Then just as Hank had said, Leon walked into the bar

around nine-thirty. As he made his way inside, he immediately noticed that the usual crowd had begun to arrive, but to his concern, he saw Diane sitting alone at the bar. Diane never sat alone—especially at the bar. She always sat at a table or booth, but never alone. She had too many friends.

Leon walked over to Diane and extended himself to give her a "hello" kiss. Diane responded with a quick smack of the lips and immediately pulled her head away saying, "We need to talk!"

Leon hand-signalled to Hank and mouthed, asking him if everything was okay while he was gone. Hank responded with a thumbs-up, no problem nod of the head. Diane then followed Leon to his office and shut the door upon their entrance with a louder-than-usual closure. It was a signal, although an unintentional one, it was a signal that "we're about to have a very serious conversation!" Needless to say, Leon had gotten the message and immediately took a seat on a nearby sofa. A million thoughts must have run through his mind. His brain synapse compartment was working overtime, sending out neurological transmitters to all available bodily transponders, asking for any information available as to what in the world could be going on to cause Diane to act so dramatically. In just a matter of seconds, all of Leon's neurological alarm circuits reported back with a guarded response:

*Warning! Bodily defense security alert system overload:*
*No known threats found; Proceed with caution.*

Diane then took her seat on the sofa near Leon.

"What's this all about?" asked Leon. "You seem stressed. Have I done something to cause you to be upset?"

"Well, I hope not," replied Diane, "but that's what I'm trying to figure out. You've been acting, for a lack of a better word, you've been acting strange lately, and neither I nor the staff members have been able to figure out why the sudden change in your appearance and your demeanor. It's been going on now for over three weeks, and the change seems to begin the first of the week immediately after you've visited a local church. Beginning Monday, your personality seems more pleasant than usual, and you seem to be concerned, in a good way, about your clothes and your personal hygiene. Then, by the end of the week, you're back to your old self, drinking, cussing, and talking down to the staff without any reasonable justification. We're all just concerned about you, Leon."

Not one to beat around the bush, Diane got straight to the point, "Just tell me. What is going on?"

"Okay," said Leon. "First of all, there's nothing to worry about. However, there is something "going on," and I've been trying to think of a way to tell you about it, but I wanted to learn more about it so that I would be more comfortable in explaining it to you."

"Leon, honey," said Diane, "you know you can tell me anything. We've always been able to resolve our differences by discussing our thoughts and opinions openly with each other. We may not always agree, but at least we know where each other stands on touchy subjects. So, tell me, what is it that you don't feel comfortable talking to me about."

"Well, you remember Lester Herron, right?" asked Leon. "He did me a big favor by getting that fire exit door installed, and for his payment for the work he did, he said that he didn't want any money, but to pay him back, I had to go to his church the following Sunday morning."

Diane's once tear-filled eyes began to return to their emerald-green sparkle. Her unnatural facial frown was recalculating back to her normal smile. Without even knowing it, she slightly turned her body toward Leon, anxious to hear more of the story about his reluctance to explain himself before now.

Leon continued, "I had Hank drive me to church that morning because I was too drunk to drive myself. I'd planned to go inside the church, find Lester and after he acknowledged that I was there, I would leave. That would be my payback for what he'd done for me.

"Well, at least that was the plan. Everybody was just so friendly at that church. They made me feel welcome and didn't seem to care about how I looked or surely how I must have smelled from the cigarettes and alcohol.

"I was so drunk that I tripped over a doorway threshold and fell flat on my face in the aisle just inside the church sanctuary. There was a band playing a country-gospel song, and they never missed a beat as I composed myself and found my way to a nearby seat. When I finally gathered all of my senses, I looked up and saw Lester Herron on stage in front of the congregation playing the guitar, looking at me and smiling big as a Chessy cat.

"At first, I thought about leaving, as by now, he'd acknowledged that I was there. Then, the band struck up a fast-paced, old-fashioned country gospel song that had everyone standing, clapping, and singing along. I enjoyed it so much that I forgot about leaving.

"After a short while, the preacher began his sermon. The first thing he mentioned was, *Where in the world are you? Where will you be in the years to come? Are you satisfied with where you are right now? Do you think that if you keep going as you are today, you'll be happy with where you are in the days and years to come?*

"Diane, it felt as if there was no one else in the room and that he was talking straight to me. I thought about where I am and where I'll be in the years to come, and I didn't like where I was and where I'll be if I keep going the way that I am today. I began to think about how bad a sinner Lester Herron had once been, and if he had not changed his life, where would he be today? The preacher continued his sermon by talking about faith and trust in the Lord and how, by the gift of the grace of Jesus, anyone, including me, can receive the joy of salvation.

"That sermon, the music from the band, and the way the

people of the church accepted me gave me hope and something to think about. I left there feeling, *I can do better than this.* In the following sermon, the preacher taught about the life of Christ, how He started His ministry preaching about the Coming Kingdom of Heaven, and how He performed miracles, including healing the sick, restoring the sight of a blind man, and even raising a dead man who had been buried for four days.

"And just last Sunday, he taught the most touching sermon I've ever heard. He vividly told the story of the brutal crucifixion of Jesus and his resurrection from the grave. He told how Jesus was the symbolic Lamb of God, who shed His blood for the remission of sins for anyone who would acknowledge Him as the Son of God and as our Redeeming Savior. He said that by Jesus sacrificing Himself on the cross, He paved the way for us to enter the Kingdom of Heaven unblemished and without sin if we truly believe who He says He is and that we have faith and trust in the Lord our God. Technically, we don't have to do anything to earn our way to heaven except to be a servant of Jesus and by being obedient to His commandments. By the way, the preacher said that he would talk more about Jesus' commandments next Sunday. Would you like to go with me?"

Diane didn't hesitate. She immediately moved closer to Leon and wrapped her arms around him, giving him a warm, loving hug. "I'd love to go with you," she said. "What time do we have to leave?"

"The service starts at eleven o'clock, but we'll talk more about that later. Right now, I want to finish what I started in my explanation of your concern about my recent questionable changes to my appearance and disposition.

"Every Sunday, I got more and more of an understanding of how I'm going about living my life in all the wrong ways. I tried hard on my own to change my appearance and my walk in life, but the sinful lifestyle I'm living, my relationship with some of the unscrupulous people around me, and even the smell and stench of the club keep pulling me back into my own little world of sin.

"I'm really trying by taking baby steps to see if I can make *my walk with Jesus* a real thing, but I'm telling you, all the bad habits and temptations around me are making it really hard for me to stay focused and maintain my self-control. Cigarettes, alcohol, drugs, you name it, this club's got it. That's why I never said anything to you. I wanted to know more about how to do the right things the right way, and I was hoping once I got a good hold on the concept that I would discuss everything I've learned and present it to you to see what your thoughts were."

Thankfully, Leon didn't have to wait long for Diane to respond. He was ready for a change, and he'd hoped she'd feel the same way. If she didn't, then he didn't know what he'd do about his future if it didn't include Diane, and more importantly, his new favorite daily exercise—his walk with Jesus.

To Leon's delight, Diane, not being one to shy away about what her thoughts were on any subject, came right out and voiced her unbiased opinion.

"Leon," Diane began, "you don't know how happy that makes me feel. I've been a ball of nerves these past few weeks, not knowing what was going on, but now it all makes sense. I have a confession to make as well. As hard as I tried, I was skeptical and suspicious of the changes in your appearance and how you presented yourself before others. I knew something was going on and that there was more than likely a plausible explanation, but still, in the back of my mind, I had a smidgen of a doubt that you may have been up to no good of some kind. And for that, I sincerely apologize. I'm so sorry that I ever doubted you. I hope you'll forgive me."

"Well, there's no reason to apologize," said Leon, "but if you think that you need to be forgiven for something that you simply thought about, then so that you may have peace of mind, I forgive you."

"Thank you, baby," said Diane. "I love you."

"I love you, too," said Leon. "Oh! My goodness! Wow!"

"What is it?" asked Diane. "Is everything ok?"

"Yes. Everything's fine. I just had an ah-ha moment," replied Leon. "You know, like when a chemist finally finds the answer to a formula he'd been working on for a long time, he *goes ah-ha, I've found it*!

"So, what was your ah-ha moment?" asked Diane.

"Well, at first, it didn't dawn on me when you asked me to forgive you of your minor transgression about me," answered Leon.

"And?" asked an inquisitive Diane.

"Well, I answered that I forgive you," said Leon. "Do you know why?"

"No," Diane said anxiously, "but I'm dying to know."

"It's because you came to me out of love, trust, and faith in me, hoping that I would feel the same about you. And you were right; I forgave you because of the sincerity in your heart and for the love that you have for me," replied Leon.

"So, what was your ah-ha moment?" Diane jokingly pleaded.

"It was when I realized that that's the way Jesus forgives us," said Leon. "When He knows that we come to Him in love, trust, and faith about anything, he reads our hearts, our minds, and our words, and when He is satisfied that we believe in Him and acknowledge that He is the true Son of God, then, *because He loves us*, our sins are forgiven. Isn't that a comforting thought?"

"Wow! It certainly is," said Diane.

They remained alone for a short while in Leon's office, sequestering themselves from the rest of the world. Leon was excited as he continued to tell her about his experiences at the church and how it was slowly but dramatically changing his outlook on life. To his delight, Diane agreed with everything he said. Little did he know, but she admitted that she, too, was also having troubling thoughts about the way they were living and how they were wasting their lives away. And like him, she didn't know if she'd be able to go on with her life without him, in case he didn't feel the same way.

This moment was the start of a new beginning for each one. Diane was excited that she would be accompanying him to the church the following Sunday.

"What time did you say we need to leave to get there on time?" she asked.

"Well, the service starts at eleven o'clock," said Leon. "It shouldn't take any longer than fifteen minutes or so. There's just one thing you need to remember once we get there.

"What's that?" asked a concerned Diane.

With a witty smile and a joking tone, Leon answered, "Just remember to step over that threshold as you enter the door."

They continued their teenage-like love banter well into the evening. Like two high school sweethearts, they laughed, snuggled, and kissed, one trying to outdo the other. There were times when they would take breaks from the "play time" to discuss serious matters about their lifestyles and what they needed to do to improve them. And, by the end of the evening, they were both reading from the same book, so to speak; in fact, they were both on the same page—they had acknowledged their worldly, sinful ways and had made up their minds that they were going to do something positive to make the necessary changes to get on the right track of life.

Things were going to be different, and others would soon see the new Diane and Leon. This was their new beginning, indeed. They finally had something hopeful to look forward to. They would soon be out of that life, living mired down in a hopeless rut and onto a path designed and prepared by God.

Once they realized that they were both dreaming the same dream, their joy and happiness ignited a spark, changing their personalities once again, from mature to less than mature, laughing, snuggling, and kissing like teenagers. Looking back now, both Diane and Leon agree that this was the first day of their soon-to-be new life. Some might even say, by the way they had conducted themselves, that this was their second first date as well, and were starting all over, this time not only in love with each other but in hopes for a potential new love in both their lives—their love for a Savior—their love for Jesus.

Chapter 33

## Diane Gets a (Spiritual) Make-Over

**The following Sunday morning,** Diane drove her car to the club to pick up Leon, who had stayed up all night drinking and playing pool. After a struggle to walk a drunken Leon to her car, she secured him in the passenger's seat; then they sped away to the Holiness Church.

Upon their arrival, Leon perked up from his drunkenness, as he was proud to show off Diane to his fellow church members as they approached the entrance to the church. Diane was amazed at how everyone seemed so friendly and accepting. Her nervousness faded as everyone around made her feel as if she was gratefully welcomed and sincerely appreciative of her first visit to their church.

When they reached the entrance to the church, Leon cautioned Diane, "Now, watch out for that threshold and make sure you step over it without tripping."

Some of the churchgoers chuckled at Leon as he protectively cautioned Diane about the raised threshold. It couldn't be determined if they were humored by his courteous reminder or if it was because he hadn't fallen flat on his face for the fourth Sunday in a row.

As Leon had previously experienced, Diane was intrigued by the music and lyrics of the gospel quartet as they set the tone for the day's sermon. After settling in, the general vibe of the spirit of the entire sanctuary made Diane feel as if there was no other place she'd rather be on a Sunday morning than with this fellowship of worshippers.

Having completed all pre-sermon formalities, the preacher began his message. "Last week, I announced that we'd be talking about the two commandments that Jesus taught while teaching His ministry about the coming Kingdom of Heaven in the days leading up to his crucifixion. During this time, Jesus participated in discussions and often heated debates about various scriptures of the Old Testament with the Pharisees and the Sadducees. Throughout His ministry, the Pharisees and Sadducees had tried, time after time unsuccessfully, to trick Jesus into getting an answer regarding a scripture wrong in the eyes of the Jewish elite in hopes of proving His teaching and ministry as being a fraud. After many attempts to entrap Jesus with their scriptural theology, the results of their schemes always ended with embarrassment to themselves. Then, they tried one last time to prove Him a false prophet by having a lawyer, one who studied and was an expert on the Jewish civilian and Old Testament law, to challenge Him.

"Take out your bibles and turn with me to Matthew 22:34-40.

*But when the Pharisees heard that He had silenced the Sadducees, they gathered together. Then one of them, a lawyer, asked Him a question, testing Him, and saying, "Teacher, which is the great commandment in the law?" Jesus said to him, "You shall love the LORD your God with all your heart, with all your soul, and with all your mind. This is the first and greatest commandment. And the second is like it: You shall love your neighbor as yourself. On these two commandments hang all the Law and the Prophets."*

"Jesus didn't hesitate, as He quoted Deuteronomy 11:13

from the Old Testament. Afterward, He also gave them another commandment that goes hand in hand with the Supreme or Great Commandment as to not only what is expected of one's obedience and servitude to our Heavenly Father but also our relationship with one another as a reward for our blessings from God.

"My friends, this is one of the principal passages in all of Scripture. It's principal because of an answer that Jesus gives to a question that is asked of Him. In it, Jesus tells all of us what our central duty, responsibility, and privilege in life are. To the degree that we fail to live up to what Jesus says in this passage is the degree to which we fail at life.

"Jesus is, in effect, telling them that the most important commandment that God gave Moses to pass on to His people was the one that they recited every day, as well as expressed by the symbolic emblems attached to their doorposts and worn on their arms or foreheads—that is, to love God with all of your heart, soul, and mind."

At that moment, Leon caught a glimpse of Diane's reaction out of the corner of his eye. To his delight, she appeared deeply moved by the spoken words of the preacher. It was obvious that something he said had struck a delicate chord. Although her facial expression showed little emotion, the look on her face told everyone around her not to disturb her. She didn't want to be interrupted in her deep thought, as she needed to hear the complete message as to what this man was talking about.

The preacher continued, "Let's examine these commandments in more detail. First, we are to love God with all our hearts. We use the *heart* to refer to the seat of the emotion, but the Hebrews used it to refer to the core of one's being. It is as one writer put it, *the hub of the wheel of man's existence, the mainspring of all his thoughts, words, and deeds.* To love the Lord with all your heart means that your life centers and revolves around Him. He is at the forefront of all that you think and do.

"To love God with all your soul does not mean to let your

emotions lead you wherever they may. There is an emotional side to our love for God and we should not be fearful to show it. There is a proper passion that we should have for our God, and especially when we gather together to worship Him, there should be a feeling there. So, sing the songs and hymns with feeling and don't be afraid to laugh or cry, say *Praise the Lord*, or shout *amen*.

"We are also to love God with all our minds. It requires mental endeavor and strength. It is loving God with all our minds that balances out our emotions and keeps them in proper check, for it is our mind that sets the direction that our souls fill with passion as our whole being pursues after God.

"Now, let's direct our study on how Jesus expects us to love our neighbors. When a person is hungry, he feeds himself; when thirsty, he gets a drink; when tired, he lays down to rest; when sick, he goes to a doctor. To love your neighbor as yourself is to care for them with the same intensity, with the same concern, with the same commitment, with the same effort, and with the same actions as you do for yourself. The simple fact of the matter is that humans are naturally self-centered, and they love themselves more than anything or anyone else. But as we learn to love God with all our being, we also learn to be *other*-centered and start fulfilling this command as well to love others the same way we love ourselves."

By now, Diane was reaching for a tissue. Her eyes were tearing up as she tried to hold back from expressing the one emotion that no one wanted to show, and that was the emotion of guilt. She was beginning to feel guilty for not loving God obediently, nor was she serving Him as being the Supreme Master of not only the universe but more specifically, in her life as well. She was also guilty of indulging in rumors, gossip, and fabrications along with her fellow associates, whom she often disguised as being her friends. In addition, her definition of love often resulted in her limited tolerance toward others. And in many cases, her compassion was repressed, and her empathy was often selective.

She kept her focus on every word the preacher spoke as he continued his message. "All the rest of the commandments in both the Law and the Prophets and technically all the Old Testament were dependent on these two commandments. Why? Because all the other commandments are only extensions of these two, being details of how to fulfill these two. True love for God will come out in loving people. 1 John 4:7-8 puts it this way:

*Beloved, let us love one another, for love is from God, and everyone who loves is born of God and knows God. The one who does not love does not know God, for God is love.*

"To truly live for Christ can only come as a response of a changed heart, a heart that now does want to love God and other people. Do you love God in this way? Do you love others in this manner? The starting point is coming to God in humility, seeking His forgiveness. From there, it extends as that humility becomes part of your life and the Lord becomes the priority of your life, and you begin to count other people as more important than yourself. I pray that this message has been a challenge to each of us this morning to love God and others in a deeper way than we ever have before."

After the service ended, swarms of people converged around Leon and Diane. Diane was overwhelmed with joy by their sincere affection and genuine appreciation of having her as a visitor. She agreed with what Leon had once told her saying, the music, the people, and the preacher's message were all factors, both individually and altogether, that would compel one to want to return to the church for another visit.

On their way home, an excited Leon began with a barrage of questions about Diane's first visit to the church. "Well, how was it? Did you like it? Was it what you had expected? Are you glad you came with me? Do you think you'll want to go back again sometime?"

Every question was one immediately after the other, giving Diane no chance of answering without interruption. "Well, it wasn't exactly what I had expected," Diane was finally able to reply. With a look of concern, Leon looked her way. "It was much better than I had expected. And yes, I would like to go back. I feel a sensation of somehow having been energized, for lack of a better word—kind of like the feeling after taking a refreshing shower after a long, tiring day at work. I feel good. I feel really good. I feel…rejuvenated."

Leon looked toward her once again as they locked eyes. He reached for her hand and softly kissed it with affection. "I'm glad you went with me. It means a lot that you feel the same way I do. Let me be the first to say that *God loves you, and I love you*."

Without hesitation, she returned the gesture by looking him in the eye and kissing his hand saying, *I love you too, Boo!*

The following week, Diane, unknowingly, presented herself in a like manner as Leon after his first visit to the church. Her walk was brisk, her posture was erect, and her countenance had a brighter-than-usual glow. But there was a problem. As the weekend approached, both Leon and Diane found themselves surrounded by their usual "friends" and good-time buddies. As the saying goes, *old habits die hard*. The temptation to drink, smoke, and swear was overwhelming. Or was it just their natural thing to do? Either way, they couldn't control their lust and did so anyway, feeling no remorse for their disobedience to God. Although they had just heard the lesson of the two most important commandments in the bible, unfortunately for them, they had not learned its importance—*love and obey the Lord thy God and love your neighbor as yourself.*

But when the following Sunday morning came around, they arrived at the church without having any guilt by association with the sin they had indulged in, in the days leading up to their visit. Little did they know that they would soon have a great spiritual awakening—a wake-up call of sorts. You might call it a theological "slap in the face." Today's message was about something they'd never considered. Fortunately for them, it would shine a light on the shadow of sin trailing each of their lives. To their surprise, this Sunday morning's message was taken from Galatians 6:7:

*Do not be deceived, God is not mocked; for whatever a man sows, that he will also reap.*

Chapter 34

## The Aroma of Iniquity

**Leon and Diane** continued attending church services every time the doors were opened for the next several months. Then, one Sunday in October of 1996, after returning to the club from a very moving, emotional sermon, both Leon and Diane were immediately repulsed by the obnoxious, rancid smell of a combination of human vomit, cigarette smoke, and soured alcohol when they returned to the nightclub. The stench inside was so overwhelming that Diane gagged to the point of almost throwing up as she bolted for the doorway to run back outside.

"Are you alright?" asked a concerned Leon as he rushed to Diane, now bent over, coughing and gagging in the club parking lot.

After a short pause, she caught her breath and gathered her composure. "I'm fine for now, but I ain't going back in there," she answered. "That disgusting stench in there has a smell of pure evil. I don't know why I haven't noticed it before now, but that odor is sickening, to say the least."

Leon, who hadn't gotten past the doorway entrance, decided to go inside and check for himself. It wasn't but just a minute before he came back outside, bursting through the door, and joined Diane in the parking lot.

"My God!" he exclaimed. "That is awful! How in the world did we ever live in an environment as disgusting as that?"

"I don't know," replied Diane, "but I know one thing; I mean it when I say I ain't never going back in there again."

"You're right, that does smell like pure evil," Leon said as he locked the door.

They both remained silent for a moment as they propped themselves against Diane's car, contemplating what to do next.

"You know what?" asked Leon.

"What?" answered Diane.

"I think the Lord has opened our noses to get our attention by showing us what kind of a nasty, miserable environment we've been so-called living in," he responded. "If sin has a smell, then that's got to be one of them. I agree with you. I don't ever want to go back in there either."

Then Leon walked across the parking lot, and took something out of his pocket and threw it as hard as he could into a nearby wooded area.

"What'd you do?" asked Diane upon his return.

"I threw the keys away," he answered.

"The keys to the club?" she asked.

"Yep," he said.

"Why'd you do that?" she asked.

"So, it wouldn't be a temptation for me or you to go back inside that God-awful, stinkin' environment ever again," he said.

"What about the other two owners of the club?" Diane asked.

"What about them?" Leon responded. "It's their club, not mine. They have their own keys. They can do with it whatever they want to do with it. I'm through with it. I've been running this club every day for the last seven years, and I'm sick of it. As

I said, with the way that thing smells, I ain't never going back in there again."

A short time later, Leon had one of the former club employees open the door for him so that he and Diane could retrieve their personal items and other club-related items that belonged to Leon. That was the last time either one of them set foot inside the club. Hurricane Central, the once high-energy, flamboyant social club/watering hole/smoke pit, was now as quiet as the aftermath of a real hurricane hitting landfall. And like any business severely damaged by the force of a powerful hurricane, this one would either need to be cleaned up and restored or functionally shut down.

As far as the other two owners were concerned, when they learned of the club having been closed without their notification, they panicked in fear of their namesakes as reputable businessmen, their dignity toward their now unemployed staff, and more importantly, the potential loss of the money they had financed in the initial business investment as well as in a nightclub with its doors now closed and no business plan to move forward.

To say their dissatisfaction with Leon was an unpleasant one is a massive understatement. Needless to say, there was a lot of back-and-forth verbal vitriol expressed by all parties in the months following the closure of the club. Without going into the particulars and details of exactly how the club's closure went down, the final results were determined by the lawyers representing each party. It was decided that since Leon had invested as much as two hundred thousand dollars worth of theatrical lighting and sound equipment in the original partnership, he would donate his part of the investment to the other two owners. And since he had approved of the use of his name, image, and likeness as being another significant part of his investment, the remaining decision of what to do with the club and the property would be up to the other two original monetary investors.

It's not sure whether the other investors made money or if they lost money in their investment, but it should be noted that with the use of Leon's name and management, the club was very successful during the seven years of its existence. After Leon locked the doors and threw away the keys, the building never opened again as a business for a nightclub. Considering all of what went down, Leon and Diane saw it as their one small victory over Satan.

In the weeks that followed, Leon and Diane continued weekly church services, but at the same time, they didn't slow down one bit with their partying, drinking, and smoking. They paid their respects to the Lord at church and, without realizing or possibly ignoring their sinful nature, they also succumbed to the influence of Satan by giving in to their unrelenting, habitual temptations. In their minds, they weren't doing anything illegal or causing harm to anyone else, besides, what was the harm in having a little celebratory fun with friends? It was almost as if they were living their lives as a country music song. They had their ups and downs during the week, raised hell on the weekends, and praised the Lord on Sundays. For the most part, life was good. Well, life was good…for a while.

The couple had gotten engaged back in July and were now renting a house together in Aiken, planning their upcoming wedding, which was to take place the following February. While Leon was sitting idly unemployed at home, Diane continued to work a full-time construction job at a nearby government Department of Defense facility. Leon's lack of interest to find a job and his ongoing anger issues and mood swings, combined with his daily consumption of alcohol, added to the pressure of Diane planning their upcoming marriage. Needless to say, the additional stress began to cause division and unrest in their relationship, especially for Diane. And as if she needed anything else to consume her mind, Christmas was just a month away, and with it would come even more anxiety and restlessness.

In addition to acknowledging the birth of Christ, the Christmas holidays are usually a time of joy and cheer for family and friends to partake in celebratory festivities. But for some, Christmas time can be a downer, a time of loneliness and depression. The additional financial stress of having to buy gifts for family and friends, having to pretend that you're having a good time with members of the family you haven't seen for some time that you really don't get along with, and other issues of personal despair, can add an unprovoked strain to one's sanity in dealing with the emotional pressures that life brings our way.

All through her younger life, Diane was one who always looked forward to the Christmas holidays. She was a people person, and she enjoyed the fun, laughter, and good times with friends and family during this time. But this Christmas was different. She'd not long been divorced and was now planning to marry again. She couldn't help but ask herself if she and Leon were rushing into marriage. Were they truly right for each other? Would it last? Her previous two didn't. This would be her third marriage, and she wanted it to be her last. Her love for Leon was undeniable, but was there something she was missing? She should be happy, but instead, she's worried sick. To complicate her nervousness and indecisiveness, Leon's anger issues and drinking, not to mention his failure to financially contribute to the bills and potential wedding expenses, added to her stress and uncertainty.

Thankfully, Christmas passed with no significant issues, but to add to their troubles, during the month of January, Diane and some of her fellow employees were laid off in the weeks leading up to her wedding. Now they were both unemployed, but still living together, and still planning a wedding. This was supposed to be the happiest time in Diane's life. What else could possibly go wrong?

Perhaps the biggest issue with Diane's unrest was brought on by her mother. Her mother had always been the love of her life, her best friend, her good time buddy, her party pal...her everything. But when Diane met Leon, the mother and daughter times together slowed down almost to a complete stop. And when Diane started going to church, her mother saw it as another distraction away from her. Diane's mother didn't care for Leon from the start of his and Diane's relationship. Leon and Diane's mother were close to the same age, and Diane's mother, in addition to Diane spending more time with Leon than her mother, thought that Leon was too old to be in a relationship with her much younger daughter. Diane's mother's best friend and party pal had found someone new. She was now left alone. A pity party was the highlight of her day. She felt betrayed and abandoned. What could Diane possibly see in that low-life Leon Everette? she thought. How dare he take my daughter away from me and ruin her life!

Now, Diane's mother was no angel, as she like to party as much as anyone, but she was a good person. She was a friend and confidant to those around her, especially Diane. More importantly, she was a loving, caring mother. She had been the one person that Diane could trust to share her innermost secrets and private matters with and vice versa. She meant the world to Diane, and it broke Diane's heart that she and Leon didn't see eye to eye on a lot of things that were going on in her life.

Finally, in January 1997, after months of a tug-of-war between a stressful, emotional pull between Leon and her mother, Diane reached her breaking point. It seemed that the two people she loved the most in her life were also the two people most responsible for the emotional pain and misery in her life as well. Her marriage was literally just a few weeks away. But her life and emotional state of mind were a mess, to say the least.

The only comfort for her peace of mind Diane could find was reading Bible verses from notes she had made while attending past sermons at her church. Scriptures like,

Psalms 34:17-20: *The righteous cry, and the LORD heareth, and delivereth them out of all their troubles.*

Philippians 4:13: *I can do all things through Christ who strengthens me.*

Romans 8:28: *And we know that for those who love God, all things work together for good, for those who are called according to His purpose.*

The Bible verses and prayer did give her hope for a better future, but as the weeks and months passed, and as the wedding date got closer and closer, the more the emotional turmoil in her life became more and more intense. Leon was pulling her one way, her mother was pulling her the opposite way, and the thought of a commitment to a potentially insecure marriage that was just weeks away became more than she could emotionally sustain.

The Bible verses didn't let her down. Her prayers didn't let her down. But the emotions of humanity and her deteriorating bodily functions, along with her struggles with the supernatural forces of Satan were trying to convince her that prayer and Bible verses were just a band-aid to an open wound. It finally got to the point that it seemed as if her direct line of the mental link between her and God had resulted in a loose or shorted connection. It seemed as if everything in her mind was going dark off and on. Although God was still on the receiving end of her prayers, Diane had become so emotionally distraught that her ability to transmit a mental prayer stopped, as if all the thought-stimulating functions in her brain had somehow been disrupted.

By now, her everyday life had become a constant struggle, just trying to live it as if it were just a normal day in her life, but as the wedding date got closer and closer, so had Diane's anxiety become more intense and unmanageable. Her once strong will to live had been overcome by a stronger repulsion to even exist.

Finally, she found temporary relief from her anxiety and panic attacks by taking anti-depressant medicine to get back control of her emotions. At first, one Xanax pill seemed to help, but after a while, it became less effective. If one could help a little, why not try three? That was better, but over time, it just wasn't enough. If three were good, but no longer effective, why not just take the whole bottle and get it over with?

And, with the last swallow from a bottle of an alcoholic beverage...*she did!*

Chapter 35

## Life Interrupted

**Leon had spent** most of the day helping Lester Herron and other church members in making electrical installations, carpentry work, and painting the walls of the new addition to their church. The church membership had outgrown the church's seating capacity and it was long overdue to expand its sanctuary footprint. They'd put in a good day's work, and after coming to a good stopping point, they decided to call it a day. After Leon and his friends said their goodbyes, Leon got into his truck and headed home.

As he pulled into the driveway, he noticed Diane's car was already parked there. Apparently, she had gotten home early from her construction job at the Savannah River Site, a Department of Defense nuclear facility. He was excited to tell her about the progress they'd made on the new church building and how it wouldn't be long before it would be ready to hold church services, allowing more people to attend.

As he unlocked the front door and pushed it partially open, he immediately felt something was amiss. The house was eerily quiet, and no lights were on. It seemed unusual that he didn't hear at least the faint sound of music, as Diane usually had either the radio, TV or some form of music or sound playing when she was alone. More troubling was that Diane would never be alone in a house with no lights on. Was something wrong? It sure seemed like it. And where was Diane?

It was mid-winter, and the darkness from the outside seemed to extend into the cold, silent living room as Leon continued to slowly open the door. It was so quiet that the only sound heard was coming from a clock mounted on a nearby kitchen wall. *Tick-tock. Tick-tock.*

Leon thought it to be unusual, as he knew the clock was there, but he'd never before noticed the seemingly haunting sound coming from the clock. But then again, the house had never been this quiet before, either. He had an uncomfortable feeling as the sound he heard was as if the clock was trying to tell him something. He knew what it was saying, but what did it mean? *Tick-tock. Tick-tock.*

"Diane," he called out.

No answer. *Tick-tock. Tick-tock.*

"Diane," he called again.

Still no answer. *Tick-tock. Tick-tock.*

He slowly moved toward the center of the house, but Diane was nowhere to be seen.

"Diane!" he called again with a louder tone.

Still no answer. *Tick-tock. Tick-tock.*

As he got closer to the master bedroom, the clock somehow seemed to get louder and more frequent.

*Tick-tock! Tick-tock! Tick-tock!*

As he approached the partially opened bedroom door, he slowly pushed it open. *Tick-tock! Tick-tock!* The room was dark, cold, and silent. *Where are you, Diane?* He thought. Then he reached for the light switch and turned it on. ***Tick-tock! Tick-tock! Tick…***then after a very short pause, and suspecting something may be wrong, he frantically shouted, "Diane! Diane! wake up!"

Diane lay motionless on her side across the queen-size bed.

Leon quickly turned her over onto her back. Then, in desperation, he violently shook her, but there was no response nor change in her facial expression, which was totally bland and emotionless.

"Diane! Wake up!" he continued, over and over. He slapped her face. Right, then left, then right again. No response. He checked for a pulse. It was weak, barely noticeable. He watched her chest for a breathing movement, but it was almost too slight to distinguish.

He paused momentarily to look around the room when he noticed an empty bottle of whiskey and an empty bottle of antidepressants. Alcohol and drugs—one's worst enemy as a casual user or one's best friend as an aid in suicide. This was no accident. Diane would never use the two together for getting high as a casual user. Lately, her life had been in turmoil, but had she done the inevitable? Had she tried to end her life? Leon wasn't taking any chances; he was taking the love of his life to the nearest hospital.

"Diane! Diane! Wake up!" he shouted, but still no response.

He quickly took her in his arms and fled across the living room floor, passing the kitchen along the way. *Tick-tock! Tick-tock! Tick-tock!* He flung the front door open, ran to his truck, and positioned Diane in the passenger's seat. Without hesitation, he drove as fast as he could to the nearby Aiken Regional Medical Center Emergency Room.

During the drive, Diane lay quiet and unmoving, her head resting on the window of the truck.

"Diane, wake up!" he shouted, over and over. No response.

When he was about to approach the hospital parking lot, he grabbed her by her hair and started snatching it in both anger and despair.

"Diane, wake up!" he cried. "Diane, please don't leave me. I love you. Please. Wake up!"

Without meaning her any physical harm, he continued jerking and snatching her hair, trying desperately to get the least response from her unconscious state. Her hands felt cold, and the color of her face was turning a grayish pale. Was he too late? Did he do the best he could? What would he do now if it was, in fact, too late? How could he go on with his life without his precious Diane? All these questions and more haunted him every second of his now slowly diminishing, hopeful demeanor.

Having reached the hospital emergency room, he quickly scooped Diane up and carried her inside. As the automatic double-door glass entryway parted, he saw two nurses headed toward him with a hospital gurney. He gave them the empty bottle of anti-depressants he'd brought from home and told them she had taken them in conjunction with alcohol. The nurses knew what to do right away and quickly escorted her to the nearest emergency operating room.

Leon waited in the visitor's waiting room for what seemed like hours without hearing anything from the nurses. He'd asked other hospital personnel about Diane's condition, but no one had any details of the life-saving procedure taking place in the operating room.

He decided to call Diane's brother to inform him. Her brother quickly sped to the hospital to check on his loving sister, where Leon described to him what he knew of the situation.

Many hours later, which must have seemed like an eternity for Leon and Diane's brother, the ER doctor appeared and reported that Diane was stable but remained in serious condition.

"Hello, Mr. Baughman, I'm Doctor Reynolds," said the ER doctor. "Diane is in recovery, as we pumped her stomach and removed all the toxicity from her system. We gave her a mild sedative, and she's resting peacefully for now.

"Mr. Baughman, can you tell me what happened from the time you found her until the time you arrived at the hospital? We're trying to assess how long she was unconscious."

"Well," said Leon, "when she wouldn't respond at the

house, I picked her up and loaded her in my truck and got here as soon as I possibly could, which didn't take long at all."

"Did she ever regain consciousness before arriving at the hospital?" asked the doctor.

"No, she never responded at all," answered Leon. "I tried slapping her face and pulling and snatching on her hair, but nothing worked. I know it sounds mean now, but I was very aggressive when I snatched and pulled on her hair on the drive over here."

"It doesn't sound mean at all, Mr. Baughman," the doctor assured. "There are times that we have to take drastic measures ourselves when nothing else will work in a life-or-death situation. As a matter of fact, you may have saved her life by doing what you did. It's possible that with the vigorous shaking and pulling of her hair, you may have set off a rush of adrenaline, causing a spike in her blood-oxygen flow to her brain.

"We'd like to keep her here for observation. We don't know for sure how long she was unconscious and whether she may have lost her normal supply of oxygen to her brain. I'm confident that she'll make a full recovery, but I would prefer to monitor her until she becomes fully aware of her surroundings. She's still not awake, but you may now go visit with her."

"Thank you, doctor," said a reassured Leon.

Upon seeing Diane, Leon teared up. Although she couldn't respond, he held her hand and spoke encouraging words of love and comfort, nevertheless. The feel of her hand was much warmer now, and the color of her face had almost returned to its normal, radiant glow.

The following day, when Diane did finally recover from being unconscious, she still had not regained her original persona. Not knowing where she was or how she got there, she awoke viciously agitated and forcefully combative with anyone around her. Although the doctors at Aiken Regional Medical Center had done all that they could for her initial medical condition, Diane was still far from being mentally stable. They had no other choice but to send her to a substance abuse rehab center at a nearby facility on the hospital's campus.

During the ambulance transfer, Diane got so violent that the hospital personnel had to call the local police to restrain her. Upon entering the Aurora substance abuse rehabilitation facility, she became so aggressive and combatant that when the Aurora personnel assessed her, they decided that she needed to be transferred to a more secure facility. With her mental state being as aggressive as she was, she needed a more advanced professional staff equipped to deal with combative patients with mental issues as well as substance abuse issues.

As the EMTs secured Diane in the back of an ambulance, Leon asked the police where they were taking her. The police told him that she was being transferred to a more secure and private facility and that he was not permitted to disclose the location of the facility to anyone. When Leon threatened to follow them, the police warned him that if he did follow them, they would have to have him arrested for disobeying a police officer's order. The police officer assured Leon that they had his contact information and that at the proper time, someone would have Diane or a staff member contact him.

Not surprisingly, Leon watched as they left, and when they got to a safe distance, he followed them to Columbia, SC, to a treatment facility called *Three Rivers Behavioral Health*. Upon their arrival, Diane still wasn't aware of what was going on and continued to behave with uncontrollable rage. After a dose of a mild sedative, she calmed down, and after weeks of professional care and therapy, she fully recovered from the most traumatic experience in her life.

During her time there, she was allowed to make a phone call to let her friends and loved ones know where she was and that she was doing much better. One morning, at around six-thirty am, a relieved Leon received her phone call. They briefly discussed what had happened, and Leon assured her that he would always be there for her through sickness and in health. Before she ended the conversation, Leon asked her if there was anything that he could do for her. She told him that she wanted him to bring her a bible. "Please, go find me a Bible," she said. "That's all I want."

During her time at the behavioral health facility, Diane had a lot of 'alone' time. It allowed her to clear her mind and reflect on what had happened leading up to the day of her admittance. There were times when she first arrived at the facility when she didn't know where she was or how she got there. She didn't know if she was in heaven or if she was in hell. When she did finally recover all her mental faculties, she spent most of her time thanking God for allowing her a second chance at life. She vowed that if she had a full recovery that she would spend the rest of her life serving Him and would never do anything remotely similar to what she had just been through.

It was during this time at the facility that she gradually became physically, mentally, and spiritually stronger. She thanked God faithfully every morning when she awakened to greet a brand new, blessed day.

On her last day at the rehab facility, she recalled one of the last Bible verses she'd read before all of this had happened, Philippians 4:13:

*I can do all things through Christ who strengthens me.*

She acknowledged that Christ had done his part, and with His help, she would honor her commitment to Him, as she had previously promised.

However, there was one more important thing that she needed His help on that would give her peace of mind if Jesus would watch over and comfort her intently for the next two weeks. By this time, she was now beginning to reclaim the happiness she had once felt before her life-interrupted, traumatic experience. Two weeks from that day, on February 22, 1997, her happiness would be fulfilled, as it was hers and Leon's blissful wedding day! To God be the glory!

Chapter 36

**The Devil Made Me Do It**

**Diane and Leon** were happily married at the Holiness Church on Highway 1 and left to celebrate their honeymoon shortly afterward. As a wedding gift, Leon's former business manager, Carroll Fulmer, invited them to use his private condominium at Sand Point Beach, Florida, for their honeymoon destination.

One afternoon, while enjoying the warm Florida sun and relaxing in a lounge chair on the beach, Diane began to appreciate her immediate surroundings. Just weeks ago, she had survived a near-death experience; now here she was enjoying the time of her life with the one she loved, surrounded by all of God's glory.

The welcoming, warm sunshine and the fresh ocean breeze offered her calmness in her leisure and restfulness. As she closed her eyes in tranquil relaxation, her unobstructed thoughts took her into a surreal daydream as she recalled one of her favorite scriptures in the Bible: the Twenty-Third Psalm. She quietly applied it to her life as David had done so eloquently centuries ago.

*The Lord is indeed my shepherd, I shall never want, as He supplies me with all of my needs; He has led me to lie on a beautiful beach beside the still ocean waters, listening to the calming of the waves as they softly ripple against the thirsty shoreline; the Lord has recently restored my soul, and now He will lead my paths of righteousness for His name's sake; yes, though I had just a few weeks ago, walked through the valley of the shadow of death, I will now fear no evil, for my shepherd is with me and I know that His rod and His staff will comfort me; He has prepared a bountiful table of healthy, delicious food before me, for all of my enemies to see and to show them just how much He cares for me; He has anointed my head with his precious, redeeming oil; I am so blessed, my cup of grace runneth over; let it be known that I am surely humbly grateful for His redeeming grace, and I know that because He loves me, goodness and mercy shall follow me all the days of my life; and because I love Him, I will dwell and serve in the house of the Lord forever.*

Suddenly, she was awakened from her deep, inspiring thoughts as the tidal waters began to climb the shores, touching her feet. As she regained her focus, she looked around at her surroundings. The sun proudly shined high in the warm afternoon sky, a radiant glow against a beautiful, unobstructed blue sky, as clouds as white as sheep's wool wandered softly about their way. The ocean breeze had gained more strength, encouraging the palm trees to gracefully sway back and forth as if happily waving to their friends of nature all along the shoreline. Graceful birds of the coastline had taken flights to get their daily exercise and perform their rituals of survival.

Feeling humbled by the wonders of God's creation, Diane recalled another one of her favorite bible verses, Psalms 118:24:

*This is the day that the Lord has made, and I will be glad and rejoice in it.*

Glad she was, and rejoice, she did. That was the day that she decided that she would commit her soul to the Lord. He had led her through the valley of the shadow of death and had restored her soul, and now she would surely follow Him all the days of her life. Hallelujah! Praise God! The Lord had made this day for her!

After a fun time and a wonderful honeymoon experience, the young couple returned home to start their new lives together. On the first Sunday after their honeymoon, Diane surrendered her life to Jesus and was saved at their home church before a joyful congregation. Her soul had indeed been restored. It was an elated congregation but not a unanimous one. For some unknown reason, Leon was the only one not celebrating her, having devoted her life to serving Jesus.

Diane would learn of Leon's attitude later in her life, as she would be made aware by divine intervention that because of her being saved, Satan had lost another soul to Jesus. He would now have to resort to using Leon to make her as miserable as possible in hopes of her losing her faith and returning to his power and authority. But Diane, being a strong and faithful Christian woman, stayed in daily contact with the Lord, praying for strength and protection for both her and Leon from Satan's lies, deception, and temptation. Since Satan isn't allowed to hear our silent prayers to God, he had no idea that Leon was being protected by the power of prayers from Diane. But that certainly didn't stop him from trying.

Clever and deceptive are not just simple words to describe the evil mannerisms of Satan—there just aren't any words known to mankind that can accurately describe his vile and wicked ways. Although some may say that Satan can't attend and disrupt a church service, he was surely present this day, and unfortunately for an ungodly Leon, his presence was manifest through him.

Leon had been known to have anger issues and mood swings all of his life, but for whatever reason, this was one of the worst that he'd ever presented himself in that way. Diane was shocked with unbelief at the sudden change in Leon's demeanor. He had been a loving and faithful husband for the past two weeks. What could have been so traumatic as to set off such a drastic change of emotions?

Most days, he would be a mild, warming companion, yet when Diane started to attend church regularly, he would go berserk, acting like a deranged madman. He wasn't physically violent, but his harsh language, loud outbursts, and hateful attitude caused an unpleasant darkness in Diane's happiness. Nevertheless, Diane maintained her devotion to God as well as to her marriage. She knew that it wasn't in her power to help Leon from his affliction, but she faithfully continued her daily prayers to God, asking Him for divine intervention.

In making matters worse, Leon stopped attending church services altogether after the wedding. Then, one day, a miracle happened. Two weeks after Diane got saved, she and Leon got into a heated argument as she was getting dressed to go visit her mother after getting home from church. She and her mama had recently reconciled their differences after Diane's traumatic, life-threatening experience, and her mother had cooked a Sunday family dinner, but Leon didn't want to go. Diane and Leon had already had a heated argument earlier that morning. Leon was mad because of all things. Diane was getting ready to go to church, and he didn't want her to go. She went anyway, and now she was home from church, changing clothes to go visit her mama and family.

"Where do you think you're going?" Leon asked with a hateful discourse.

"I'm getting ready to go see my mama. Where did you think I was going?" answered a stern Diane.

"Oh, no, you're not!" demanded Leon.

"Oh, yes, I am, and you can't stop me," replied Diane.

When Diane finally got ready to go, Leon followed her to her car, stomping, cussing, and berating her all along the way.

As he watched her drive away, he continued to fuss and act out. When she was finally out of sight, he returned to go back inside the house, but the door was locked. He went around the house and checked all the doors and windows, but they were all locked as well.

It was mid-winter and a bright sunny afternoon, but a very, very cold day. To make a bad situation a worse situation, Leon was barefoot and dressed in only his undershorts. He thought about breaking one of the windows to get out of the cold weather but changed his mind when he saw something in his backyard. It was the reflection of the sun shining on a metal storage shed. It appeared to be his best choice for keeping warm for at least the next few hours. That did work fine for a while, but the shortened winter days meant the coming night darkness would replace the warm sunshine with its cold companion.

As the sun slowly removed itself from the winter's sky, so did the warmness lose its place from the comfort of the shed. Then, just when the sun was about to call it a day, Leon saw headlights coming up the driveway. It was Diane, returning home from her mama's house.

Diane was shocked at what she saw as she brought the car to a stop. It was Leon standing barefoot, with no shirt, wearing only his undershorts, slightly bent over with his bare arms crossing his chest as if he were hugging himself.

She knew right away that he'd locked himself out of the house. She expected an argument when she got out of the car, but she also knew that she had him right where she wanted him, as she was the one with the key to the house, and he was the one who'd been fighting the cold for the last few hours. There was no way he was going to take control of this argument, as she would come out vocally locked and loaded.

"Are you crazy?" she exclaimed. "Don't you know you can catch a cold in weather like this? And why don't you have any clothes on?"

Leon was almost too cold to respond, but as he began to

snap back at her, she interrupted, "Move out of my way. I have to change clothes, and I don't want to be late," she ordered.

"Where do you think you're going now?" asked an irate Leon.

"I'm going to church. Move, I said," insisted Diane.

"Oh, no, you ain't!" demanded Leon.

"Oh, yes, I am! Now, get out of my way," Diane said with heated passion.

As Diane made her way to the door, she unlocked it and went inside. Leon followed closely behind but was not quick enough to get inside as Diane closed the door and locked it behind her, as the argument continued.

"Where do you think you're going?" asked a clever Diane.

"I'm coming inside," answered Leon.

"Oh, no, you're not," said a demanding Diane.

"I need to come inside, Diane; I'm freezing," said a pitiful Leon.

Diane paused for a moment as she watched him shaking from the cold and rubbing his arms, trying to create warmth. As he began to pace back and forth along the driveway, she couldn't help but smile and silently laugh. *This is what you get for being so mean to me,* she thought. If she wasn't in a hurry to get ready for church, there is no telling how long she would have made him suffer. But for now, she thought maybe he'd learned his lesson.

"Well, if you change your attitude and come to church with me, I'll let you in," Diane assured.

"I ain't going to church; you can forget that!" said Leon.

"Ok," said Diane, as she slowly began to walk away from the door.

Just as she was about to walk out of his sight, Leon cried out, "Wait! Wait!"

Diane stopped and turned around, looking at him with discontent.

"Ok. Ok," said a whining, freezing Leon. "I'll go to church, but I ain't changing my attitude for nobody, not even you. I am what I am."

Diane paused for a moment, then chuckled, "Ok, Popeye," in a reference to the cartoon character's famous words, "Come on in but hurry up. I don't want to be late."

Diane opened the door to allow him in, and before his first foot hit the floor, he started cussing and stomping until he reached their bedroom at the back of the house. Any other time, Diane would have been upset with him, but this time, she smiled, holding back laughter, as she followed him along the way.

On the drive to the church, Leon adamantly insisted, "I agreed to go to church, but I ain't stayin' all night. If you decide you want to lollygag around after the service talking to old ladies, then I'm liable to act up and embarrass you."

"Oh, you won't embarrass me, Leon," replied Diane. "I'm used to it. If anyone gets embarrassed, it'll be you."

"Well, all I'm sayin' is when the preaching's over, I want to go home," said a toned-down Leon. "I don't want to be here in the first place, and I sure don't want to be here any longer than I have to."

Upon reaching the church, Diane and Leon went straight into the sanctuary and took their seats without stopping to talk to anyone along the way. The gospel quartet started off the service, singing a few heartfelt songs as if warming up the congregation for a Holy Ghost Revival. Then, on the last song, the preacher was so moved by the Holy Spirit that he got up from his seat and started preaching over the music, praising the Lord and welcoming His Spirit into their presence.

Soon the people in the congregation also began feeling the presence of the Holy Ghost and began singing, waving their hands, clapping, speaking in tongues, and dancing and swaying in holy, ceremonious jubilation. Everyone in the room was going about their own way of giving praise to the Lord, thanking Him for His blessings and His presence in their lives. Everyone, that is, except for Leon.

Leon sat alone in his seat, his head down and his body slumped over, displaying an appearance of despair. Everyone around was so into their own spirit with the Lord that no one noticed Leon sitting alone and unmoving. Then Lester Herron looked out into the congregation and noticed Leon for the first time. Lester put down his musical instrument, walked over, and sat down beside Leon. Lester put one arm around Leon and held him close, but didn't say a word, but in reality, he was quietly saying a prayer for Leon's sake. The two men sat alone for a short while when suddenly, Leon was stricken by the Holy Ghost. The power of the Holy Spirit was so intense that Leon sprung from his seat and ran straight to the prayer altar at the front of the congregation. That was the very moment that Leon Everette Baughman surrendered his life to Jesus.

Leon had not been aware, but Diane, Lester, and the whole membership of the church had been praying for some time on his behalf. To some, Leon seemed like a lost cause, but having faith in Jesus, they continued their prayers in the hope that God would remove the blinding sin in his life and allow him to see the light of righteousness. The devil had once again been defeated and another lost soul had finally come home to the Lord.

Leon received praise and prayers from all around and was even teased by some, calling him "Spiderman" for the way he jumped from his seat and landed at the altar. Having been a fan of Spiderman, Leon quoted a famous line from one of his movies, "With great power comes great responsibility." It was the perfect response for the moment. He now had the power of the Holy Spirit with him, and now it was his responsibility to use that power to help other lost souls find their way to salvation.

It was a great moment. It was a great transformation. Some say it was a miracle. Good had once again conquered evil. Just a short time ago, a man filled with bitterness and without hope had been saved from a sinful life with Satan to a redeemed life by the grace and forgiveness of Jesus. Leon would later recall one of his mama's favorite sayings, *for all things are possible with God.*

Diane was elated, to say the least. This was the last thing that she had expected from going to church that night. Just a few short weeks ago, her happiest moment was at their wedding. She and Leon had left the church united for life. Now, they were leaving the same church, united for eternity. All the way home, she and Leon sang the uplifting gospel song, *Oh, Happy Day.* It was a happy day, indeed.

After they arrived home and had settled in, Diane and Leon purged their home. They went around the house and prayed in every room, asking the Lord to bless their house and rid it of all evil and ungodly spirits. They continued the purge by burning all non-God-related materials, including vinyl albums, magazines, books, etc. The last thing they did for the purging was to pour out all alcoholic beverages down the sink. When Leon tried to hide one last bottle of whisky for what he called "insurance," Diane scolded him on the spot.

"What are you doing?" she asked in anger.

"I'm just saving one bottle, just in case," Leon innocently replied, as if he were a child that had gotten caught with his fingers in a cookie jar.

"Just in case of what, Leon?" she demanded. "You just turned your life over to the Lord and He has accepted you based on your faith. Is this how you plan to serve Him? Remember what the bible says, Leon, *man cannot serve two masters.* You have to completely stop drinking alcohol, or it will torment you for the rest of your life. If anything, it's a liability, and it sure doesn't serve anything as insurance except for damnation."

Leon apologized to Diane with sincerity, then said a prayer out loud, asking for forgiveness from both God and Diane.

Diane forgave Leon, then said a prayer of her own on behalf of Leon. In their final act of purging the house together, they poured the last bottle of alcohol down the drain in the kitchen sink, then said one final prayer, asking for God for strength to protect themselves from the tempting powers of Satan.

Alcohol is one of the most potent bodily toxins available to mankind. Its addictiveness can be life-consuming, often resulting in divorce, friendship, employment, and even death. The year was 1997, and neither Diane nor Leon has had a drop of alcohol since that fateful night. Leon also quit cigarette smoking that night as well. Diane struggled with cigarettes for another six months before she, too, quit cold turkey. Hallelujah! Ain't God good!

Chapter 37

## Somewhere Over the Rainbow

**In early 1997,** Diane was approached by a friend of hers at work who wanted to demonstrate a home appliance product that he was selling. The name of the device was a revolutionary bagless canister vacuum cleaner called the 'Rainbow'. The predecessor to the Rainbow, originally called the 'Rexair,' was invented in 1929 but was upgraded and redesigned in 1955, resulting in the unit as we know it today. The Rainbow vacuuming system, although known for being somewhat pricey, also offered low monthly payments, making it a buyer-friendly product. Its powerful suction, durability, and ability to contain dust and dirt inside a water-filled, sealed canister added to its selling appeal.

Diane's friend, Ted, was new to the Rainbow company and needed experience in an in-home demonstration of his product. Diane talked it over with Leon, and Leon said that he didn't mind allowing him to practice his selling technique, but that he wasn't interested in buying a new vacuum cleaner.

Ted was excited and appreciative of the opportunity, and a couple of nights later he showed up at Diane and Leon's home right on time. As he made his opening spiel, he demonstrated the quality construction and all the available attachments which were included in the package sold with the unit. He went through all the particulars of how each attachment made it so much easier and user-friendly for the person responsible for home vacuuming. The demonstration was quite impressive, as both Diane and Leon agreed with Ted that they liked what they saw, but Leon still insisted that he wasn't interested in purchasing one.

Then Ted did something they weren't expecting. As he was about to bring his demonstration to a close he said, "I know you're not interested in buying my product, but I just want to let you know that I really appreciate you letting me practice my sales pitch with you.

"But there's one more thing I'd like to show you if you don't mind before I go."

"What's that?" asked Leon.

"Do you have a vacuum cleaner that you use regularly?" asked Ted.

"Yes, we do," answered Diane.

"Would you mind getting it for me? I have one more demonstration I'd like to practice if you don't mind," said Ted.

"Sure," said Diane, "I'll be right back.

When Diane returned with her bagging system vacuum cleaner, Ted unexpectedly poured out a small amount of old vacuum dust and debris from a small bag he had in his pocket. Diane and Leon looked at each other with suspicious uncertainty as to what his intentions were. Why was this man pouring dirt on their freshly cleaned floor?

Ted didn't hesitate to continue with his demonstration as he said, "Now, don't panic or get upset, I promise you I'll clean this mess up and more than likely, it'll be cleaner after I'm through or at the very least it will be just as clean as it was before."

Ted plugged their vacuum into a wall socket and turned it to the on position, and when he did, as the bag filled with air, a visible cloud of dust immediately appeared from the bag's contents. As he continued to operate the vacuum, he showed them that as the vacuum slightly hit a wall or piece of furniture, the dust continued to fly out of the supposedly concealed bag. As he finished the demonstration, he cleaned up all the dirt and debris that he had just dumped on the floor. Diane and Leon agreed that the floor looked as clean as it was before he'd dumped out the bag of dirt. Not knowing what was coming next, Diane and Leon looked at one another as if to say there was nothing so special about the demonstration except for the disappointing fact that their vacuum cleaner emitted dust into the atmosphere.

While they waited, Ted disconnected their vacuum cleaner and wrapped up the cord, and returned it to its original configuration, then handed it off to Diane. As he then began to plug in the Rainbow vacuum cleaner, he continued his sales dialog, saying, "This is my final demonstration. Now, don't get me wrong, but I've proven how your vacuum cleaner, which is a very good unit, can work against you as it puts out dust while you're trying to clean your house. Now, watch this."

Ted turned the Rainbow system on and vacuumed the entire floor, including the spot where he'd dumped the dirt and debris. When he finished, he showed Diane and Leon all of the dirt and debris inside the clear plastic canister that their vacuum had missed. The difference between the two vacuums was impressive, to say the least. Ted's vacuum system was indeed far superior to theirs.

As Ted was gathering all the parts of his vacuum system to take back to his car, Leon unexpectedly and to Ted's delight asked, "How much does one of those things cost?"

Ted described all the functional parts and attachments that came with the unit's package, including the warranty, sales literature, literature showing how to make a sales representative's profits grow, etc., then added, "I'd like to sell you this unit, but I have a much better offer for you if you're interested."

"I'm always interested in a better offer," Leon said jokingly.

"Well, I can sell you this unit for what we discussed, or you can save money on the unit by signing up as a sales representative and begin making money doing the very same thing that I just showed you. As you can see, it's not difficult at all, and all you need is a list of friends and/or referrals to help get your business up and running. By doing what I did in asking Diane for a *free*, in-home demonstration, once you get inside someone's home, the product actually sells itself, don't you agree?"

Diane looked at Leon, and they both shrugged their shoulders as if they did, in fact, agree with what he had said.

"Tell me the truth," said Ted, "You weren't really sold on anything that I said until you saw my last demonstration, were you?"

Diane and Leon both smiled and shook their heads in agreement.

That was the night that Diane and Leon decided to start their own Rainbow vacuuming system home-based business. During the final months of 1997, they sold only a few units, but in 1998, they made their small business a priority as a source of income and were named sales team of the year for having sold more units and have made more money than any other Rainbow sales team, not only in South Carolina but in all of the southeastern United States.

Diane gives credit to Leon's sales approach as being the force behind their success. Leon, on the other hand, gives credit to Diane, as she was the one who made the cold calls and talked to people in person about setting up appointments for a *free*, in-home sales demonstration. Together, they made the perfect sales team.

Leon tried several times to follow the literature and script and general theory provided by the Rainbow sales department, but when he saw that their approach wasn't working as he had expected, he completely disregarded nearly all the company's guidelines and procedures and decided to try selling them using his own, unwritten methods. The strategy worked, as their sales and referrals increased exponentially over the course of the following year.

On one occasion, Diane had made an appointment with a fellow co-worker at a Department of Defense facility in South Carolina. Her friend's name was Archibald Polaski. 'Archie,' as Diane called him, was a mechanical engineer for Westinghouse, a well-known subcontractor at the site, and was exceptionally good at his job.

Now, Archie was very smart; in fact, some people shied away from having to deal with him because of his over-the-top vocabulary and extensive knowledge about things that weren't interesting to most people. For instance, if you asked him what time it was, he would tell you, but first, you would have to listen to him describe how his Swiss movement, twenty-four timing gear wheels, six axial rotation springs, and among other parts, a two-piece regulator with a pointer makes the watch keep perfect time in any hemisphere and any climate. What he wouldn't be interested in was whether the Atlanta Braves won their game last night.

Archie was hesitant at first, but Diane was persistent, and he liked Diane because she would take time to listen to his opinions about job-related subject matters and, among other things, how happy he was to be married to his lovely wife, Jane. Although most people thought him to be boring, Diane thought he was amusing and would tell him things to say and do to keep his wife happy and how to make their marriage an ideal one.

As they were on their way to meet the Polaskis, Diane reminded Leon that although they may seem peculiar, to try and overlook their social awkwardness, as from everything

Archie had told Diane, they were a truly genuinely nice young couple.

Archie met Diane and Leon at the door to his and Jane's home, and as he opened the door, he welcomed them in while at the same time looking down at the floor mat just inside the doorway. Diane immediately caught his drift and motioned to Leon to wipe his feet before going inside.

Leon's first impression of Archie was complex, to say the least. Diane was right in her assessment. He was an odd-looking character, but he presented himself as having a kind, welcoming demeanor. Nevertheless, for the moment, Leon was the one in the room feeling socially awkward.

The first thing you noticed about Archie was his oversized, thick, black-framed glasses with lenses slightly thicker than a normal glass lens. Archie's black hair appeared as if it had more than a little dab of Brylcreem and was parted in a perfectly straight line from front to back on the left side. The long side of the part was a straight left-to-right combing that extended across his head, landing with a perfectly even cut well above his right ear. He was dressed in dark-colored polyester trousers with a long-sleeve white shirt buttoned up to his protruding Adam's apple. His shoes were plain black leather lace-ups with grooved slip-resistant rubber soles covering his white athletic crew socks.

As Archie introduced his wife, he might as well have introduced her as being called by the name 'Plain Jane.' Jane was dressed in a short-sleeved, below-the-knees, flowery cotton dress with a flat-laced, semi-circular collar that looked like it was once a popular style in a lady's clothing catalog from the 1950s era. There was, however, something very appealing to her outward appearance. She wore her hair in a tight bun, and her complexion was surprisingly pristine, but she had a slight dental overbite that probably couldn't pull a leaf of lettuce from a BLT sandwich. Her skin was fair, and her body was petite but shapely, and she had a most pleasant, cordial disposition. She was somewhat shy at first but warmed up after a short, friendly conversation. All in all, she demonstrated the perfect model of a fifth-grade middle school teacher, which was what she did in her profession.

As Leon began preparing for his presentation, Archie offered everyone a six-ounce bottle of cold Coca-Cola. As he delivered the sodas to each person, he carefully and strategically placed a coaster beneath each bottle to prevent any possibility of creating a water ring on the furniture.

Archie watched close as Leon began attaching the hose and attachments to the Rainbow canister. When Leon returned from having filled the plastic canister with water, Archie began to speak in engineering vernacular.

"Leon," asked Archie, "how long is that hose, and what is its diameter?"

"I'm not really sure, but if I recall correctly, it's ten feet long and one and a half inches in diameter," answered Leon.

"Well," continued Archie, "with a ten-foot hose, having a diameter of one and a half inches, powered by one hundred twelve watts of electricity, how many psi, that's pounds per square inch, of suction do you think it generates by the time it deposits the dirt and debris into the canister holding about a half-gallon of water?"

Leon immediately stopped what he was doing and turned toward Diane with a look of *help me out here* on his face. But Diane just sat straight up, smiled, and shrugged her shoulders as if to say, *I have no idea what to tell you.*

Then Leon paused, and not to be out-witted, responded, "Archie, I don't know how many psi, that's pounds per square inch, this vacuum with suck, but I can guarantee you that it's so powerful that it'll suck the freckles off the face of a thirteen-year-old, red-headed choir boy with no problem, whatsoever."

Diane burst out laughing as she noticed Archie looking out into space as if imagining the physical forces and scientific dynamics behind Leon's colorful description. Leon quickly broke Archie's concentration by saying, "I was just messing with you, Archie. It has great suction power, but it's not that powerful."

Archie looked at Jane, raised his head, and nodded as if he'd just gotten the gist of the joke as both of them chuckled with a burst of short laughter. Then Leon got everyone's attention with an unexpected demonstration, one that even Diane wasn't prepared for.

Archie and Jane had just had a brand new, bright white, Berber-cut, low-pile carpet installed in their living room. It was spotless and as pristine as if it were just installed that very day.

Leon looked at Archie and asked, "Archie, although we just met, do you think that you can trust me?"

"Well," replied Archie, "I trust Diane, and since you came with her, I suppose I can trust you. Why do you ask?

"Well," Leon replied, "since you're an engineer, you probably, without even realizing it, need proof of how things work mechanically. Would you like to see how much suction this vacuum has? You can take my word for it, or I'll be glad to demonstrate it for you. What'll you say?"

Archie answered, "I trust you, and I'll take your word for it, but as you said, having the mind of an engineer, I really would like to see it in action."

"You said that you trust me, is that right?" asked Leon.

"Yes, I trust you," answered Archie.

"Well, watch this," said Leon.

Leon then grabbed his Coke and poured it out onto the brand-new, bright white carpet. With their mouths opened wide, Archie, Jane, and Diane all gasped in unison with an unexpected shock on their faces.

Without hesitation, Leon grabbed Diane's Coke and poured it out onto the floor. For a moment, no one said a word as they just stared at the seemingly ruined carpet.

"Y'all watch this," said Leon, as he turned the Rainbow vacuum cleaner onto the Coke-stained carpeted floor. Surprisingly, after about two minutes, the carpet was restored to its original sheen and dryness.

"Feel that floor where the Coke stain was, Archie," said Leon.

Archie kneeled down and ran his hand across the formerly wet and stained spot on the floor.

"It's dry. You can't even tell it was ever wet," said a relieved Archie. "And it's as clean as it was before you poured the Coke on it."

Leon smiled and said, "I think we're done here. We don't want to take up any more of your quality time together, but we really appreciate you allowing us into your beautiful home to demonstrate our product to you. We've enjoyed our visit, but we don't want to overstay our welcome. The time you've allowed us to visit with you means a lot to Diane and me, as it has allowed us to perfect our sales techniques, and we want to thank you both for your gracious hospitality."

As Leon was disassembling the hoses and attachments and putting them back into their storage box, Archie suddenly spoke up, "Y'all don't go just yet. How much does one of those units cost?"

"Well," said Leon, as he gave them a brief overview of the entire product's package price. "But I can save you some money on this unit by showing you how you and your wife can actually make money on this product by setting up your own Rainbow home-based business."

Shortly thereafter, Leon and Diane left the happy couple's home having made yet another successful sale and a potentially new business partnership with Archie and Jane. Diane and Leon had left the home, not only as a happy couple but also as happy entrepreneurs in their home-based business.

This sale was a special one. This was the sale that put them over the top for good, having for the *third year in a row*, as having been named the Rainbow's top sales team for the entire southeastern United States.

Whenever people would ask them how and from where they got their keys to success, Diane would always answer, "Having faith in God and giving Him all of the glory for allowing us to succeed is *how* we explain our success; as far as *where* we get our blessings, it's someplace, wherever God may be, possibly…somewhere over the Rainbow."

Chapter 38

## This Church Runneth Over

**Diane and Leon** continued doing very well with their Rainbow vacuum home business well into the twenty-first century, that is, until September 11, 2001, when terrorists attacked the World Trade Center in New York. After that date, the lack of trust and safety in having strangers come into one's home for a demonstration of their product became less effective. On the other hand, it was also uncomfortable for Diane and Leon to go into a strange home as well.

One day, Leon was coming home from a positive and potentially productive meeting with an acquaintance from his past. Jose Alvarez and Leon had just met by chance while both were shopping in a local grocery store. The two old friends and former high school classmates exchanged pleasantries and caught up with each other's past life history. Jose told Leon how he had started a landscaping business in Aiken County, SC, and now had more business than he could manage with the four-man crew with which he was working. Leon, now in the process of ending the Rainbow vacuuming business, was unemployed and jokingly asked, "You wouldn't happen to be hiring, would you?"

Jose was caught off guard by Leon's question and couldn't tell if Leon was joking or if he was serious. Here he was talking to a local legend, a former popular country music entertainer, and Leon was asking him for a job. Now, Jose wasn't a deceptive person, but he was a clever entrepreneur. In his mind, he thought that if Leon was, in fact, joking, then they'd both just have a good laugh. But, on the other hand, if he was serious, Jose imagined the potential for even more business with someone as popular as Leon working for him.

The two men continued their conversation in the store's parking lot for almost an hour. Jose told Leon all about his landscaping business, including the cost of running the business and the benefits and rewards for hard work, pleasing a satisfied customer, and more importantly, looking back on the work he'd done in making the earth a more beautiful place to live.

At one point, Jose made an unexpected comment, "Leon, it just so happens that I've been thinking lately about having someone partner up with me. This business has grown so much that I'm now struggling to keep up with just myself and my small crew of workers. I have a proposition for you. If you're serious about coming to work for me, why don't you try it out first, say for a couple of weeks or months, or whatever you prefer, then decide if you think this opportunity is the right one for you. Trust me when I say I've already done the groundwork, no pun intended, and I already have a good following in Aiken County, and the potential for this business is unlimited. If you decide it is not right for you, then I will understand, and we can still walk away as friends."

Leon tried not to show his emotions as he heard Jose's proposal. Sure, he'd been joking about a job, but at the same time, he was kind of interested. Landscaping could be difficult, but he was one to never shy away from hard work. On the other hand, planting trees, flowers, and shrubs has been known to be excellent therapy for some people in helping them control their anger and anxiety issues. He smiled inside himself, thinking: *I wonder, if I could plant a whole forest of tree saplings, would that be enough therapy to help me with my anger issues?*

With that same smile now showing on his face, Leon said, "Thank you, Jose, I really appreciate your offer. I am interested, but before I give you my final answer, I'd like to discuss it with my wife."

"Okay," said Jose, "y'all talk it over and let me know what you decide. I look forward to hearing from you soon. It was good to see you. Take care, Leon."

"Thanks, Jose," replied Leon, "and you, as well. I'll be in touch."

When Leon got home, he told Diane about his conversation with Jose. Diane seemed to have noticed a tone of excitement in his voice and told him that it sounded like a good opportunity, and if things didn't work out, then the two men could always part ways on good terms, as Jose had suggested. After about two weeks, Leon decided to give landscaping a try and quickly discovered that working with his hands outdoors was indeed good therapy for his anger issues. For some reason, he felt that working outside in the open air, making lawns, flowers, trees, and shrubs more beautiful, gave him a good sense of well-being.

Their business did grow over time, and after several years of working together, Leon and Jose amicably parted ways. Leon decided that he wanted to start a landscaping business of his own, and he's been successfully running it ever since.

During this time, Leon started back playing his gospel music at local churches. At one such performance, he met a down-on-his-luck, homeless biker at a church primarily consisting of hardcore, but Jesus-loving motorcyclists. Leon befriended the lost biker and began to witness to him on a regular basis. Now, this particular biker was unshaven and rugged looking; his clothes were old and ragged, and his personal hygiene was less than desirable. However, his soul was lost, but he wanted to be saved by the grace of Jesus.

Having learned this, Leon became excited, as he had been witnessing to him about the process of salvation for some time. Leon immediately made arrangements to have his head deacon meet with the biker, as was the church protocol. The deacon agreed, and a date was set to meet the lost soul before the actual baptismal ceremony.

Well, to say the least, things didn't go God's way that day. Leon showed up with his biker friend and about six other bikers from their local church. All of the bikers were clean and respectable, but their outer appearance was a big turn-off for the head deacon.

They were dressed in jeans that were well-worn, holey, and frayed. They wore leather vests with their club logo embroidered on the back, identifying them as *Bikers for Jesus*. Their footwear was traditional biker boots, and their headwear consisted of what is called a 'do-rag,' which consisted of a scarf or decorative cloth with its ends or corners tied in the back.

When the deacon saw what he later called *a gang of bikers* pull up in the church parking lot, he made a point to greet them at the entrance of the church. Then unexpectedly, he asked Leon to come inside and for the others to wait outside. Needless to say, the conversation that followed between Leon and the deacon would likely not have been one to be blessed by the Pope or any other religious hierarchy.

The deacon berated Leon and scolded him for *bringing trash in from the street*. Leon had a few words of his own, but nothing like what came out of the deacon's mouth. Leon pleaded with the deacon that the man was broken and was looking to get back on his feet. He wanted to surrender his life to Jesus, and with the help of his Christian biker friends, he was certain that he could turn his life around.

But the deacon was adamant. He would not let the bikers into his church. He was afraid of what other church members might think of him by letting what he called *the low life* mingle with *the holier-than-thou* church crowd. What he failed to do was ask himself, when confronted in a situation such as this, *what would Jesus do*? Leon tried to remind the deacon that Jesus saves according to what's inside someone's heart and not to someone's outer appearance, but the deacon rebuked him, nevertheless.

From that day on, neither Leon nor Diane ever went back to that church again. Instead, they started a church of their own in their home living room. The first services consisted of about a dozen or so people, or about the number of the disciples and Jesus had at many of their religious discussions. With Leon leading the music and delivering the weekly message, the home gathering eventually outgrew its seating capacity.

A search committee was formed to find another location, and they ended up using the Ward, SC community center, which could accommodate up to about seventy-five people. Within about a year, the community center became too small for the growing congregation. Their next move was to a building at a Batesburg, SC, church campsite, but in time, it too became overcrowded. The congregation prayed and prayed, but they couldn't find anything of the size that they needed for the price they could afford. Then, one day, God said, *that's about enough— it's time for a miracle.*

One day, Leon was driving on Highway 1 when he noticed a *for sale* sign on the property of a former business establishment —*Hurricane Central*. The thought ran through his mind that that was a good location, and it certainly had enough room to accommodate his congregation, but in his mind, things had ended on such a bad note between himself and the other two investors that it would take an act of God to make that building available. *Just wishful thinking*, he thought, as he continued driving past the vacant, dilapidated property.

Not long after, Leon began having nights of restless sleep. Then, on one unsuspecting night, he was suddenly awakened by a voice saying, *call Curtis Carlisle*. The voice awakened him around three o'clock that morning and he passed it off as being a strange dream. He tried going back to sleep but only tossed and turned. Finally, he was wide awake and still hearing the same voice with the same message, *call Curtis Carlisle.*

*Curtis* Carlisle was the original and present owner of the building once called Hurricane Central. After Leon quit managing the nightclub and threw away the keys, he and Carlisle became archenemies. There was no way Leon was going to call Carlisle, no matter how badly they needed a building for their church. Besides, he'd convinced himself that the building was too expensive anyway.

But the voice wouldn't stop. *Call Curtis Carlisle* became like a repeating mantra in Leon's mind. *Call Curtis Carlisle.* The voice continued into the late morning and finally, Leon got up and went to the living room and prayed alone to God. Leon had never been nervous before in asking God for anything, for he knew that *with God, all things are possible.* Then, in a surreal moment, Leon engaged in conversation with God. But this wasn't just any ordinary prayer or conversation with God—that was the night that Leon Everette got into an argument with the Almighty God.

Chapter 39

## One Call That's All

**Leon's heart grew** heavy. Here he was about to go into prayer, and of all things, challenge God's authority, knowing very well that disobedience meant disrespect to the very God that he loved and worshiped. Then he recalled how Job, in a much more difficult set of circumstances, had argued with God, questioning His authority and commands. It didn't go well for Job, and if he were to disobey God, then it would certainly not go well for Leon either. Leon recalled the harsh rebuke that God gave Job for his direct, absurd line of questioning concerning his wisdom and decision-making. Job 38:2-4 describes the conversation:

*2 Who is this who darkens counsel by words without knowledge?*
*3 Now prepare yourself like a man; I will question you, and you shall answer Me.*
*4 Where were you when I laid the foundations of the earth? Tell Me if you have understanding.*

To put it mildly, God disciplined Job harshly by paraphrasing, "Who do you think you are, man that I made, in a universe that I created; if you're so smart, where were *you* when I laid the foundations of the earth? Just tell Me, Job, if you think you've got it all figured out and think you know better than Me. How dare you question my wisdom and authority!"

With this in mind, Leon began to pray, "God, I'll do anything that you want or need me to do, but if this is indeed your voice that I'm hearing, then I am not comfortable with calling Curtis Carlisle. We're archenemies; I don't like him, and he doesn't like me. I'm sorry, God, but there's no way I'm calling Curtis Carlisle."

"What are you so afraid of, Leon?" God asked. "Are you afraid that he might hurt your feelings or that you might hurt his feelings? I don't think that you're afraid at all, Leon. I think you're using fear to disguise your pride. Yes, that's it. Your pride is holding you back, and you don't want to admit it, do you? You're too proud to do the right thing. You're too proud to call a man and tell him what's on your heart because you would be the one who blinked first by contacting him before he contacted you. You think that you would look weak in his eyes and that he would think that he got the better of you. That's it, isn't it, Leon?

"Well, Leon, you know what I think about someone with a proud heart, don't you? Let me remind you as it is written in James 4:6: *God opposes the proud but gives grace to the humble.* And here's another one, Philippians 2:3: *Do nothing from rivalry or conceit but in humility count others more significant than yourselves.* And finally, this is one of my favorites, James 4:10: *Humble yourself before the Lord, and He will exalt you.*"

"But, God," Leon pleaded, "I can't. It just doesn't seem right for me to have to call him. It's that simple."

"I disagree, Leon," said the Lord, "that's not your heart talking, that my son, is your pride. Let me refresh your memory about the origin of pride. Do you recall what it was?"

"No, I don't recall," Leon replied. "Remind me."

"Most people think that the first sin was when Eve ate the

forbidden fruit in the garden of Eden. That was the first human sin and is the direct result of sin in the world today, but the first sin was pride. There's a proverb that describes it in very simple but very specific terms; it's Proverbs 16:18: *Pride goes before destruction, a haughty spirit before the fall.* Many laymen say it this way, *Pride comes before the fall.*

"When you have time, I want you to go back and read Isaiah 14:12-15; it tells how Satan was disqualified from living in heaven. He was so full of pride that he wanted to elevate himself above all of my creations, including Me. I created him; he was, at that time, my greatest creation; he was perfect in every way; he was beautiful and charismatic; he was given command over legions of angels, but nothing I could do was enough to satisfy his self-serving ego. So I cast him out of heaven, as referred to in your bible as *Satan's fall from grace.*

"Pride, Leon, is the root of all other sins. Pride is your greatest enemy. Humility is your greatest friend. So, My son, humble yourself before Me, swallow your pride and do what you know is the right thing to do. Call Curtis Carlisle, not with pride, but with a humble heart. If he rebukes you, then that's on him, not you. You need a place to hold your church. I've gotten you this far, and I'm not going to abandon you now.

"So, gather your composure. Get some nourishment and make yourself whole. Take a shower and refresh yourself; then, when you're ready, make the call. The hardest part is picking up the phone and dialing that first number. If you can get that far on your own, I will take it from there. Deal?"

Then Leon was awakened from his deep thoughts as Diane had come to check on him.

"What's wrong, Leon?" she asked.

"I've got to call Curtis Carlisle," he said.

"You've got to call who?" she sternly asked.

"Curtis Carlisle," he said. "I've got to call Curtis Carlisle."

"Have you lost your mind?" she asked with sarcasm.

"No, I mean it," said Leon, "God told me to call Curtis Carlisle."

"Well, good luck with that," she said with mockery.

"No, I'm serious," he said. "You know how restless I've been the last few nights, right?"

"Yeah, so?" she asked.

"Well, I had another restless night again last night. I thought I had a dream, and someone was telling me that I needed to call Curtis Carlisle. I tossed and turned for the longest time and kept hearing that same command over and over. When I finally got up and was fully awake, I continued to hear that same voice telling me to call Curtis Carlisle.

"So, I came in here to pray and ask God if that was his voice telling me to call Carlisle, and lo and behold, I believe that it was. When I was praying, it felt like I was talking directly to God, and He was engaged in the conversation with me. He opened my eyes to reveal to me that it was my pride that was causing all my emotional distress. He said that if I humble myself, He will help me make the call. So, at nine o'clock this morning, I'm going to call Carlisle's office, and I want you here with me. And I'm going to tell you right now that if he gives me a hard time, then I'm going to give it right back to him."

"I'll be here for you, but that doesn't sound like a humble attitude, Leon," Diane consoled him. "If God said to be humble, then put down your prideful defenses and initiate that call with a tone of gentleness and sincerity. If Carlisle responds negatively, then just politely end the call and be done with it. You may not get the conversation you were hoping for, but at least you will have made the conversation as you and God agreed on."

"Yeah," replied Leon, "you're right. I'll do my best to control my emotions. His office opens at nine o'clock, and I'm going to call at one minute past nine."

After Leon had completed all the preparations that God had suggested, at one minute past nine, he picked up the phone. At first, he was hesitant, but when he composed himself, he looked at the dial on the phone and cautiously entered the ten-digit code to Carlisle's office.

"Hello, Mr. Carlisle's office, how may I direct your call?" answered a polite, professional-sounding lady's voice.

"I'd like to speak with Curtis Carlisle, please," said a nervous but confident Leon.

"Please hold; let me check to see if he's arrived yet," she answered.

After a short pause, the secretary returned to the phone call.

"I'm afraid he's not available right now, may I take a message and have him return your call?" she asked.

"Ma'am, I mean no disrespect to you, but I'm a former business partner of Curtis, and I've known him for years, and I know all his habits, including his morning routine, and I'm sure that he's in and probably just doesn't want to discuss business at this early hour. He more than likely hasn't had his first cup of coffee to start his day, which is what he usually does before he either makes or takes the first phone call of the morning. Would you please tell him that Leon Everette would like to speak with him? Thank you."

"One moment, please hold, Mr. Everette," she said.

Leon looked at Diane, both waiting in anticipation, not knowing what to expect. This man and Leon had been each other's nemesis for years. They expected as much as a hellfire and brimstone tone of voice and language that would embarrass a sailor. What they hadn't prepared for was this:

"Leon Everette! I've been meaning to give you a call," Carlisle answered, surprisingly. "It's good to hear from you. How in the world have you been?"

Leon paused for just a quick second, pulled the phone away from his ear and looked at the receiver as if the phone was playing a trick on him. Either that, or he'd possibly called the wrong number. Then Diane nudged him to continue with the conversation.

"I'm doing very well," answered Leon, "and I hope that you are, as well."

Before Leon could continue, Carlisle interrupted, saying, "I don't know if you've heard, Leon, but I have turned my life around since we last talked, or should I say yelled at one another. But as far as I'm concerned, all that hate and disrespect between us is in the past. Since our last misunderstanding, I've remarried to a wonderful Christian woman who has opened my eyes and made me realize a lot of things that I had been missing in my life. I've come to learn that life isn't all about money, and wealth was my idol for all my life until she taught me about Jesus and salvation, and how *the love of money is the root of all evil.*

"Well, enough about me. I apologize; I didn't mean to take over the conversation. You called me. Tell me, to what do I owe to deserve this phone call?"

Leon and Diane both let out a sigh of relief as the phone call continued.

"Well, to be honest," Leon began, "Diane and myself have been saved as well. As a matter of fact, that's why we left the club the way we did all those years ago. But I don't want to bring up bad memories right now."

As Leon was talking, he was also thinking that since Carlisle had told him about his life's transformation from serving money to serving God, he, too, would like to tell Carlisle why and what happened in his life to make him walk away from their once successful business venture. Now that Carlisle understood the meaning of giving up everything in life to serve the Lord, he would be more receptive to Leon's motive at the time, and hopefully, the two men could put their corrupted pride and disdain for each other in the past and move forward as mutual friends. Knowing that may have been wishful thinking, Leon proceeded with the call.

The reason I'm calling is that I saw a *for sale* sign in front of the old Hurricane Central property. Me and Diane are members of a church that is experiencing growing pains. We've grown from our home living room to the Ward Community Center, to the Batesburg Church Campsite, and now we have to find another place large enough and for a price that we can afford.

I know we can't afford to buy the building at Hurricane Central, but I was wondering if you would consider leasing us enough space to hold our church services until you get a contract on the property."

"Well, I'd rather sell it to you," Carlisle said.

"I know we can't afford it, but how much are you asking?" asked Leon.

"Four and a half million," Carlisle replied.

"Four and a half million," Leon laughed. "Thank you, but no thank you."

"Okay, I'll tell you what I'll do; since it's you, and it's for a church, I'll let you have it for what I owe on it. How's that sound?" Carlisle asked.

"So, how much do you owe?" Leon asked.

"Only eight hundred thousand dollars," replied a confident Carlisle.

"Eight hundred thousand dollars," Leon sighed. "I appreciate the offer, but we're a small group, and we don't have anywhere near that kind of money."

"Okay, I'll tell you what I'll do. Let me make a couple of phone calls to see if I can shuffle some finances around, and I'll get back to you," answered Carlisle. "Better yet, how about when I've got my figures together, I'll call you, and you and Diane can join my wife and me for lunch one day at our home in Woodside Plantation?"

Leon looked at Diane, who was listening in on the conversation, as she nodded her head affirmatively.

"That sounds good, Curtis," Leon replied. "It was nice talking to you, and I look forward to hearing from you soon."

"Believe me, it was my pleasure, Leon," replied Carlisle. "I will be in touch before the end of the week. It was nice to hear from you as well."

If ever two wrongs would ever make a right, then Leon and Curtis would be their names. Two formerly hard-hearted, prideful souls, after years of animosity and bitterness toward one another, had finally come together to make amends in a humbling, civilized way. It's not sure if either one of them realized it at the time, but they had both succeeded in accomplishing one of the main reasons for Jesus' life here on earth: to live a righteous life where good overcomes evil, as stated in Romans 12:21:

*Do not be overcome by evil, but overcome evil with good.*

As things turned out, the two men were more alike than they had ever imagined. Both of them had remarried, and their wives were the main influence in their acceptance of Jesus as their Lord and Savior. They'd both quit drinking and smoking. They were both instrumental, though in different ways, in their church. May Jesus have all the glory, as both men had overcome evil with good, because as it says in 2 Corinthians 5:17,

*Therefore, if anyone is in Christ, he is a new creation. The old has passed away; behold, the new has come.*

Chapter 40


**Just Give Me What You Think Is Fair**


**Just as he** had promised, Carlisle called Leon a couple of days later and set up a luncheon at his home the following day. As they pulled into the driveway of Carlisle's home, Leon and Diane were amazed at the gorgeous, sprawling landscape setting the grounds for a magnificent, ten-million-dollar mansion. Just because Carlisle was now serving the Lord didn't mean he had to neglect the benefits of being a successful businessman. Besides, now he was giving God all the glory and credit for his many financial successes. And, to his credit, his tithes reflected his appreciation for his many blessings.

As they entered the courtyard at the rear of the mansion, Leon and Diane were taken aback as they saw what appeared to be an Olympic-size swimming pool surrounded on all four sides by a marble promenade covered by a full walk-around balcony, supported by an array of tall, elaborate granite columns. Exquisite statues and a variety of colorful flowers and exotic plants decorated the entire aquatic panorama. The walls and the floors were as pristine as a hospital emergency room, and the art deco furniture offered a warm, relaxing appeal. The low-level steam emitting from a heated jacuzzi presented itself as a welcoming invitation to a whole-body or a simple foot-dipping, gentle hydrotherapy massage. At the end of the pool, nearest the entrance to the home, was an outdoor kitchen that even the great chef, Emeril, would envy. The high-quality stainless-steel cookware and appliances were contained by natural, earthen stoneware, topped with a flawless matching, elegant granite countertop.

Carlisle had previously asked Leon what he and Diane preferred to eat, but Leon said that he and Diane were not picky to surprise them. Not one to disappoint, Carlisle didn't take any chances, as he had his private chef cook up some prime Angus rib-eye steaks from cattle that had been massaged with a livestock therapeutic machine, roasted free-range chickens that had only been fed natural, non-steroid, and chemical-free food, and live Maine lobster, in case someone had a taste for succulent seafood. For dessert, everyone was allowed to make their own ice cream sundaes from a variety of flavors of ice cream and fruit, as well as an assortment of toppings.

After a series of cordial conversations between the two couples, one of which included Leon and Diane explaining their reason for leaving Hurricane Central in the manner they did. Carlisle and his wife seemed pleased that they were forthcoming as they justified their actions as not being disingenuous but out of their obedience to Christ.

As they continued to eat their sundaes, Carlisle and Leon got down to business about Leon's interest in finding a place for his church to hold Sunday services.

"Well," Carlisle began, "The property has been on the market for some time now, and I haven't had any serious offers at all. Truth be told, you're the first to approach me about it in over a year. I know the asking price is high, but you must admit, it's a prime location for future commercial development."

"As I told you on our phone call the other day, I got with one of my accountants, and he's shown me a way that I can owner-finance the whole shebang, including the entire property and building for a small down payment and whatever you and I can agree on per month after that."

"How much of a down payment would you need?" asked Leon.

"For you, fifty thousand dollars," said Carlisle with a smile.

"Whew!" said Leon, "That's a generous offer, and I appreciate it, but that's way out of our range."

"Well, can you do twenty-five thousand?" asked Carlisle.

"Thank you, Curtis, but we're a small church with a really low-budget congregation," Leon replied.

"Well," chuckled Carlisle, "What can you afford? Can you afford five thousand?"

"Now, I want you to know that I'm sincere when I say we're low on funds, but I think we can do the five thousand. That is very kind of you, and you can't imagine how thankful I am to make this deal with you," said an appreciative Leon.

"Then we have a deal," said Carlisle. "I'll get the paperwork started and will contact you when I've got a date for signing the official documentation. In the meantime, you're welcome to start making the place ready to suit your needs for a new church. Here are the keys. I wish you and your congregation all the best."

Chapter 41

**Epilogue**

**Leon's story was** originally meant to end after the completion of the new church building, but Jimmy Adams and Little
David Wilkins had other unforeseen plans for Leon. Jimmy and
David were once acquaintances of Leon during his career as a
country music entertainer in Nashville during the 1980s. Jimmy
was working as an agent and promoter, as well as in other executive positions in the music and entertainment business. David
was a popular singer and songwriter, and over time, both men
became good friends with Leon.

In 2018, David wrote a new song entitled *I Stand the Tallest
When I'm Down On My Knees*. He was especially excited after
finishing the song, but to make the song complete, he felt as if
he needed another male vocalist to accompany him to get the
best solo and harmonic dynamics possible to complete the song
in the way that he had intended. After he had exhausted all his
ideas and couldn't decide on a second vocalist for his song,
David reached out to his friend, Jimmy Adams.

After hearing David's solo version of a demo of the song,
Jimmy knew right away who the perfect person David needed
to complete his song was—Leon Everette. But Leon had been

away from the Nashville scene for some thirty years, and it seemed as if no one knew where he was or how to find him. He wasn't on social media, and an internet search only offered that he was last known to be living in a small town in rural South Carolina called Ward.

After many unsuccessful attempts to find Leon, Jimmy conducted a search on Facebook for Everette, Leon's stage name, and Baughman, Leon's true last name. Unfortunately, there were no results for a Leon followed by either of those two last names; however, there was a result under the name of Diane Everette Baughman. Could she possibly know the Leon Everette he was looking for? Jimmy wasn't one to give up easily, and he wasn't about to stop now, as he reached out by sending her a private message, right away.

"Excuse me," he wrote, "I hope you don't mind, but are you related to or do you know a man named Leon Everette by chance? He's an old friend of mine that I've been trying to get in touch with, but I have lost all forms of his contact information. If you don't know him, please accept my most sincere apologies. Thank you."

Upon receiving the private message, Diane showed it to Leon, as she had never heard of anyone named Jimmy Adams.

"Yes, I know Jimmy Adams!" Leon exclaimed. "He's an old friend of mine from my Nashville days. We go way back. Send him my phone number. I'm excited to see what he wants."

Shortly after receiving Diane's reply, Jimmy gave Leon a call.

"Hey Leon, it's Jimmy Adams; how are you?"

After a brief exchange of pleasantries and after discussing old times as friends in Nashville, Jimmy said, "I've got someone that I'd like to join with us on a conference call if you don't mind."

"No, I don't mind," Leon responded. "Who is it?"

"I'll let him introduce himself," replied Jimmy.

"Hey Leon, it's Little David Wilkins! How are you doing, my friend?"

"David, it's good to hear from you! I'm fine, and I hope that you are as well," Leon responded.

After another brief discussion of past and present life experiences, Jimmy and David got down to the purpose of their call.

"Leon," David began, "I've recently written a country/gospel song, and I'm looking for another male vocalist to help me complete it. I reached out to Jimmy in hopes that he might have someone in mind, and right away, he suggested you. After giving it a considerable amount of time and thought, and not being able to think of anyone else who meets your vocal skills, we've decided to invite you to come to Nashville and record the song with me."

"Me? Come to Nashville?" Leon laughed. "I appreciate the offer and the kindness behind your invitation, but there's no way I'm going back to Nashville. I swore over thirty years ago that I'd never go back to that God-forsaken place, especially to do a studio recording."

"I understand," consoled David, "but it's just one song, Leon. Come and help me finish the song, and then you can go right back home—no strings attached."

"David, I'm honored that after all these years, you chose me to record the song with you, but I'm going to have to respectfully decline the invitation for personal reasons," Leon replied.

"Leon," Jimmy intervened, "I understand your frustrations with Nashville. I was there when all the stuff went down back during the prime of your career. But things are a lot different now. I'm in discussions with a prominent record label that gives me a lot of flexibility to make decisions based on my opinions without internal interference. Why don't you come up and let me show you around, make the recording with David, and afterwards, if you're not completely satisfied with the way things are going, then you can go back home with no hard feelings whatsoever."

After a brief pause, Leon replied, "The invitation is both appreciated and intriguing, but I've still got a bad taste from my last experience in Nashville, and I just don't have any desire whatsoever, to go back there. But I do hope you find someone else, and I also hope the song will be a successful one."

The phone call ended on both ends, from a joyous hello to a less-than-idyllic goodbye. Old friends, not having contact in over thirty years, finally were able to rejoice in having been reconnected by voice, only to end with the possibility of not being able to reconnect in person. But Jimmy Adams and Little David Wilkins were professionals in their trade and knew that they had a hit song and would not give up their efforts to make it public without further attempts by way of personal ambition and positive persuasion.

For the next few weeks, Jimmy and David would call Leon at all times during the early morning hours. To make the annoying phone calls more distressing, Nashville time was one hour behind Leon's home in Ward, SC. Needless to say, Leon's pleas for them to stop the late-night phone calls fell on deaf ears. Jimmy and David were on a mission, and they weren't going to quit until they got what they wanted. One way or another, they were going to bring Leon back to Nashville.

Finally, after weeks of unsuccessful late-night calls, David decided to send Leon a demo copy of the song, including a copy of the lyrics. Upon receiving the demo, Leon laughed, thinking, "What will they try next? I'll listen to the song as a courtesy, but there's nothing they can do to convince me to go to Nashville."

When he finally got around to playing the demo, Leon was immediately blown away by David's vocals, the song's melody, as well as the accompanying lyrics. Leon knew a hit song when he heard one, and this was one of them. As Leon listened to the song and read along with the lyrics, he began to sing the duet position. For the next few days, he couldn't get the song out of his mind. Everywhere he went, he was singing the song over and over to himself. The lyrics were genuinely heartfelt, and the melody was pleasantly all-consuming.

After letting Diane listen to the song, she and Leon agreed to go to Nashville with two stipulations—Jimmy and David would have to stop calling at all hours of the night, and after making the recording with David, they would return home as they had promised, with no strings attached.

Upon hearing Leon's terms and conditions, there was no hesitation, as both Jimmy and David agreed to stop calling after hours. Furthermore, if Leon would come up for at least a day and record the song with David, then he could either go back home or stay as long as he liked.

Upon their arrival in Nashville, Jimmy had made accommodations at a five-star hotel for Leon and Diane to stay in. The next day, David and Leon recorded the song at the Hilltop Studio, and to Leon's surprise, he was elated to have been in a recording environment once again.

Leon didn't realize until now what he'd been missing all those years after leaving Nashville. As they say, he had suddenly gotten *that old-time feeling* once again. Music was in his heart, and perhaps Nashville wasn't so bad after all. The duet with David made him realize just how much he truly missed recording and performing, and now he found himself beginning to want it back more than ever. Afterward, they all went to a party that included other musicians, their friends, as well as elite members of the Nashville music industry.

Leon was pleased to see for himself that the business atmosphere in Nashville was just as Jimmy had described. Under Jimmy's management, there was no *our way or the highway* system but rather a flexible approach to meet the individual needs of all vested parties. Jimmy also let it be known that he was also open to hearing formidable suggestions and insightful ideas with all ongoing music collaborations, a prior condition that had very strict and limited access from Leon's last experience in Nashville.

Jimmy's down-to-earth style of professionalism gave Leon a sense of trust and confidence in his managerial skills and his knowledge of talent. There was no doubt that Jimmy Adams was a member of the *Who's Who* club among the Nashville music elite, as over the next two weeks, he introduced Leon to other up-and-coming musicians, musicians that were already well-established, as well as new and notable music industry administrative professionals.

The original plan for an overnight stay resulted in an exciting, fact-finding two-week endeavor. But Jimmy still had more unexpected business propositions for Leon. Because of his personal trust and professional affection for Jimmy Adams, in the weeks that followed his trip to Nashville, Leon signed a contract designating Jimmy as his music business manager and industry agent.

By signing with Jimmy, Leon would once again, after over thirty years of leaving the music industry, be signed under contract to a new, prestigious recording label—MC1/Sony. History was made on that day, as MC1/Sony would sign one of the oldest artists ever to sign a contract under its reputable record label. Because they believed in his vocal talent as well as his commitment to music, Jimmy Adams and MC1/Sony took a chance on signing the seventy-three-year-old entertainer to a new country/gospel record label contract.

Not long after the ink had dried on the contract, Leon's first recording, *Would Jesus Be Welcome There,* began to immediately climb the music charts as well as being a favorite on popular music download channels. To the joy of everyone involved, the song reached the number one spot on the Itube 247 inspirational/country music chart ahead of the likes of Blake Shelton, Dolly Parton, and Carrie Underwood, who were also listed in the top ten at the time. In addition, his duet with David Wilkins on *I Stand the Tallest When I'm Down on My Knees* peaked at number five and stayed in the top ten on the inspirational/country charts for five weeks.

While on his drive back home, Leon began thinking about all the exciting events and unexpected blessings that had taken place in the past few weeks. He then realized that all the late-night phone calls, pleas to return to Nashville, and the surprising results of that all-inspiring trip were because of the blessings of his Lord and Savior, Jesus Christ.

Was God instrumental in having Jimmy and David call night after night during the early morning hours and waking a sleeping Leon and Diane? Well, one would have to admit, the results of the moment could be reasoned as being a miracle of faith or a coincidence of chance, and God certainly doesn't act out of coincidences. Besides, if they had called during the daytime hours, their purpose for having Leon come to Nashville may have had different results. After all, having them stop the late-night calls was one of the reasons for getting Leon's attention about going in the first place.

Leon then recalled a story as recorded in the book of Genesis, Chapter 17. Abraham made a covenant with God when he was ninety-nine years old. In paraphrasing, God said *if you do as I say and be perfect in all of your ways, I will multiply you exceedingly, and you will be the father of many nations, and I will be their God.* Among other conditions, God told Abraham that he would also bless his wife, Sarah, with a son and that she would be the mother of nations. Abraham laughed, but not in a mocking way, and asked, "How can a man who is one hundred years old and a woman who is ninety years old bear a child?" In his heart, Abraham knew that there was no need for an explanation as to how God would perform any miracle. If God said He was going to do something, He would always keep his word. God kept His word, and the nation of Israel and its descendants are the direct results of that special covenant that the Jewish people celebrate to this day.

Now, Leon didn't necessarily have a covenant with God in the way that Abraham did, but he was a faithful, obedient servant, and he had, at one point, promised God that he would never go back to Nashville to record or perform country music that had any message whatsoever, that included adultery, alcohol consumption, or any other inappropriate content. For over thirty years, Leon kept his promise to God, and in return, God blessed him beyond his means with a Godly wife and healthy marriage, their precious dog named Punkin, whom they cherish as being their loving daughter, a steady, profitable landscaping business, a new church, and church family, and now, at seventy-three years old, a new recording contract by one of country music's industry leaders, MC1/Sony.

While this may be the end of the book, the story of Leon Everette continues. With the guidance and partnership of Jimmy Adams, Leon is now officially under contract with Jimmy's personal media group—MC/JAM (Music City/Jimmy Adams Media). In 2023, Leon, with the help of MC/JAM, re-launched his music and entertainment career by recording new songs, playing live venues, and giving his personal Christian testimony to anyone who will listen. "I'm having more fun than ever before," says Leon, "because now, I have Jesus in my band."

He was born a boy of humble beginnings from the rural South Carolina countryside, who at just seventeen years old, dropped out of high school to join the Navy. After serving two tours of duty in Vietnam and having learned to play the guitar aboard a Naval Aircraft Carrier, the USS Coral Seas, after his service he endured hardships and struggles in his marriage as well as his new beginnings in his life once again as a civilian.

After finding steady employment and having made positive improvements in his marriage, he formed a local band performing at weddings, special engagements, and finally venturing into the local nightclub scene. Then, after months of unsuccessful attempts to find a way on his own to get an audition or interview with recording label executives in Nashville, on the eve of his quitting his local nightclub entertaining, he met a complete stranger who would help him achieve his goal of becoming a country music superstar.

While performing at a local nightclub in Augusta, GA, a self-made millionaire named Carroll Fulmer was in the audience when he first heard Leon Everette perform. Carroll was so blown away and impressed by Leon's vocal talent and his allure from the audience that he convinced Leon to let him take the lead in his music career. In less than a year's time, with Carroll's influence and guidance, Leon's music was not only entering the top ten in the country music charts, but he also became the newest member of the RCA Record Label family.

After a successful music career and having established a devoted fan base, the stress of commitments as headliner of the band *Hurricane*, the long, tiring pressures from being on the road and making deadlines for recording contracts led Leon to turn to alcohol to cope with his anger issues. In the end, it came down to disagreements on his future career decisions with recording label executives that resulted in his retiring from the music industry. To add insult to misery, several years later, he and his wife, Kathy, divorced.

After years of being a successful small business entrepreneur, he agreed with two other investors to open a nightclub using his name and image as part of their agreement. After managing the club for seven years, he met a man named Lester Herron, who witnessed to him about Jesus. Leon and his then fiancé, Diane, began attending church, and over time, both became disciples of Jesus Christ. Leon's faith and obedience to God led him to start a new church, and of all places, he found the perfect location—the building that was once the nightclub that he had managed in the past—*Hurricane Central*—*Once a place for sinners to play, it was now a place for sinners to pray.*

Leon is now an ordained minister, church administrator, and minister of music in the church that he was instrumental in founding in 2018. When he's away from his church responsibilities, he continues to record music and play venues for audiences who have a love for country and gospel music. As the old saying goes, *he's still alive and standing,* but now, *he stands the tallest when he's down on his knees.* And wherever he goes, and with every opportunity that comes his way, he proudly shares his life's story as well as his personal relationship with his Lord and Savior, Jesus Christ. He never holds *anything* back, as he humbly and faithfully tells it all—THE GOOD, THE BAD, AND THE BLESSED!


## THE END

Chapter 42

**Bonus Reading**

**Before any writing** had begun, Leon told me that he wanted to tell the story of his whole life, including his childhood experiences, as well as his post-country music career. It was important to him for his fans to know more than what a search would find on the internet.

There are, however, a few stories that didn't make it into the main storyline due to inconsistencies with chronological events. At the request of Leon, I've included them as bonus material for your reading pleasure.

Although it was originally a part of the Bonus Reading section, *Not Just Another Day* (Chapter 1) was my first story written for the book. It was kind of a "trial run" to see if Leon would be interested in my writing style. It tells the story of how he was involved in a near-death automobile accident at just three years old. It was the first of many of his near-death experiences up to the age of fifteen years old. Leon agreed that using this story at the beginning of the book would be a good indicator to the reader, to no fault of his own in this case, of how his often wild and reckless style of living started out.

The very first day I approached Leon about telling his life

story, his wife, Diane, told him to tell me about how he got his first guitar. *A Boy and a Guitar* starts at a concert at Wembley Stadium in England. As he's getting ready to go on stage, he stares into his dressing room mirror and recalls the day, as a seven-year-old boy, he was walking to school and found a one-string guitar in a trash can along the way. He's had a passion for music ever since.

His life story wouldn't be complete if it didn't involve some form of fighting. The *Fightin' Side of Me* is the story of his first-ever fight, which took place in a city park near his home in Queens, New York. It seems that one of the Yankee schoolyard bullies didn't like the way the new southern kid in town talked. Unfortunately for him, he wouldn't like the way the southern boy fought either.

I suppose you could call *Murder in New York* a near-death experience as well. It's the story of two young boys delivering newspapers on their daily routes in the city of Queens, New York. One morning, as they entered a high-rise apartment building, the two boys entered twin elevators to their respective floors. Two went up, but only one came down.

*Uneasy Rider* is one of my favorites. At fifteen years old, young Leon takes his dad's *brand-new* Harley-Davidson motorcycle out for a ride while his dad is away at work. Needless to say, it wasn't a good idea. Yep, another near-death experience.

Chapter 43

## A Boy and a Guitar

**Wembley Stadium, the** pride of London, England, 1983. Known for its many sporting events and traditional concerts, it was now ready for a new class act—country music. Various high-demand performers from the hills and plains of the southern region of the United States would soon adorn the same historic stage already accustomed to not only competitive sporting events but also rock, opera, classical, and other popular forms of entertainment.

The locals proudly called their stadium the Crown of England. But not to be outdone, the press and media would feature it, at this time, as the Grand Ole Opry of England. The English faithful had been waiting eagerly for months to attend this momentous occasion. They could hardly wait to hear the twang and charm of the spoken southern drawl but were, at the same time, also aware that it was often hidden when heard through the musical vocals and instrumental acoustics.

Nevertheless, it wasn't just the country music singers that they longed for; it was the intriguing sounds of banjos, harmonicas, steel guitars, as well as snare drums that seemed to also have a southern twang-like, pounding resonance. All of this is what they had been craving. The Day had finally arrived. And now they were about to get a very good dose of enchanting southern hospitality, musical and comedy entertainment, and more.

A knock on the dressing room door was followed by a brief announcement in an old English vernacular. "Excuse me, Mr. Everette, just a gentle reminder that you're scheduled to make your way to the stage in precisely forty-seven minutes, please."

"Thank you very much," replied the South Carolina native, "I'll be retty ta go."

"What a charming, southern voice. I quite like it," said the assistant to himself as he scurried off to his next point of contact.

From inside the dressing room, just a few English meters from the stage, Leon Everette Baughman, stage name—Leon Everette, was preparing himself for this long-awaited moment. The overflow crowd of fans had already gathered, and he could tell by the applause and laughter that they were enjoying the moment as they were already well-entertained.

He checked off all of the preparation boxes in his head as he went through them one by one. Guitar-strung and tuned? Check. Backup singers ready? Check. Musicians accounted for and ready? Check. Sound systems tuned and monitors properly stationed? Check.

As he began to dress for the part, he thought, "These folks want to see the country in me, so I'm gonna give'm some real, down-home country." He reached down and pulled on his favorite tight blue jeans and wrapped himself in a bright red, high collar, rhinestone decorative shirt. He topped off his jeans with a two-inch wide, white patent leather belt with a buckle so big that it could easily be seen from the opposite side nosebleed section of the stadium.

He then checked his wardrobe closet for his cowboy boots. "Now, which ones should I wear?" he pondered. He had quite a selection to choose from, so he narrowed his search to his three favorite styles. The Dingo Harness, the Laredo Leather, and the Cold Grey and Black Reptilian style. "Heck, these people want country," he chuckled, "they're going to get my favorite, the grey and black snake-lookin' thangs."

Looking into the mirror, he made sure his long, wavy dark hair was well-groomed. That's when he realized that he still had one last item to "top it all off"—his cowboy hat. He reached upward to a nearby shelf holding several hat storage boxes. From one of the boxes, he carefully removed a black felt, wide-brim, western-style cowboy hat and strategically positioned it on his head.

After donning the hat, he stopped and looked intently into the well-lit dressing room mirror. "This is me", he said. "You look good. You're ready for this. This is what you've been working for all your life. You will not let your fans down because this is not only your moment but theirs as well."

He then sat down in the padded seat, hard-backed dressing table chair and continued to stare into the lighted mirror. Suddenly, there was a momentary pause and quietness from the concert arena as one performance was ending, and another was about to begin.

While still embraced in the gaze in the mirror, his thoughts stealthily took him back in time to his first encounter with a guitar. It was, in some sort of poetic way, the beginning of his illustrious career. From a seven-year-old boy finding an old beat-up guitar in a trash can by the roadside, with only one string and singing Elvis Presley's "You Ain't Nothin' but A Hound Dog" in front of his class at grammar school to ending up here at Wembley Stadium was quite a leap of faith, to say the least. Yep, just a boy and a guitar. Who would ever have imagined that this simple, innocent, and unremarkable occasion would lead to becoming the story of how the legend of Leon Everette would begin? As Leon continued to stare into the mirror, a memory of his mama came to mind:

* * *

"Leon, come on and eat some breakfast. You don't want to be late for school," said Ms. Baughman, Leon's mother. Leon heard her call but didn't immediately acknowledge it because he was fixated on watching his favorite morning TV show, Captain Kangaroo. A static disturbance had blurred the black and white TV screen, and he was hastily trying to adjust the "rabbit ears" antennae to find an unobstructed, clear picture. He had to get that picture clear soon, as one of his favorite characters on the show was about to be introduced—the Dancing Bear.

"Leon, come on and eat, honey," said Mrs. Baughman, "Your breakfast is going to get cold, and you don't want to be late for 'show and tell' at school today."

The TV show continued and was featuring the Captain and Mr. Green Jeans talking about the Dancing Bear's song and dance routine coming up soon, but the TV interference just would not clear. Finally, he thought to turn the adjusting knob behind the channel selector. Presto! The picture cleared up, and there he was, the Dancing Bear coming into view.

"Leon Everette Baughman! Don't make me come in there and turn that TV off!" demanded Mrs. Baughman, "Get in here right now!"

Oh, my goodness, Leon thought; she's used the mama's code for 'this is your last warning,' calling me out by my full name. Well, at least I got to see the Dancing Bear, if only for just a moment.

As Leon sat down to eat, his mama saw the disappointment on his face. She knew how much he liked singing along with that "darling" Dancing Bear. Without hesitating, she rushed back into the living room and turned the TV up loud enough to where Leon could at least hear it while he ate his breakfast. After all, that's the least a loving mother could do for her seven-year-old son.

Leon's ears popped up as soon as he heard the sound from

the TV. The Dancing Bear was singing one of his favorite songs, and he knew every word of it. He sang along and swayed back and forth to the rhythm of the music as he ate his breakfast.

If they could just come up with a way to where you could watch it again somehow at a time when you wanted to watch it, Ms. Baughman thought. I mean, they make movies and TV shows and play them when they want to. Why can't Leon watch The Dancing Bear anytime he wants to? If only there was a way to record it and watch it later. My poor dear.

After finishing eating his breakfast, Leon got ready for school, grabbed his show-and-tell object, and headed out the door, but not before giving his mama a goodbye kiss.

"You be careful, Leon," his mama said, "And have a good day at school. And have fun with the show and tell today. I love you."

"I love you too, mama," Leon said as he closed the door and began his short walk to school.

The second-grade class at Leon's school was holding a "winner take all" prize for the best show-and-tell presentation. Each student was to bring in an item from home and present a brief talk about it in front of the class. The winning prize? A Whiffle Ball and Bat for the boy winner and The Most Happy Family Doll set for the winning girl.

The year was 1956 and the city was Pittsburgh, Pennsylvania, and these two items were among the most popular toys for boys and girls at the time. Show and Tell was also a favorite competition for grammar school students throughout the city, as well.

"I really want that ball and bat," Leon thought. But he wasn't sure if his show-and-tell object would be interesting enough to discuss before the class. After all, almost everybody in class already had a Slinky of their own.

Most of his friends loved the Slinky. It was just a loosely coiled spring that you could sort of juggle from one hand to the other, and although it was a simply designed toy, it was fun to play with. One of the coolest things about the Slinky was watching it walk end-over-end by itself down a flight of stairs.

As he started his walk to school down the unevenly paved sidewalk, he began thinking of a way to convince the class that his Slinky toy was the most interesting of all the other show-and-tell objects. Oh, how he desperately wanted that Whiffle ball and bat!

He took notice as he walked along his route to school that it was trash pick-up day in the city. The curbs along the streets were lined with big, metal trash cans in front of almost every house along the way. They were topped off with a large, round metal lid with a handle on top for easy opening and closing.

As he passed by the trash cans, he began kicking the sides and banging the lids, creating somewhat of a musical, rhythmic beat. "That's it!" he exclaimed, "I can sing the Slinky jingle and have the class join in with me. I'm sure they all know that song."

> It's Slinky, it's Slinky, for fun, it's a
>     wonderful toy.
> It's Slinky, it's Slinky, for every girl
>     and boy.
> Everyone knows it's Slinky.
> Everyone knows it's Slinky

He continued his walk, singing along and pounding and kicking the trash cans along the way, when all of a sudden, he noticed one trash can without a lid on it with an object protruding out the top. As he got closer, he saw that it was an old, beat-up, one-string guitar. He grabbed it by the "handle" and examined it closely. It only had one string, but to him, it sounded pretty dog-gone good.

"Wait a minute!" he thought, "This would be a great show-and-tell object. I'll bet no one else has a guitar. Even if it only has one string, it still makes a good sound. I'll play it for the class and sing a song. Now, what song would they like to hear? Surely, not the Slinky song. This has to be a real guitar-playing song. I'll have to think of something before I get to school."

Upon his arrival at school, his teacher, Ms. Jones, finished calling the roll for her second-grade class. All were present and eager for show and tell day.

Bobby Rogers was first with his Play-Dough demonstration.

"Boring!" Leon thought.

Next, it was Susan Wright's turn. She showed her Raggedy Ann doll and how to change her shoes and comb her hair.

"Boring!" Leon sighed.

Classmate after classmate continued with one boring routine after another. Then, he heard his name called.

Giggles were heard from his classmates as he grabbed his tattered, one-string guitar and made his way to the front of the class, positioning himself alongside the teacher's desk in front of the unblemished blackboard.

"My show and tell object is my new guitar," he said, "At least, it's new to me. I just found it in a trash can on the way to school."

His comments were met with roaring laughter from everyone except for Ms. Jones.

Seeing the shyness and embarrassment on his face, Ms. Jones immediately said, "Well, Leon, I can hardly wait to hear you play and sing. What song will you be performing?"

"I'm gonna sing, 'You Ain't Nothin' but A Hound Dog,' by Elvis Presley, Ms. Jones," he replied.

The laughter continued once again, but Ms. Jones quickly shushed them and said to Leon, "I'm excited to hear it, Leon. Please, the 'stage' is all yours."

With his feet slightly spread apart and one hand firmly gripping the neck of the guitar, the other hand began to strum the one crucial string. As he sang the lyrics, he was unaware of his swaying movements to the melody, but whatever it looked and sounded like, it was a crowd-pleaser. The whole class reacted with joy, clapped, and responded very favorably to his "song and dance."

"Thank you. Thank you very much," he said.

To say the least, this was by far the best show and tell of all time. Needless to say, Leon won that coveted Whiffle ball and bat. And more importantly, his mama would be so proud!

* * *

"Mr. Everette," called the Wembley employee, "It's time for you to approach the stage. Is there anything I can do to assist you, sir?"

The employee waited patiently, but there was no response.

"Mr. Everette, it's your time now, sir. Are you ready?" asked the employee with a slightly louder tone.

The second announcement jolted Leon out of his deep thoughts about his past. It was showtime, and he needed to compose himself and get back into his pre-performance routine.

"Thank you, sir," Leon replied, "I'm retty. I'm coming. Please lead the way."

"Right this way, sir. Please follow me," said the employee.

As he approached the stage, Leon noticed that all the musicians and backup singers were just finishing taking their places. The Leon Everette fans in the audience were aware that he was next on the entertainer's card and began shouting in unison, "Leon! Leon! Leon!"

The master of ceremonies readied his announcement when he saw Leon approaching: "Ladies and gentlemen, all the way from Aiken, South Carolina, please give a warm England welcome for Leon Everette!"

As he topped the stairs and began his way across the stage, the band struck in unison into a fast-paced, foot-stompin' can't sit in your seat song that everyone in the audience was already familiar with.

As Leon continued toward his prearranged position on the

stage, a stagehand walked toward and met him and handed off his guitar, neither one slowing down nor missing a step along the way.

When Leon approached the microphone stand, he tried in his best English accent and called out, "Good day, England. It's good to see y'all. Are y'all ready to boogie? Alright, let's have a jolly good time, then." And, of course, his fans went wild!

Up until this moment, the audience hadn't seen a performer close to the excitement and charismatic allure that Leon would bring. He had the moves of Elvis, the suave voice of an erotic angel, and the good looks of a Casanova. His open shirt, exposed chest, and lavish cowboy attire made him look like a centerfold model in *Rodeo Monthly* magazine. He was more than a singing cowboy. He was not only a crooner but also a fun-style but not-over-the-top hell-raiser, pleasantly trapped in a complex world of both country and rock music. He was the complete package, and many of the other performers that were to follow always cringed, knowing they had to be at their very best when following a performance as authentic and pristine as his.

Chapter 44

**The Fightin' Side of Me**

**A young southern** boy growing up in Queens, New York, could be challenging at times, to say the least. It was no different for Leon, who, at ten years of age, moved there with his parents in 1958. His daddy, Albert Baughman, was a union electrician from Langley, SC. Al was more than eager; he was excited to take on the responsibility of being the primary financial supporter for the family. At the time, even though there were jobs available close to home, he was smart enough and adventurous enough to move into unchartered territory to find the best source of income to support his young family. After hours of research and conversations with his fellow union brothers, Al found a very lucrative opportunity in the state of New York.

Leon's mama's name was Eula Lee. She was not only the cook and homemaker but also the maternal glue that held the family together with her loving affection, emotional stability, as well as her spiritual walk with God. Young Leon was the pride of her life. She loved him beyond words. She had spent her whole life growing up and living in the South, but she would do anything for the betterment of his young life, even if it meant moving from a quiet, comfortable family home in rural South Carolina to the noisy and busy streets of Queens, New York.

Leon was the new kid in town when he settled into his fifth-grade class at Queen's Elementary School. His unique southern drawl was charming to the girls in his class yet fuel for fun for some of the boys. He was also a young walking, talking individualistic paradox. Some of his characteristics were appealing to some, yet envious to others. For his age, he was tall, dark, and handsome. And the young ladies adored him. His physical appearance was thin but well-toned, but his long, dark, wavy hair was easily his finest feature. Unfortunately, and to no fault of his own, it was his southern accent that would be responsible for the first fight in his young, innocent life.

Back in those days, the schools had what they called recess. It was a time for the students, as well as the teachers, to take a restroom break. The students were also allowed to go outside and play and take a break from the stress of the classroom environment. It was a good and healthy way to relieve stress, as well as to intermingle and have fun with friends and other classmates. It was good for the teachers, as well, as all the physical activity of their students would help to lessen the anxiety and hypertension and help bring calm to their over-active mannerisms.

One day, while at recess, Leon and his friend Johnny were playing catch with their baseball and gloves. They were having a good time talking and tossing the ball back and forth to one another when suddenly, while the ball was in mid-air, big Jim Logan snatched it and ran away with it.

Jim Logan was physically obese for his height and age. I mean, he had a lot of soft, malleable tissue. He was one of the tallest, if not the tallest, boys on the playground. His cheeks were puffy and rosy red. His hair was cut close in a modified flat-top and crew-cut style. When he spoke, his voice had an unnerving deep bass pitch to it and was usually loud enough for everyone on the playground to hear, whether they were being spoken to or not. You guessed it. Big Jim was The Bully on the playground. Furthermore, he was extremely jealous of the sleek, handsome, and smooth-talking new kid, Leon Baughman.

Leon frantically chased after him, demanding he give the ball back. Needless to say, Big Jim was slow on the run. Leon quickly caught up with him as Big Jim bent over, gasping to catch his breath.

"Give me back my ball," demanded Leon.

"You want it, you take it, hillbilly," said Big Jim.

"I don't know what a hillbilly is, but I do know I want my ball back. Now, give it to me," Leon insisted.

"A hillbilly is a stupid, funny-talking, mama's boy crybaby," said Big Jim.

"I might be a mama's boy, but I ain't no crybaby. Now give me my ball, or I'm gonna tell the teacher," said a persistent Leon.

Leon suddenly noticed that they had been encircled by all the kids on the playground. Having never been in a situation like this, Leon thought to himself, "I've got to end this somehow without embarrassing myself and without any physical confrontation, but I want my ball back."

"Oh, you're going to tell the teacher. You're a sissy. "Leon is a sissy. Leon is a sissy," Big Jim chanted over and over.

In the meantime, while relaxing in her classroom, Ms. Taylor, Leon's teacher, noticed that the playful noise from the playground had suddenly stopped. Not knowing what might have happened, she rushed for the door and fled outside, only to see a crowd of children surrounding two boys in the playground. It did not look like a fight at this point, but she rushed toward them before one could get started.

"What's going on here?" she demanded.

"Big Jim and Leon are about to get into a fight," said one of the boys.

"Nobody is fighting in my schoolyard," said Ms. Taylor. "Big Jim, Leon—stay here. Everyone else—inside. Now!"

Looking at both the boys, Ms. Taylor asked, "Now, what is going on here?"

"Big Jim took my ball and won't give it back, Ms. Taylor," said Leon.

Seeing the ball in Big Jim's hand, she asked, "Is that Leon's ball?"

"Yes, ma'am," said Big Jim.

"Did you take it without his permission?" she asked.

"Yes, ma'am," said Big Jim.

"Then give it back," she said.

Reluctantly, Big Jim handed the ball back to Leon.

"Now, apologize," she insisted.

Big Jim's full face soon matched the color of his already rosy cheeks. It was so red that it looked like one big round cheek with a hole in it where his mouth was. He didn't apologize to anyone, especially a low-life hillbilly.

"I said to tell him you're sorry. Say it. Now!" she commanded.

Big Jim took in a slow, deep breath and quietly, but insincerely, said, "I'm sorry."

"Oh, no!" said Ms. Taylor, "That's not good enough. Tell him you're sorry as if you mean it."

Big Jim suddenly had a feeling that he had never experienced in his young life. His body had gone numb, and his nerves were uncontrollable, and that deep, fearful voice was now merely a whimper. He shook with fear. Not only was he scared, but he was also angry beyond description. But he knew that if he did not obey Ms. Taylor, she would probably tell his dad, and that could result in more harsh punishment for his bad behavior.

One last time, he breathed in, gathered his composure, and in a gentle, squeaky, whimpering voice, uttered, "I'm very sorry, Leon."

"Thank you. That's better," said Ms. Taylor.

"Now, what do you say, Leon?" asked Ms. Taylor.

Without hesitation, Leon responded, "I accept your apology."

Looking at both with a foreboding stare, she asked, "Are we good here?"

"Yes, ma'am," the boys replied in unison.

"Good. Now get back in the classroom, and I better not have any more trouble out of you two. Do you understand me?" she said.

"Yes, ma'am!" The boys replied.

Not surprisingly, as she led the two young boys back to the classroom, Big Jim couldn't help himself.

Looking at Leon, he mouthed without saying, "I'll get you later, hillbilly."

The rest of the school day resumed its normal routine. As for Leon, everything was back to normal. He had genuinely forgiven Big Jim for his bullish actions toward him. He hoped that Big Jim would feel the same toward him, as well. But deep down inside, he knew there were still more potentially unpleasant interactions yet to come, for he alone could only control his actions.

He'd never been in a fight, and he certainly didn't want to get into one. To make matters more difficult, he couldn't suppress a haunting thought that he couldn't overcome and one that wouldn't go away—the one that kept reminding him that Big Jim most likely didn't feel the same way.

After school, Leon went home, changed clothes, had a snack, and then went to a nearby park to meet up with his friend Johnny. Leon and Johnny's friendship was genuine. He and Johnny got along very well and enjoyed each other's company. They began playing hit-and-catch. One boy would take the ball and bat and hit grounders for the other to catch. They'd do this for some time, then switch positions. After a short time, they heard an unexpected shout nearby.

"Hey, hillbilly, who said you could play in my park?" Big Jim yelled.

"This is the city's park, not yours, and I don't want any trouble, Big Jim," Leon responded. "But if you want to play with us, you can."

"I don't have a glove," Big Jim replied, "Besides, I don't play with hillbilly sissies."

As Big Jim moved closer, Leon reminded him, "Big Jim, I don't want any trouble from you."

Alongside Big Jim were Henry and Alfred, his two human bookends. They weren't bullies, but they befriended Big Jim so he wouldn't bully them. Usually, whenever you saw Big Jim, Henry and Alfred were close by. Normally, they weren't troublemakers, but they acted like tough guys when they were in public with Big Jim. They were a lot of talk and absolutely no action.

"Give me that ball, hillbilly," Big Jim demanded.

"Get your own ball. Why do you want mine?" asked Leon.

"It ain't that I want your ball, hillbilly; I just don't want you to have it," said Big Jim.

"What's wrong with you, anyway? You're always making trouble," said Leon.

"I don't make trouble," boasted Big Jim, "I am trouble. Now, give me that ball."

Before Leon could respond, Big Jim hit him in the face, and Leon fell to the ground moaning. Big Jim then reached down, took his ball, and threw it over the park fence.

The unexpected punch in the face was an experience like Leon had never had. It hurt, but that was the least of the pain. It was the embarrassment and humility that taunted him. Besides, Big Jim had his backup crew with him, and he was unaware of what they might do next.

"Get up, sissy," said Big Jim. "If you want your ball, it's somewhere over the fence."

"I said, get up!" Big Jim shouted. He then kicked Leon in the ribs with a forceful thrust.

"Leon is a sissy. Leon is a sissy," chanted Big Jim.

Henry and Alfred chimed into the chorus, making it three times as painful for Leon.

Johnny stood by helplessly, but Leon didn't blame him. They were outnumbered, and they didn't want any sort of physical altercations whatsoever.

Leon laid in agony on the sandy soil, softly crying more from embarrassment than anything.

"Leon is a crybaby. Leon is a crybaby," chanted the three harassers.

"Johnny, go home!" Leon cried out as he didn't want them to get him involved.

Big Jim looked at Johnny, and Johnny begrudgingly turned and ran away.

As Big Jim reached down to hit him again, Leon sprang up, grabbed his glove, and ran home.

As he was running away, he could still hear them chanting, "Leon is a crybaby, Leon is a crybaby."

By this time, Leon's daddy was just getting home from work when he saw Leon crying as he got closer to home.

"Leon, are you okay? Are you hurt?" he asked.

Leon was very reluctant to tell him the truth, but he knew he had to.

"Leon, what's wrong? Talk to me," said Albert.

"I'm not hurt. I just got beat up in a fight at the park with Big Jim," said a whimpering Leon.

"Did you start the fight, Leon?" asked Albert. Albert knew he didn't, but he had to ask.

"No sir," said Leon, "Big Jim did."

"Are you sure you're not hurt?" asked Albert.

"No sir," said Leon, "Just embarrassed, I guess."

"Then what in God's name are you crying for? We don't have crybabies in this family," scolded his dad.

"Let me put my lunch box in the house. We're going back down to the park, and you're going to make this thing right. You're going to make him apologize. Do you understand me?" asked Albert.

"Yes, sir," Leon responded.

As Albert went inside the house, Leon couldn't help but recall the event that took place at recess earlier that day. He knew how hard it was for Big Jim to apologize in front of Ms. Taylor, but now he had to apologize to him alone. Hopefully, his daddy would be there to back him up and make it easier to accomplish an almost impossible feat.

As Albert came out of the house, he gathered himself and sat down on the steps to talk with Leon.

"I'm not mad, son," said Albert, "But I'm disappointed that you came home crying. I know it's hard, but you're going to have to learn to take up for yourself because Mama and Daddy won't always be there to defend you. Do you understand what I'm saying?"

"Yes, sir," a reassured Leon replied.

"Okay, here's what we're going to do. We're going to go to the park and hope that Big Jim is still there, and if he is, you're going to walk up to him and look him straight in the eye and demand that he apologizes. Don't worry, I'll be right behind you. But, whatever you do, do not look back at me because if you do, he will think that you are weak and that you have to depend on me to intervene for you. Do you understand?"

"Yes, Daddy," answered Leon.

"Okay, let's go. Now compose yourself before we get there," said Albert.

"You ready?" asked Albert.

"Yes, sir!" Leon confidently replied.

As they approached the park, Leon spotted Big Jim, Henry, and Alfred near the swing and slide area.

"There he is, right there," Leon pointed.

"Okay, son, you can do this. I'll be there for you. I have faith in you, son. Just do what I said, but whatever you do, do not look back at me! Find the courage to just look him in the eye and show that you aren't scared and tell him that he owes you an apology. Do you understand?" he insisted.

"Yes, sir!" said a confident Leon as he then began his approach to the swing and slide area.

Before he could get there, Big Jim and his companions started walking his way.

"I guess Daddy was right," Leon thought confidently as the three boys got closer. "They see Daddy behind me, and they must want to get this over with as bad as I do."

But that mode of thought changed almost as fast as he thought it.

"Here comes the hillbilly, boys," laughed Big Jim.

"Why do you always call me hillbilly, Jim?" asked Leon.

"Because you talk funny," Big Jim responded, "Besides that, your mama and daddy talk funny, too. You're just all a bunch of low-life hillbillies."

That was all it took. Leon had had enough. He didn't have time to think. All he heard was, "Your mama's a funny-talkin' hillbilly," to get an instant reaction.

Without hesitation, he punched Big Jim in his stomach, and as he gasped and bent down to catch his breath, Leon responded with a left uppercut to his nose, sending him to the ground.

Leon stood over him and said, "I didn't want to hit you, Jim, but nobody makes fun of my mama. Now apologize, or you're going to get another one."

As blood began to trickle from Big Jim's nose, Leon looked around at Henry and Alfred. Without hesitation and without Leon saying anything, they both fled, leaving Big Jim lying on the ground, still gasping and crying in pain and embarrassment.

In a squeaky, high-pitched voice, Big Jim uttered, with

sincerity, "I'm sorry, Leon. I won't pick on you anymore. I promise." cried Big Jim.

"I accept your apology…again. Now get up and go home, and let's forget this ever happened, okay," said a reassuring Leon.

"Okay, Leon, I'll see you at school tomorrow," said Big Jim as he slowly walked away, with his head uncontrollably looking downward.

Leon turned quickly to see his daddy's reaction, only to see him walking toward him from afar off across the playground.

As his daddy got closer, Leon frantically asked, "Daddy, I thought you said that you would be behind me all the way!"

Albert kneeled, put his hand on Leon's shoulder, and said in a fatherly tone, "Son, I'll always be behind you in whatever you do. I said what I said as a figure of speech, hoping it would reassure you to help you build confidence in yourself. It worked, Leon, and I'm very, very proud of you. Now, let's go home and see what mamas got for supper. You hungry?"

"You better believe I'm hungry. After all this, I'm starving!" smiled Leon as he proudly hugged his daddy.

Chapter 45

## Murder in New York

**To be at work** at two o'clock in the morning as a newspaper delivery boy wasn't always easy for Leon, but the determined thirteen-year-old made it his passion to be on time or earlier for his job at the Long Island Daily Press to fold and roll his papers as he prepared for his assigned delivery route. One group of papers was simply folded once in half, then placed in a stack, and was primarily used for door-to-door apartment buildings. The rolled papers were tightly rolled and held together with a small rubber band and were used for riding along the sidewalk or street on his bicycle, to be tossed to the nearest porch or doorway of assigned houses and / or businesses along the way.

After finishing his job preparing the papers, he loaded up both his front and rear baskets attached to his vintage Schwinn Suburban newsboy bicycle. "Old Blue," as he called it, was his pride and joy. Both wheels used narrow tubes with wide white-wall tires that were well supported with standard spokes. Factory-installed supports were mounted to the front and rear forks and fenders to ensure safety and stability. The hand brakes were located on the left handlebar, as was a rear-view mirror. A hand clutch was attached to the opposite right handlebar. Decorative tassels were attached to the end of the rubber handlebar sleeves that gave a sporty look when blowing in the wind as the bike would ride by. Just for fun, Leon also attached a toy horn toward the center of the handlebar. Not to be outdone, sometimes he would place a clothespin to a folded playing card and attach them to the rear wheel spokes to make a sound that resembled a small motorbike.

Although it came with a factory-installed kickstand, Leon also installed a rear-wheel kickstand for more stability to handle the cumbersome load of the newspapers. This kickstand consisted of a piece of metal that flipped down from the frame on each side of the back tire, touching the ground below the wheel. Just gently pulling the bicycle rearward allowed the bicycle to lock in position without leaning, thereby maintaining balance for his loaded baskets of newspapers.

He'd always check the air pressure in his tires and oil the chain before starting his route to make the ride smoother and faster. Speed was important to a newspaper bicycle route, as you had to return to the news building every time you ran out of papers to restock your supply.

The speedy bike was also a valuable asset to Leon's paper route delivery, as the route manager would organize periodic contests to see who could deliver the most papers within a timed event. On several cold New York mornings, Old Blue and Leon would speed through the route, win the contest, and proudly claim the grand prize of "drum roll please," a box of Nestle Crunch chocolate bars.

Although there was no way Leon could have realized it at the time, these fast-paced contests may have been the catalyst that would spark his interest in his future love of motorcycle racing. As he would grow older, his overwhelming desire for a "need for speed" evolved into an uncontrollable craving like a starving lion rushing to consume a long-awaited meal.

Leon and his co-worker Tony DeAngelo only knew each other from their place of employment. They didn't live in the same neighborhood, nor did they come from similar back-grounds, but they did share a lot of things in common, i.e., bicy-cles, comic books, and competitive bicycle racing. They were about the same age and had a good on-the-job working relation-ship, as Tony was also a bicycle-riding newspaper delivery boy.

Early one dark winter Sunday morning, the two boys loaded up their bicycle baskets and headed out to the streets of Long Island to deliver their newspapers. It just so happened that they shared their first point of delivery at a nearby apartment complex called the Piedmont Apartments. It was a multi-family dwelling, designed and utilized like many others throughout the city.

As you entered the towering structure of the Piedmont building, you'd immediately walk across a small vestibule with tenant mailboxes on either side. Opposite the entryway was a lobby with a double elevator with overhead dimly lit characters indicating the basement to the seventh floor.

The manager of the paper routes had pre-planned the boy's delivery at the Piedmont building by assigning each boy half of all the apartments on each floor. Relative to the elevators, one boy would take one side, and the other boy would take the other, all the way to the seventh floor.

This morning was just like many others they were accus-tomed to as they would begin their routes. They both drove their bikes to a corner in front of the apartment building and parked them next to a nearby light pole. After securing their bikes to the light pole, they both retrieved a stack of newspa-pers from their bike baskets and headed for the elevator lobby.

Since it was still only about four o'clock in the morning, the boys always had the plan to use the elevators independently of one another. Since it was so early, there was usually no elevator traffic to speak of. Each boy took a designated elevator and began their deliveries. After finishing delivering their papers on each floor, they would return to hopefully, a waiting elevator.

As Leon and Tony departed for their door-to-door destinations, they said their goodbyes and went about their business of delivering newspapers. Little did they know that this would be the last time they would see or speak to one another.

When Leon finished delivering all his papers, he returned to his bicycle and prepared to head back to the news building to re-stock his supply. He noticed that Tony's bike was also still there, but that wasn't uncommon, as each boy would finish before the other from time to time, only to continue their respective routes accordingly.

After reloading his baskets, Leon headed out to finish his route across the city. As he passed by the Piedmont building, he noticed Tony's bike was still tied to the light pole. He thought that it was strange that he hadn't left yet, but maybe he got held up by talking with one or more of the apartment tenants. Sometimes, the little old ladies liked to talk to someone, and even though the boys had work to do, it was hard to say no to a lonely person or to just engage in a casual conversation in general.

Leon continued his delivery riding down main thoroughfares and side streets hitting all the predetermined houses and businesses along his route. When he had finished, he headed back to the news building before going home to check in with his supervisor, as he was required to maintain accountability of their department personnel.

As he approached the Piedmont building, he noticed a gathering of police cars, ambulances, and a large crowd at the front entrance. He then saw that Tony's bike was also still tied to the light pole. It appeared that it hadn't been moved since Tony parked it earlier that morning.

Leon's curiosity got the best of him, so he asked a police officer what had happened, and he said someone had been murdered. Rumors in the crowd were that someone had killed a young newspaper boy in one of the elevators. He had been brutally stabbed repeatedly with a knife. The young boy didn't have a chance, as he was carrying a stack of papers and was defenseless to the perpetrator. It looked like a robbery gone bad, but Tony didn't carry any money. He wasn't selling newspapers, as he was simply delivering papers that had already been sold by pre-paid subscriptions.

To say the least, Leon was devastated. Tony was a good person and wouldn't do anything to harm anyone. He was a good employee and a dedicated newspaper delivery boy, who was always on time and never missed a day of work.

Needless to say, Leon had a hard time getting over the death of his co-worker. Although he didn't know Tony very well, he knew him well enough to know that he was a kind, polite, and trustworthy person. Although both Leon and Tony were merely thirteen years old at the time, the murder of his favorite, loyal co-worker still haunts him to this day. But the eeriest thought is that it could have just as easily been him if he had only chosen the other elevator that morning—*Tony's elevator.*

Chapter 46

**Uneasy Rider**

**The FL Duo-Glide** was one of the most popular selling motorcycles in the long history of the Harley-Davidson Motorcycle Company. Although its name was proudly stamped on several obvious parts of the motorcycle, as with other models preceding it and among Harley-Davidson owners, it was known simply as the "74." The number 74 referred to the 74 cubic inch twin engine that came as standard equipment for that particular model. The 74 was the elite industry standard and the pride of motorcycle owners for its superior power, good looks, and rugged durability. And Leon's dad, Al Baughman, was one of those proud owners.

Al had been a motorcycle enthusiast and owner for most of his adult life. His love of motorcycles and his desire to help others maintain theirs enabled him to become president of the Aiken Motorcycle Club in Aiken, SC, in 1963, the same year he purchased his very own brand-new 74.

Al beamed with pride every time he saw the excitement on the faces of other members of the club as he drove up for a motorcycle rally. He didn't necessarily have to describe much about it, as the general appearance of the motorcycle told its own story. It was Hi-Fi Red, a patented Harley-Davidson brand color, which was similar to the resulting blend of a mixture of Fire Engine Red with Candy Apple Red.

The single "sprung" seat was one of its most distinguishing features. It didn't come with a passenger seat over the rear fender, but one could squeeze on the back of the oversized driver's seat, depending on how badly they wanted to ride. Nevertheless, Harley-Davidson owners knew without explanation that the single seat was intentionally meant for one person —the driver.

Accenting the red gas tank and front and rear fender was chrome galore. Chrome beamed on almost everything metal that wasn't painted red, including the front forks, wheel spokes, handlebar, twin-engine, muffler, shock absorbers, and even some of the stabilizing supports throughout its ruggedly gorgeous frame.

Sometimes, in glistening sunlight, it was like looking at a motorcycle made of rubies, dazzled with diamonds, and crowned with a black onyx seat and rear fender soft leather saddlebags accented with rhinestones. All this luxurious motorcycle bling was supported and transported by front and rear high-quality Dunlop tires to make any ride seem like you were gliding effortlessly on air.

Besides good looks and performance, there is one other important attribute to Harley-Davidson motorcycles—the bikes sound when started. Al's bike was no different. If there was such a thing as a motorcycle opera, Al's bike would be the fat lady singing the closing song of the performance. Everybody wanted to hear the delightfully dramatic and pleasantly satisfying sound of a gripping vocal melody, and nobody wanted to leave until that song had ended. This was Al's pride and joy. This was Al's "Big Red".

Al pampered that motorcycle like a baby. No dirt, bug rash, or oily residue was ever seen by anyone else but him, as he cleaned and polished it every chance he got. Although his home had a two-car garage, one section was specifically designated for Big Red to protect it from the elements, as well as theft. Big Red sat isolated in the unoccupied portion of the garage with plenty of room to prevent anyone from accidentally bumping into it or any object from damaging it. If there was one rule in Al's household, it would be "Keep away from Big Red."

Al's twenty-mile commute to work in Augusta, GA was primarily by automobile, as he reserved Big Red for the weekend and leisurely travel only. It gave him peace of mind to know that while he was away, Big Red was protected from damage or theft from the outside world. However, what he failed to take into consideration was a potential threat from someone inside his own home.

One day, while Al and his wife Eula were at work, their son Leon became bored and restless, as he didn't have anything to do to keep himself occupied. It was summer break from school, and for a fifteen-year-old boy, the great outdoors was far more appealing than being couped up inside a house.

Leon opened the front door and felt the warm sunshine and a cool morning breeze on his face. It was a perfect day for a motorcycle ride, he thought. He then looked toward the kitchen, where, on a wall, he saw the key to his Harley-Davidson Sportster. But what caught his eye was the key right next to it—Big Reds. The more he looked at Big Red's key, the more it seemed to be begging him to go for a ride.

Leon then recalled a haunting memory. It was about one year ago that he'd wrecked his dad's other motorcycle at Caesars Head Park and Campground in the northwest mountains of South Carolina. While motorcycle racing one of his dad's friends, he badly missed a turn and flew over the side of the roadway, crashing down the side of a mountain and hitting countless boulders and trees along the way.

When EMS arrived, they had to call for a wrecker with an extended boom and cable to retrieve him in the rescue attempt. Although he remained conscious throughout the ordeal, there was nothing he could do to help himself, as he was too far down the mountain to climb and even more so, too badly injured to move.

Leon ended up in a hospital in Greenville, SC, and the motorcycle ended up and remains in what Leon calls Never-Never Land, somewhere at or near the bottom of the mountain. Although the near-death experience caused him to be hospital-ized for two days, and as bad as the circumstances ended, at least Leon had his dad's permission to ride his bike on that fateful day.

Nevertheless, Leon couldn't take his eyes off Big Red's key. As he continued to stare at it, his unrelenting emotions began to take over his ability to make a rational decision about taking Big Red for a ride. He knew his dad wouldn't allow it, and he knew that he would be violating his paternal trust, yet the urge to ride was trying to convince him that it would be just a leisurely ride and that there was nothing to worry about. No one would know. How could they?

Leon fought through his trance-like fixation and quickly closed the front door. Just a few steps away and to the right was the kitchen, which led to the garage where the Sportster was stored.

He methodically passed through the kitchen and grabbed the key to his Sportster. As he opened the garage door and turned on the garage light, the first thing he saw was a beautiful but lonely-looking Big Red, just sitting there. Just like him, he thought, Big Red wants to go for a ride, too. Big Red needs to be ridden, he thought, trying to convince himself of any guilt or wrongdoing.

He walked toward the garage entrance and raised the large exterior door. Once again, he saw the clear blue sky and felt the warm sunshine and refreshing morning breeze. He didn't need to convince himself that he was going to go for a ride; the alluring weather demanded it.

He looked into the garage at a nearby corner and saw his

Sportster. I'll just take the Sportster, he thought. That way, he could relieve his urge to ride without any guilt toward his parents or potential harm to Big Red. Riding the Sportster would be a much safer and more practical decision, he concluded.

As he re-entered the garage to go to get the Sportster, Big Red once again demanded his attention. All of a sudden, Leon stood as rigid as a rock. His eyes became fixated, staring intently at Big Red. His self-control was becoming unmanageable, and he quickly went into another hypnotic-like trance. The desire to ride Big Red was persuasively overwhelming him.

"Ride me! Ride me!" he imagined Big Red pleading. "It's a perfect day for a motorcycle ride, and we've never ridden together. Come on, Leon, let's go for a ride!"

Leon fought hard to take back his self-control, but Big Red was just too demanding. I'll just take it for a spin, and when I get home, I'll clean off any dirt or residue and park it back in the same spot that I drove it from, he thought. But what about the odometer? That would be the only evidence of Big Red being violated. Would it be worth the risk, he thought? Maybe I'll just sit on it and get the feel of it. What's the harm in just sitting on a bike?

So, he slowly climbed on Big Red and balanced himself, placing a foot on the concrete floor on each side. As he raised the kickstand, he slowly moved the bike back to the open-air driveway.

As he gripped the handlebars and felt the potential power of the motorcycle, he thought oh my goodness, how can you not take this bike for a ride? Just sitting there on Big Red gave him emotions that he'd never experienced before. He felt like someone that had complete control and power over the highway. It truly felt like he was king of the road, and Big Red was his ethereal throne.

Like an addict needing a fix, Leon couldn't restrain himself from the unshakable urge to ride Big Red. Without any further hesitation, he hurried back to the kitchen, where the keys were waiting. He snatched Big Red's key off the wall, dashed to the garage, and grabbed his Bell motorcycle helmet somewhere along the way. "Lookout roadways," he said out loud, "here comes me and Big Red!"

As he slammed his right foot down to apply pressure on the kick-starter, Big Red's engine roared like a lion and then idly purred like a seductive kitten. After a few warm-up throttles, they were ready to go.

Leon carefully maneuvered the bike around the neighborhood and then onto a nearby thoroughfare, making sure to avoid the high-traffic major highways. After a short ride, he approached a convenience store, where he saw one of his riding buddies, Randy Courson, filling his Sportster with gasoline.

As Big Red pulled into a nearby parking spot, Randy's eyes grew wide open, and his chin dropped with absolute astonishment.

"Leon," Randy called out, "Is that your bike? It's gorgeous! That's the baddest-looking bike I've ever seen!"

"No, it's not mine," said Leon. "It's my dad's."

"Wow! What an awesome bike, Leon. I'm headed to Snipes Pond Road," said Randy. "Some other bikers are hanging out over there. Why don't you come with me and show them your dad's new bike? I'm sure they'll love it."

"I don't know," said Leon. "That's a dirt road, and I don't want to get it dirty. I'm not even supposed to be riding it. My dad would kill me if he found out that I took it without his permission."

"Don't worry, Leon," said Randy, "I'll ride back with you and help you clean it when you get home."

"Ok," said Leon. "But you promise you'll help me clean it, right?"

"For sure!" replied Randy.

So, off to Snipes Pond Road they drove.

Sure enough, upon arriving at Snipes Pond Road, there were

about six other young bikers doing doughnuts, wheelies, and drag racing. But all the reckless activity stopped when Leon and Big Red drove up.

Everyone stopped and stared as the big red machine slowly and deliberately approached like motorcycle royalty. In unison, they all "oohed" and "aahed." Some even playfully bowed down as the beautiful behemoth came to a stop.

Needless to say, Leon's head grew two hat sizes as he began to feel the tightness inside his well-padded Bell helmet.

After admiring Big Red for a short time, they resumed their reckless motorcycle games, doing doughnuts, wheelies, and drag racing up and down the long red dirt road.

Once again, Leon's emotions began to get the better of him. It just so happened that racing was one of his weakest vices. He loved to just flat out go fast and watching them race was enticing him more and more to join them. But at least he had sense enough to know that the potential of wrecking was greater with other bikers involved.

Then, he had an idea. He would go to the bottom of the hill and race up the road by himself. He wanted to feel the ultimate power and to see just how fast Big Red could go. Besides, showing off was his specialty, and although he had already made an impression by riding up on Big Red, he wanted to give them more.

He yelled out and hand signaled for everyone to clear the road. As they aligned themselves along the roadway, he shouted, "I just want to see how fast this thing will go, y'all. After that, the roads are all yours."

He slowly pampered Big Red to the starting point at the lower end of the roadway. The dirt roadway in front of him slightly increased in grade as it approached the finish line of the designated raceway. He'd raced this road many times on his Sportster and had complete confidence that Big Red could match or outperform the Sportsters proven speeding ability.

He snugged his Bell helmet chin strap tighter and began

racing Big Red's throttle as if to say, "I'm about to release the beast!" Big Red's roar commanded everyone's attention as the throttle revved up and thundered out to the waiting crowd. There is no other sound like a Harley-Davidson motorcycle's engine, and Big Red's 74 had one of the most dynamic tones in the county.

Leon gave one last high-performance throttle as the "all clear" signal was given by Randy to go. A sudden full blast of the throttle and a quick release of the clutch made Big Red's rear tires spew a seemingly endless trail of red dirt as it began its climb up the sloping incline. The odometer very quickly read 35 mph, 45 mph, and then 65 mph as Leon completed the execution of the four forward gears.

75, 80, 90 mph, the beast roared as it passed the excited bystanders. Then suddenly, without warning, an unexpected washout from a recent rain appeared directly ahead. The shallow trench was unavoidable, as it extended the entire width of the road and beyond. In addition, the hazard appeared too quick and too late for Leon to react. The speeding bike rammed into the washout with the front tire penetrating a sun-dried deep rut, causing the rear end of the bike to somersault high end over end before hitting the hard ground and rocks, tumbling over and over and finally coming to rest around a distant pine tree.

During the tumultuous tumbling, Leon fought hard to maintain his grip on the handlebar, but the bike continued to spiral violently out of control, taking him along with it. Then, without any way to maintain control, Leon's air-born body came down hard against the handlebar. At the very time, the bike made a vicious landing from one of its flips, forcibly impacting the ground one against the other.

The impact of the handlebar crushed Leon's right lung, causing him to lose his breath. His head was bleeding profusely from a gash in his skull. In addition, the impact on his head caused a concussion, causing him to lose total consciousness.

His intestines were also badly dislodged and mangled from the many brunt forces of the hard ground and rocks as he tumbled uncontrollably along the path of pain. His Bell helmet, one of the safest motorcycle helmets made for the industry, was completely demolished as his head was pounded over and over before finally coming to a rest against a huge boulder.

Big Red ended up being a total loss, entangled around a sturdy pine tree. Its short-lived motorcycle life was over. What was once a proud replica of motorcycle art was now just a bulky mass of mangled metal. The once highly esteemed 74 had been reduced to an unenviable status of less than zero.

Leon's initial assessment wasn't much better, but for now, at least, it appeared that he wasn't a total loss. He was still breathing, but barely. His pulse was weak, and blood was oozing from all parts of his body. His face was unrecognizable, as blood from the huge gash in his skull was covering it. To make the scene even more horrific, brain matter could easily be seen protruding from the huge opening in his head. Bones were surely broken, but it was hard to tell how many and which ones as his body lay limp, unmoving, and unresponsive.

The frantic young bikers fought through the emotional trauma they had just witnessed and finally gathered their thoughts. After a short discussion, Randy sped away to get medical support as the rest did their best to attend to a bleeding, unconscious Leon.

Finally, after about half an hour, which must have seemed like an eternity for the young bikers, medical support arrived. The paramedics assessed Leon's condition and equipped him with a fresh supply of oxygen, then secured him on a stretcher, boarded the ambulance, and sped away to the nearby Aiken Hospital.

Leon's frail body was taken directly to the emergency department, where several doctors worked together to repair the damage to his battered body. The most critical, as well as the most obvious injury, was determined to be to his skull. The surgery was long, complex, and lasted long into the early morning hours of the following day. Finally, one of the doctors arrived at the waiting room where Leon's parents were nervously waiting.

"Mr. and Mrs. Baughman?" I'm Dr. Howington, said the surgeon. "Leon's injuries were very significant, but his vital signs are stable for the moment. Unfortunately, the trauma to the head caused him to lose consciousness, and he's in a coma. It's hard to say at this time how long that situation will last, but the body has a miraculous way of healing itself, but unfortunately, it will be a slow, drawn-out process."

"There's no easy way for me to tell you this," the doctor continued, "but based on my experience with this type of injury, even when he awakens from the coma, the probability of him returning to his normal state of being is very unlikely. If and when he comes out of the coma, his brain will, in all probability, be in what we call a vegetative state.

"I know that's a lot for you to take in, but it's my responsibility to inform you, nevertheless," continued the doctor. "I also know it's hard for you not to worry, but I assure you that we will do our best to make him as comfortable as possible and will use all of our medical expertise to do our best to restore him to his normal state of health."

"If you'd like," said the doctor, "you may follow me, and I'll take you to where we're holding Leon at this time and explain in more detail what we did during the surgery."

The shaken young couple held hands and followed the doctor down a long corridor leading to the Intensive Care Unit. Upon entering the ICU, the first thing they saw was someone's heavily bandaged head wrapped with gauze and an arm and lower extremity in a cast lying on a bed that was unnervingly enclosed in a clear, thick, plastic tent. Initially, the patient was unrecognizable, but as they got closer, they realized that it was their son, Leon.

Before the stunned parents could say anything, the doctor

calmly explained, "I know that you seeing him this way comes as a shock, and unfortunately, there's no way I can make that any better for you, as we've already done our very best for his condition. Please allow me to explain what I mean.

"The plastic tent that you see is what we call a Confined Ventilative Enclosure. During the accident, Leon suffered massive trauma to his chest area, causing his right lung to collapse. Unfortunately, the damage to the lungs is irreparable. In addition, he lost a significant amount of blood from his bodily wounds, as well as an extensive injury to the skull. The purpose of the ventilation tent is to provide a secure, low-pressure enclosure to maintain a controlled volume of oxygen to the whole body. This technique assists him with his breathing and will allow him to get the proper levels of oxygen and blood to all the vital organs, in hopes of helping the body heal over time."

The doctor then politely, yet discerningly, offered the couple to sit in a chair just outside the plastic enclosure. The news that he had already told them was catastrophic, to say the least, but the news he was about to tell them was even worse.

The doctor then sat in a chair across from the dazed and traumatized couple. In his best, soft-spoken doctor's voice, he began to explain the worst of the worst of Leon's injuries.

"As I told you earlier," Dr. Howington continued, "Leon suffered a very traumatic blow to his head. When he arrived, there was massive bleeding from the skull, as the skull had been shattered on one side. In addition to an extensive loss of blood, the other bad news is that brain tissue was exposed outside the cranial cavity. The good news, if there is any, is that the opening in the skull acted as a vent and decreased the possibility of further swelling of the brain. Upon further extensive examination, we saw no lacerations or visible evidence of damage to the brain itself. It goes without saying that that is great news!

"However, due to the extent of the damage to the skull, we will, in time, have to perform a craniotomy. Here's what we'll have to do. For now, we'll monitor his brain function and swelling, and in time, when the brain activity shows significant improvement, we'll have to remove part of the skull and install a thin titanium plate to cover the damaged area of the brain. Later, we'll re-install the skull and reconstruct and repair the damaged area of the skull. I know this sounds like a lot to take in, and it is," said the doctor, "but it's a necessary procedure due to the complex nature of his injuries.

"During our examination, we also found that his intestinal tract was badly contorted due to the extensive trauma to his body. We surgically reconstructed his intestinal tract, and fortunately, did not see any signs of tears or lacerations. Lastly, other non-life-threatening injuries include a broken wrist and a broken ankle. We've secured them in a cast and don't expect any complications from the extent of their injuries.

"Do you have any questions for me? If not, I'll leave you as a comfort to your son, Leon. Please don't hesitate to call my office and ask any future questions; plus I'll make sure you're notified of any changes in his condition as they become available. God bless you both."

"Oh, Lord! Oh, my Lord!" cried a tearful Eula Baughman. "Albert, even if he recovers, he may never be the same."

"I know, dear," said Albert as he tried his best to comfort his loving wife. "All we can do is hope and pray now, honey. The doctors have done all they can do at this time. It's hard not to worry, but trust in the Lord for now, and we'll deal with whatever He decides as time goes by. Leon's well-being is in the Lord's hands now."

Days, then weeks, passed as Leon continued his struggle to survive, yet he remained in a lonely, comatose state. Leon's mother would visit as often as possible. She would hold his hand and talk out loud, praying, consoling him, and just reading books that she knew he would enjoy. The doctor had told her that even though he was in a coma, he might be able to hear her, and if he could, he might be able to use her voice as a comfort and a will to become stronger. Needless to say, she spoke to him as often as she could.

At some point during the long wait, Albert was approached at home by a member of the South Carolina State Patrol office. "Mr. Baughman," the officer began, "I'm Sgt. Mole of the South Carolina State Patrol office, and I'm deeply sorry for you and your wife and even more sorrowful for your son, Leon. I'm here to provide you with a copy of the accident report as required by law.

"We did a thorough investigation of the accident, and according to the eyewitnesses I interviewed and the details of the evidence at the scene, my investigative team determined that Leon was going approximately 102 mph at the time of impact with a washout stretching across the dirt road. The motorcycle was, in my opinion, a total loss and in no way, could be used for future transportation purposes.

"Since there were no other parties involved in the accident, we found it unnecessary to charge your son with a citation of reckless driving. Here's your copy of the accident report. As you present it to your insurance provider, I hope it'll help to reimburse you for the damage to your motorcycle, to say the least. Again, I'm sorry I have to be here to deliver this, but it's part of bringing this incident to an end for you and your family. I hope for the very best for you and your wife and for a miraculous and quick recovery for your son, Leon. Y'all have a good day, now."

After the officer left, Albert read over the accident report. As he read the report, his heart was broken in two places—his love for his critically injured son and his love for his most prized material possession, his Harley-Davidson 74. His hurt for the loss of Big Red was painful, but the survival and the love of his son were much more important. He could always buy another motorcycle, but he could never replace his son, Leon.

As time slowly passed by, Leon's condition started showing promising results. Al's depressing thoughts about his lost motorcycle were also on the mend, as he was able to finally put that painful experience in the past. Even in losing a long lost love, it seems that time has a way of healing the most heart-breaking experiences and emotionally difficult situations. It was no different for Al. He knew that sulking over a motorcycle wasn't doing anyone any good. He prudently manned up, put the motorcycle incident behind him, and put his full emotional energy into supporting his wife, Eula, and his critically injured son, Leon.

After thirty-three long, painstaking days, Eula received a call from the doctor's office. The news was good. Leon's critical condition had been upgraded to a stable condition. In addition, Leon had awakened from his coma and was responding favorably.

"Hallelujah! Thank you, Lord!" Eula cried out. "Albert, get ready. We have to go to the hospital. Leon's awake!"

Upon their arrival at the hospital, they found a weak but alert Leon. The plastic tent was still intact, and his bandages were all the same as when they last saw him. His vital signs had improved significantly, and although he couldn't speak, he was aware of where he was but didn't remember how he got there. He would figure this out later, but for now, he had a lot of healing to do.

After a few days, he grew stronger and stronger. The doctors removed most of the bandages, leaving the head wrap and casts to the wrist and ankle intact. His breathing had improved, but he was still too weak to breathe on his own. His skin color was returning to normal, and his dark, swollen eyes were almost back to their natural appearance. His voice was squeaky, but at least he could finally communicate for short periods before losing his breath.

His mama gave him a long, warm, motherly hug and kissed him on his forehead. "Welcome back, baby," she said as tears of joy slowly rolled down her cheeks.

"Mama," said a weak-toned Leon, "it was dark, and I didn't

know where I was or what had happened, but I could hear your voice sometimes. I couldn't see you, but I knew it was your voice, and I tried and tried to find you, but I couldn't get past the darkness."

"Well, I'm here now, honey," said the grateful mother. "You've been through quite a lot lately, but by the grace of God, you're here with me now. So, get some rest, and hopefully, in the days to come, you'll be able to go home and be with your family."

As Leon grew stronger, Al explained what happened, and as he heard the news, a teary-eyed, soft-spoken Leon told his dad how sorry he was. Al did his best to assure Leon that the motorcycle was a fond memory, but for now, it was time to focus on getting him well.

Finally, the day arrived when Leon would go home and complete his recovery. The hospital sent a team of experts to install an in-home ventilation tent over Leon's bed. By this time, his brain activity was responding very favorably and to his parent's delight, the doctors reported that there were no indications that he would end up in a vegetative state after all.

During his recovery, Leon's grandmother watched over him while his parents went back to work. The days were long and boring, to say the least. All he could do was just lay there and stare at the ceiling and watch TV.

At some point, he began recalling how this was his third time being hospitalized in less than two years. The first time was at a local Jay Cee Rodeo in Orangeburg, SC, where he was competing in a barrel race. He was only thirteen years old and didn't have any learning experience on how to ride a horse. As it turned out, he was a natural on a horse, and the excitement of competing in a rodeo was a challenge he couldn't refuse. He would go on to win many cash awards, ribbons, and trophies, but his last ride didn't result in the praises and accolades that he was used to.

During a barrel race, where a rider on horseback races

around barrels strategically placed apart in hopes of rounding the barrels in the fastest time without falling off the horse or touching the barrels, he had an unpleasant and unexpected result. For reasons unknown, the horse that he was riding began acting up and became impossible to handle. Leon did his best to hold on, but somehow, the horse was able to sling him off sending him headfirst into a pole supporting the rodeo broadcast crew's booth.

His head hit the pole with a force so hard that the pole broke, causing the broadcast booth to tilt to a severe angle, and was fortunate to not fall to the ground. The broadcast crew and other rodeo personnel hurried to Leon's rescue. An on-the-scene ambulance crew hurried Leon to the Orangeburg Hospital, where he was treated for his head injury and kept overnight for observation. Fortunately, there were no significant injuries, and he returned home the next day. Needless to say, that was his last rodeo.

The other time he recalled was the motorcycle accident he had at Caesar's Head Park and Campground. He ended up in a hospital in Greenville, SC, on that occasion but was released after a couple of days. But this time was different. This was a life-and-death situation. It could have gone either way. By the grace of God, it turned out very favorably for the "titanium" hard-headed Leon.

During his recovery, his friend Randy was very supportive, bringing him comic books, candy, hamburgers, fries, and milkshakes. One day, Leon's grandmother had to run an errand to the grocery store, and Randy agreed to stay with him until she returned.

After a short time, Randy asked Leon if there was anything that he could do for him. To his surprise, Leon responded, "As a matter of fact, yes, there is."

"What do you need, Leon?" Randy asked.

"Go see if my Sportster is in the garage, and if it is, see if it has any gas in it," Leon replied.

"Leon, you can't be serious!" said a concerned Randy. "Leon, you're on a breathing apparatus, your wrist and ankle are broken, and your head is still wrapped with gauze and has a newly implanted titanium plate in it. The last thing you need to be doing is going for a ride on a motorcycle!"

"Yeah, I know it," said Leon, "but I'm tired of just laying here all the time. I really need to get out and go for a short ride. The urge to ride is killing me. Please, Randy!"

"Think about what you're saying, Leon," Randy said. "The last time you had the urge to ride a motorcycle, you almost killed yourself. I don't think it's a good idea."

But a pitifully pleading Leon defiantly argued so much that he gave Randy a guilt trip, convincing him that he was an accessory to his torture by not letting him have a little helpful therapy by merely going for a short ride on a motorcycle.

A reluctant Randy moved the Sportster from the garage and parked it as close to the front door as possible. He then went back inside and helped Leon get out of bed and out of the plastic enclosure. *This is really a bad idea,* he thought. *But if this will help Leon, then I'll do whatever I can to make things better for him.*

He placed Leon's good arm around his shoulders and neck, supporting him while Leon hobbled toward the door on one foot. Once outside, he carefully placed Leon's good foot on one side of the motorcycle and placed his good hand on the handlebar as Leon positioned himself on the motorcycle seat. He then carefully swung Leon's leg with the broken ankle over the gas tank onto the ground on the opposite side of the bike. Assuring that Leon was well-balanced, he placed his injured hand on the other side of the handlebar. Not surprisingly, Leon refused to wear his motorcycle helmet. Nevertheless, it probably would not have fit anyway due to the mass of bandages on his head.

Randy carefully raised the kickstand as Leon acclimated himself and balanced the bike. Randy then engaged the kick starter and held on to the bike while assuring that Leon was prepared for him to let go. With a simple nod of the head by Leon that he was ready to go, the bike slowly sped away. To say the least, Randy was immediately beside himself as he began praying out loud and walking in circles around the front lawn.

As Leon maneuvered the bike slowly around the neighborhood, neighbors along the way would do a double take as he passed by. All they saw was a quick look at a figure of a person dressed in pajamas with his head wrapped like a mummy, a bone cast on one arm and another cast on one foot, riding down the road on a Harley-Davidson motorcycle. What they may not have seen was Leon blissfully smiling from ear to ear.

Leon was in motorcycle heaven. This was the best therapy he could have ever hoped for. The weather was perfect, with a clear blue sky, warm sunshine, and a cool breeze on his gauze-wrapped face.

Suddenly, it reminded him of the day he last drove his dad's brand-new motorcycle. It was the last day that the motorcycle took anyone for a ride, and it was almost his last ride, as well. This has been fun, he thought, but I suppose I should get on back home now. He drove the bike into a neighborhood cul-de-sac, carefully turned around and headed back home to a relieved Randy anxiously waiting for him.

Randy quickly grabbed the bike as it came to a stop in the driveway. As he held the bike, Leon was able to slowly unseat himself and balance himself with one hand on Randy and the other on the bike. Randy engaged the kickstand, allowing the bike to stand alone, helped Leon back to his bed, and then secured the Sportster as if nothing ever happened.

"Thank you, Randy, you're a good friend," said a grateful Leon.

"You're welcome," Randy said with nervous laughter, "I may be a good friend, but in reality, I'm a stupid good friend." The two were finally able to laugh out loud as the motorcycle therapy was a complete success.

When Leon's grandmother finally returned, Leon and Randy said their goodbyes. As he left the house, Randy finally had peace of mind that Leon's health was improving more and more by the day. Not only was his physical health improving, but so was his unique desire for adventure and danger. In a weird, unconventional way, evidenced by the irresponsible events that occurred that day, he thought this was also a true sign of improvement in Leon's mental health as well.

On his way home, Randy smiled, shook his head, and thought to himself that if Leon would do something that careless as a critically confined in-home patient, recovering from a near-death motorcycle accident, being kept alive by means of a ventilation tent, what will he do when he's completely healed and able to ride at his own free will again. That remained to be seen for now, but whatever the circumstances may be, he would always be there for his beloved, daredevil friend.

# ACKNOWLEDGMENT

During Leon's early career, he had the opportunity and privilege to open shows for the legendary country music artist Hank Williams, Jr. It was a well-known fact that during this time, Hank Williams, Jr. did not personally endorse other artists' albums due to his own personal reasons. Leon was humbly thankful and greatly appreciative that Ole Hank would make an exception for his newest album, simply entitled "Leon Everette." It's an honor and a pleasure that Leon will cherish for the rest of his life.

# ALBUM ACKNOWLEDGEMENT

Circa 1982

No doubt about it, Leon Everette is a tough act to follow. Since he began touring with us at the end of last year, Leon has torn up every audience—and I don't think you can fool today's audiences for one minute. They expect hard-rocking, no-bull country music, and I'm here to tell you they aren't willing to settle for second best. With Leon, they never have to. His stage shows are great, his music is original, and I think this new album proves that Leon Everette is on his way.

**Hank Williams, Jr.**

Elektra Records

**The Leon Everette Baughman Family
Leon, Diane, and Punkin**

Hey Y'all, this is Leon Everette and I'd like to invite you to follow me at **LeonEveretteMusic** on Facebook. I'll be there to answer any questions you may have concerning my upcoming concert dates in your area as well as any other music related news happening in my life. While there, check out my new as well as my older CDs and other Leon Everette merchandise.

I hope you enjoyed the book. Just to let you know, I'm not slowing down in my professional music career nor my relationship with Jesus. Who knows, in time I may have gotten into more (well-intended) mischief—perhaps enough to make a sequel to the book.

Ain't God Good?

Leon

# ABOUT THE AUTHOR

 Hal Reeves lives in a quiet, rural community in Evans, GA. After graduating from Evans High School in 1968, he enlisted in the United States Marine Corps. Upon completing his tour of duty at the rank of sergeant E-5, he went to work for his father as a plumber and pipefitter.

In 1990, at the age of forty years old and not satisfied with his accomplishments in life, he decided to go back to school. He spent two years of study at Aiken Technical College in Aiken, SC, and graduated with honors with an associate's degree in Nuclear Engineering. While there, he also achieved the outstanding student award for "Who's Who" among elite college students in America for his academic achievements.

After graduating from Aiken Technical College, he enrolled as a student at the School of Radiation Therapy at the Medical College of Georgia in Augusta, GA. As fate would have it (he calls it a blessing), after graduating from MCG in 1995, he was offered a job as a Radiation Therapist at the Cancer Care Institute of Carolina, in Aiken, SC, the very next week. He was happily employed at the CCIC until his retirement in 2012.

It was during his time in college at Aiken Technical College, that his English literature professor was so impressed with his essays, that he was encouraged to consider focusing on becoming a published author. During his retirement he did just that and continues to do so to the present day.

www.ingramcontent.com/pod-product-compliance
Lightning Source LLC
Chambersburg PA
CBHW071301140726
47996CB00005B/1579